Routledge Revivals

A Book of Broadsheets

This book, together with *A Second Book of Broadsheets* makes up an anthology of the 1915 broadsheets distributed by *The Times* to members of H.M. Forces serving in the trenches of World War I. The volume contains a wide variety of rich literature from before the war and was designed to give soldiers entertainment. It includes extracts from the works of Thomas Hardy, Rudyard Kipling, William Shakespeare, William Wordsworth and Charles Dickens.

A Book of Broadsheets

With an Introduction by Geoffrey Dawson

First published in 1928
by Methuen & Co. Ltd.

This edition first published in 2015 by Routledge
2 Park Square, Milton Park, Abingdon, Oxon, OX14 4RN
and by Routledge
711 Third Avenue, New York, NY 10017

Routledge is an imprint of the Taylor & Francis Group, an informa business

© 1928 Methuen & Co. Ltd

All rights reserved. No part of this book may be reprinted or reproduced
or utilised in any form or by any electronic, mechanical, or other means,
now known or hereafter invented, including photocopying and recording,
or in any information storage or retrieval system, without permission in
writing from the publishers.

Publisher's Note
The publisher has gone to great lengths to ensure the quality of this
reprint but points out that some imperfections in the original copies may
be apparent.

Disclaimer
The publisher has made every effort to trace copyright holders and
welcomes correspondence from those they have been unable to contact.

A Library of Congress record exists under LC control number: 29002956

ISBN 13: 978-1-138-90136-0 (hbk)
ISBN 13: 978-1-315-69778-9 (ebk)

A BOOK OF BROADSHEETS

WITH AN INTRODUCTION BY
GEOFFREY DAWSON
EDITOR OF 'THE TIMES'

METHUEN & CO. LTD.
36 ESSEX STREET W.C.
LONDON

First Published in 1928

PRINTED IN GREAT BRITAIN

CONTENTS

		PAGE
I.	A CHOIR PRACTICE: Thomas Hardy, O.M.	1
	(From *Two on a Tower*, by courtesy of Messrs. Macmillan)	
II.	POEMS OF ENGLAND: Rudyard Kipling	4
	1. PUCK'S SONG	
	(By courtesy of the author and Messrs. Macmillan)	
	2. SUSSEX	
	(By courtesy of the author and Messrs. Methuen)	
	3. THE ROMAN CENTURION'S SONG	
	(By courtesy of the author and the Clarendon Press)	
III.	ST. CRISPIN'S DAY: Shakespeare	10
	(From *King Henry V*, iv, 3)	
IV.	ON BIRDS AND TROUTS: Izaak Walton	12
	(From *The Compleat Angler*)	
V.	A GAME OF CRIBBAGE: Charles Dickens	16
	(From *The Old Curiosity Shop*)	
VI.	ENGLAND AT WAR: Lord Macaulay	22
	(*The Armada*)	
VII.	DAVID HARRIS, CRICKETER: John Nyren	25
	(From *The Cricketers of My Time*)	
VIII.	PARTRIDGE AT THE PLAY: Henry Fielding	30
	(From *Tom Jones*)	
IX.	THE LAST FIGHT OF THE *REVENGE*: Sir Walter Raleigh	34
X.	THE WINCHESTER COUNTRY: William Cobbett	38
	(From *Rural Rides*)	

		PAGE
XI.	NINE SONGS FROM SHAKESPEARE.	43
XII.	MR. MICAWBER'S TRANSACTIONS: Charles Dickens	47
	(From *David Copperfield*)	
XIII.	JOHN CAVANAGH, THE FIVES-PLAYER: William Hazlitt	52
	(From *The Indian Jugglers*)	
XIV.	THE MEN IN BUCKRAM: Shakespeare	56
	(From *I Henry IV*, ii, 4)	
XV.	TWO LETTERS OF CHARLES LAMB	60
	1. TO WORDSWORTH	
	2. TO COLERIDGE	
XVI.	DAVID AND GOLIATH	63
	(From *I Samuel xvii*)	
XVII.	A QUARREL WITH THE CAPTAIN: Henry Fielding	67
	(From *The Journal of a Voyage to Lisbon*)	
XVIII.	BALLAD OF AGINCOURT: Michael Drayton	71
XIX.	THE RIVER OF DEATH: John Bunyan	75
	(From *The Pilgrim's Progress*)	
XX.	AMYAS THROWS HIS SWORD INTO THE SEA: Charles Kingsley	81
	(From *Westward Ho!*)	
XXI.	THREE BALLADS	86
	1. THE WIFE OF USHER'S WELL	
	2. SIR PATRICK SPENS	
	3. THE LOWLANDS O' HOLLAND	
XXII.	ABRAHAM LINCOLN	91
	(Inaugural Address, March, 1865)	
XXIII.	MR. TONY WELLER ON LITERATURE: Charles Dickens	93
	(From *The Pickwick Papers*)	
XXIV.	A NIGHT ATTACK: Michael Scott	98
	(From *Tom Cringle's Log*)	

CONTENTS

		PAGE
XXV.	THE QUEENSFERRY DILIGENCE: Sir Walter Scott (From *The Antiquary*)	102
XXVI.	L'ALLEGRO: John Milton	107
XXVII.	1. ADMIRALTY INSTRUCTIONS RELATIVE TO HORSES AND DOGS.	111
	2. COMMODORE TRUNNION'S HUNT: Tobias Smollett (From *Peregrine Pickle*)	113
XXVIII.	1. THE UPPER THAMES: William Morris (From *News from Nowhere*, by courtesy of Messrs. Longmans)	116
	2. 'O JUNE': William Morris (By courtesy of Messrs. Longmans)	119
XXIX.	MR. PECKSNIFF AT THE BOARDING-HOUSE: Charles Dickens (From *Martin Chuzzlewit*)	119
XXX.	JOHN GILPIN: William Cowper	124
XXXI.	KING WILLIAM ENTERS EXETER: Lord Macaulay (From *The History of England*)	131
XXXII.	THE GREEN SPECTACLES: Oliver Goldsmith (From *The Vicar of Wakefield*)	135
XXXIII.	FROM WORDSWORTH 1. LINES WRITTEN IN EARLY SPRING 2. THE SOLITARY REAPER 3. THE DAFFODILS 4. 'MOST SWEET IT IS'	139
XXXIV.	1. SIR ROGER AT CHURCH: Joseph Addison (From *The Spectator*)	142
	2. THE VICAR: W. M. Praed	144
XXXV.	FROM BURNS 1. MY BONNIE MARY 2. A RED, RED ROSE 3. MARY MORRISON 4. JOHN ANDERSON	148

		PAGE
XXXVI.	A NIGHT AMONG THE PINES: R. L. Stevenson (From *Travels with a Donkey in the Cevennes*, by courtesy of Messrs. Chatto & Windus)	150
XXXVII.	MR. COLLINS PROPOSES: Jane Austen (From *Pride and Prejudice*)	154
XXXVIII.	MR. JORROCKS ON 'UNTING: R. S. Surtees (From *Handley Cross*)	159
XXXIX.	MRS. WILFER'S WEDDING-DAY: Charles Dickens (From *Our Mutual Friend*)	164
XL.	THE FAMOUS BALLAD OF THE JUBILEE CUP: A. T. Quiller-Couch (From *A Cornish Window*, by courtesy of the author)	169
XLI.	SAINT GEORGE OF ENGLAND: William Caxton (From *The Golden Legend*)	176
XLII.	RIDING TO SELL: G. J. Whyte-Melville (From *Market Harborough*, by courtesy of Messrs. Ward, Lock)	181
XLIII.	MY FIRST PLAY: Charles Lamb (From *Essays of Elia*)	186
XLIV.	THE LANDLORD'S DEBT: George Borrow (From *Lavengro*)	191
XLV.	THREE SONGS FROM LOVELACE 1. To Lucasta. Going to the Warres 2. To Althea. From Prison 3. The Grasshopper. To my noble friend Mr. Charles Cotton	196
XLVI.	LONDON OF THE STUARTS: Lord Macaulay (From *The History of England*)	199
XLVII.	HOME-COMING UP THE CHANNEL: Joseph Conrad (From *The Nigger of the Narcissus*, by courtesy of Messrs. Pinker)	204
XLVIII.	THE LOTOS-EATERS: Alfred, Lord Tennyson	207

CONTENTS

		PAGE
XLIX.	THE DEATH OF THE RED FOX: R. L. Stevenson	213
	(From *Kidnapped*, by courtesy of Mr. Lloyd Osbourne)	
L.	SIR JOHN MOORE	218
	1. HIS CHARACTER	
	(From *The History of the War in the Peninsula*, by Sir William Napier)	
	2. HIS TOMB	
	(From *The Bible in Spain*, by George Borrow)	
	3. HIS BURIAL	
	(By Charles Wolfe)	
LI.	ENGLISH-GROWN TOBACCO: Sir J. M. Barrie, O.M.	221
	(From *My Lady Nicotine*, by courtesy of Messrs. Hodder & Stoughton)	
LII.	POEMS FROM BLAKE	226
	1. INTRODUCTION	
	2. NURSE'S SONG	
	3. THE LAND OF DREAMS	
	4. THE TIGER	
	5. THE LITTLE VAGABOND	
	6. AH! SUN-FLOWER	
	7. THE CLOD AND THE PEBBLE	
	8. AUGURIES OF INNOCENCE	
LIII.	THE SOLITARY FARMER: Daniel Defoe	232
	(From *Robinson Crusoe*)	
LIV.	THE BATTLE AT RAMOTH-GILEAD	236
	(From *I Kings xxii*)	
LV.	THE BOW STREET RUNNER AND THE ROMANY CHAL: George Borrow	239
	(From *Lavengro*)	
LVI.	THE ELECTION AT EATANSWILL: Charles Dickens	244
	(From *The Pickwick Papers*)	
LVII.	SONGS FROM PEACOCK	248
	1. THE WAR-SONG OF DINAS VAWR	
	2. 'THOUGH I BE NOW A GREY, GREY FRIAR'	
	3. THE MEN OF GOTHAM	
	4. THE GRAVE OF LOVE	
	5. THE POOL OF THE DIVING FRIAR	

		PAGE
LVIII.	GILBERT WHITE ON BIRDS	253
	(From *The Natural History and Antiquities of Selborne*)	
LIX.	FROM 'ADONAIS': P. B. Shelley	258
LX.	MRS. BATTLE'S OPINIONS ON WHIST: Charles Lamb	263
	(From *Essays of Elia*)	
LXI.	1. THE GLORIES OF OUR BLOOD AND STATE: James Shirley	267
	2. THE VISION OF BELSHAZZAR	268
	(From *Daniel v*)	
LXII.	THE SECOND LINE OF DEFENCE	270
	1. THE CAPTAIN OF VOLUNTEERS	
	2. SUNDAY MORNING DRILL	
	(From Thomas Hardy's *The Trumpet Major*, by courtesy of Messrs. Macmillan)	
LXIII.	1. THE RED ENSIGN: Joseph Conrad	275
	(From *Some Reminiscences*, by courtesy of Messrs. Pinker)	
	2. HOME THOUGHTS, FROM THE SEA: Robert Browning	279
LXIV.	A MAN AND A GOOSE: W. H. Hudson	279
	(From *Birds and Man*, by courtesy of Messrs. Duckworth)	
LXV.	CLOUD AND STORM ON MONT BLANC: John Tyndall	283
	(From *The Glaciers of the Alps*)	
LXVI.	A COUNTRYMAN IN LONDON: Tobias Smollett	287
	(From *Humphry Clinker*)	
LXVII.	CHRISTMAS IN THE ANTARCTIC	292
	(From *Scott's Last Expedition*, by courtesy of Messrs. Murray)	
LXVIII.	THE MELLSTOCK CAROLS: Thomas Hardy, O.M.	296
	(From *Under the Greenwood Tree*, by courtesy of Messrs. Chatto & Windus)	

INTRODUCTION

THE anthology contained in this volume differs from others of the kind in having a definite historical interest. It is a reproduction—not indeed complete, but sufficiently representative—of the pocket literature provided by *The Times* for the men in the trenches during the early days of the War. The selection therefore is neither a new one, as in most anthologies of the kind, nor the work of any one individual. Every item in it was printed during the autumn of the year 1915 in the form of a 'broadsheet'—a single page of thin paper suitable for inclusion in a letter—and distributed in hundreds of thousands to the forces in the field or at sea. Moreover, though *The Times* may claim some credit for the organization and production of the scheme, it had its origin elsewhere and was kept alive by innumerable volunteers. No more than three bound collections of the original Broadsheets are known to be still in existence, and their reproduction now, at the end of the first decade of peace, affords a welcome opportunity to pay tribute to some of those who invented and furthered the project, assisted it with their suggestions, and in certain cases waived valuable copyrights in so good a cause.

The idea, like many others, sprang from the fertile imagination of Mr. Lionel Curtis, who recalls that he first conceived it when some young soldiers, home on leave from the trenches in the early days of August, 1915, were discussing in his house their favourite passages in English literature. Some of these passages were read aloud by Sir William Marris, who was also of the party. 'As he read,' writes Mr. Curtis, 'we all felt as though a great wind was sweeping away the clouds and the sunlight was breaking through.' One of the officers present exclaimed that 'it was a thousand pities that such stuff could not be read in the trenches,' and from that moment the Broadsheets had their beginning. The practical possibilities were discussed at once. A letter from Mr. Curtis two or three days later inquired whether *The Times* would undertake the necessary organization. Mr. Bruce Richmond, then as now in charge of *The Times Literary Supplement*, was promptly and willingly brought into the scheme and bore much of the burden of it for many months afterwards. Sir Walter Raleigh, Professor of English Literature at Oxford, was suggested as an ideal colleague in the choice of extracts, and responded to the invitation with enthusiasm. To these two, more than to any others, the present volume owes its range and its variety.

Variety indeed was Raleigh's chief preoccupation from the beginning. 'I covet infinite variety,' he was telling a friend on August 17 in one of the letters published after his death.

'I wish you would send references of anything that occurs to you, from bits of the Book of Job to accounts of a prize-fight. No standard except "good of its kind." There is room for every one's pets, except elephants. So, for a time at least, I've got a job.'

By the end of the month the scheme was ready for announcement, and Raleigh was invited to explain it in a letter to *The Times*.

'What is wanted,' he wrote, 'and what you have generously undertaken to supply, is a numerous and various selection of the best passages, grave and gay, from English verse and prose, to be printed on flyleaves or broadsheets, and sold in mixed sets at a very low price. One of these broadsheets can be enclosed in a letter, without adding to the cost of postage. Whole assortments of them can be sent to officers and distributed according to taste among the men of their command.'

INTRODUCTION

And he added a passage which might well stand alone for the introduction to the present collection.

'I confess I like the idea of this library. Apart from its main use, it seems to me to symbolize the cause for which we are fighting. The Germans are right when they call us frivolous, if it may be permitted in the name of politeness to assume that by frivolous they mean playful. They are right; we have playful minds, and they have not, so that we are often embarrassed in our converse with them. They are full of a simple unquestioning faith in Germany, in things German, in the great deeds they have done and the great deeds they are about to do, in all that is large, heavy, solid and persistent. They think of these things, if their own account is just, relentlessly and eternally, without mitigation or fatigue. They do not want Heine in their trenches; there is a danger that he might not be serious. We could not think of ourselves as they do, magnificently, for years together; some one would be sure to laugh. We are not very good at hating, and we do not believe in hate. We continue to believe in life, and in the variety and surprise of life. If we submit ourselves to rigid discipline, as we are quite willing to do, it is not that we wish to be like them, but that we hope to save life from being crushed under their machine. We believe in freedom, and we mean to keep it. We will fight as long as we can stand, so that the world may still be a place where spontaneous and playful persons, especially women and children, may lead a life free from fear. There is no better expression of freedom, in all its senses, than English literature.'

The first series of broadsheets, thirty-six in number, was published on August 30. They were divided into sets of six, each set being sold in an envelope for a penny, with special rates for large quantities, such as were purchased and distributed by the Camps Library and other organizations of the kind. The price can hardly have covered the cost of production, but it was announced from the outset that, if there should be any small profit, it would be devoted to the Red Cross Fund which *The Times* maintained throughout the war. Among the broadsheets now reprinted are to be found most of those which were Raleigh's first selection—the story of David and Goliath (XVI), for instance, and *The Armada* (VI), the Game of Cribbage from *The Old Curiosity Shop* (V), Cobbett's account of the Winchester Country (X) and Hazlitt's picture of Cavanagh, The Fives-Player (XIII), two letters of Charles Lamb (XV), and the

Adonais (LIX). These set the standard, and from the moment of their publication a flood of suggestions for future packets began to pour into Printing House Square. Within a week the game of choosing subjects for broadsheets, which Raleigh had described as 'better fun than I knew,' was being played wherever *The Times* was read.

Neither space nor memory would suffice to tell the names of all those whose ideas were adopted in the thirty sets eventually produced in the autumn of 1915. Some of the most interesting came from the trenches—among them a demand for certain extracts from Hardy and for 'passages on scientific subjects.' Men of letters, publishers, prelates, correspondents of every sort and kind made their contribution to the common stock. But it is permissible, perhaps, now that both are gone from us, to record that two of those to whom *The Times* owed much help and encouragement in those days were Dean Ryle of Westminster, and Professor W. P. Ker of All Souls (who was deeply concerned in the broadsheet now printed as XXVIII), while for another reason special acknowledgment must be made to Mr. E. V. Lucas, who not only took his share in the work of selection at the time but is the originator as well as the publisher of the present volume.

The work of distribution, though largely and intentionally left to individual correspondents, was also carried out in bulk by a number of agencies concerned with the welfare of the troops in the field, afloat, and in hospital. Among these —in addition to the Camps Library, already mentioned— were such bodies as the Y.M.C.A., the War Library, the Overseas Club, and the Church of England Temperance Association, and to them also recognition is due. It was thanks largely to their co-operation that by September 8 (just a week after the scheme was launched) *The Times* was able to announce that the sale of the first series of broadsheets had reached the round figure of one million. A little later Lord Derby was arranging a consignment for those Lancashire battalions in which he was interested—an example which was followed in other instances—while the National

Institute for the Blind, headed by Mr. Arthur Pearson, was busily engaged in reproducing the broadsheets in Braille type for the use of blinded soldiers. Meanwhile the work of production went forward fast. Within the first six weeks twenty-four sets, or 144 broadsheets, were selected, printed, and published. By December these figures had grown to thirty sets of 180 broadsheets, and the series was crowned with a special Christmas set which is represented in the present anthology by its two final extracts—the story of Scott's last Christmas in the Antarctic (LXVII) and the Mellstock Carols (LXVIII).

There was never any question of the popularity of the broadsheets among those for whom they were originally put together. In the archives of *The Times* are many treasured letters of gratitude—one, for example, which describes a 'prosaic sergeant, painfully recapturing' a familiar poem of his youth, and 'annoying those around him by intoning the stanzas as he moved up and down the trench'; another complaining that the writer had been compelled to read aloud Mr. Micawber (XII) twice over to the men in his dug-out and the Game of Cribbage (V) three times; another inspired to compare the broadsheets to 'a cool spring rippling through an arid sand-waste'; another moved, more practically to 'take the Izaak Walton one (IV) to the 86th on the Tigris.' 'The beggars are so keen on fishing,' he explained, 'that they make rods of the centre rib of the date palm.'

Was it equally worth while, after ten years of peace, to preserve the collection for other readers under wholly different conditions? To that question also the answer is preserved in a contemporary letter, written in December, 1915, from 'A Hospital, Somewhere in France.'

'It would be interesting,' it runs, 'to have all these broadsheets, and whatever are to follow, bound in one volume, as an example of English literature's beguilement, comfort and sustainment for the warrior. Such a volume, I suppose, cannot be published, but if ever I get back and am able to preserve them (and yet how can I, when every decent motive dictates that I must pass them on to others?) I shall see that mine are stitched into a cover. Another reason for binding the Broadsheets is that, as it happens, the collection would not be very different had the desire been to amuse and hearten not men of war but men of peace.'

This *Book of Broadsheets* is an attempt to fulfil that ambition—and to let others share in its fulfilment.

GEOFFREY DAWSON

September, 1928

A BOOK OF BROADSHEETS

I

A CHOIR PRACTICE

THERE was a noise of horse's hoofs without, a stumbling against the door-scraper, a tethering to the window-shutter, a creaking of the door on its hinges, and a voice which Swithin recognized as Mr. Torkingham's. He greeted each of the previous arrivals by name, and stated that he was glad to see them all so punctually assembled.

'Ay, sir,' said Haymoss Fry. "Tis only my jints that have kept me from assembling myself long ago. I'd assemble upon the top of Welland Steeple, if 'tweren't for my jints. I assure ye, Pa'son Tarkenham, that in the clitch o' my knees, where the rain used to come through when I was cutting clots for the new lawn, in old my lady's time, 'tis as if rats wez gnawing, every now and then. When a feller's young he's too small in the brain to see how soon a constitution can be squandered, worse luck!'

'True,' said Biles, to fill the time while the parson was engaged in finding the Psalms. 'A man's a fool till he's forty. Often have I thought, when hay-pitching, and the small of my back seeming no stouter than a harnet's, "The devil send that I had but the making of labouring men for a twelvemonth!" I'd gie every man jack two good backbones, even if the alteration was as wrong as forgery.'

'Four,—four backbones,' said Haymoss, decisively.

'Yes, four,' threw in Sammy Blore, with additional weight

of experience. 'For you want one in front for breast-ploughing and such like, one at the right side for ground-dressing, and one at the left side for turning mixens.'

'Well; then next I'd move every man's wyndpipe a good span away from his glutchpipe, so that at harvest time he could fetch breath in's drinking, without being choked and strangled as he is now. Thinks I, when I feel the victuals going——'

'Now, we'll begin,' interrupted Mr. Torkingham, his mind returning to this world again on concluding his search for a hymn.

Thereupon the racket of chair-legs on the floor signified that they were settling into their seats,—a disturbance which Swithin took advantage of by going on tiptoe across the floor above, and putting sheets of paper over knot-holes in the boarding at points where carpet was lacking, that his lamp-light might not shine down. The absence of a ceiling beneath rendered his position virtually that of one suspended in the same apartment.

The parson announced the tune, and his voice burst forth with 'Onward, Christian soldiers!' in notes of rigid cheerfulness.

In this start, however, he was joined only by the girls and boys, the men furnishing but an accompaniment of ahas and hems. Mr. Torkingham stopped, and Sammy Blore spoke—

'Beg your pardon, sir,—if you'll deal mild with us a moment. What with the wind and walking, my throat's as rough as a grater; and not knowing you were going to hit up that minute, I hadn't hawked, and I don't think Hezzy and Nat had, either,—had ye, souls?'

'I hadn't got thorough ready, that's true,' said Hezekiah.

'Quite right of you, then, to speak,' said Mr. Torkingham. 'Don't mind explaining; we are here for practice. Now clear your throats, then, and at it again.'

There was a noise as of atmospheric hoes and scrapers, and the bass contingent at last got under way with a time of its own:

'Honwerd, Christen sojers!'

'Ah, that's where we are so defective—the pronunciation,' interrupted the parson. 'Now repeat after me: "On-ward, Christ-ian, sol-diers." '

The choir repeated like an exaggerative echo: 'On-wed, Chris-ting, sol-jaws!'

'Better!' said the parson, in the strenuously sanguine tones of a man who got his living by discovering a bright side in things where it was not very perceptible to other people. 'But it should not be given with quite so extreme an accent; or we may be called affected by other parishes. And, Nathaniel Chapman, there's a jauntiness in your manner of singing which is not quite becoming. Why don't you sing more earnestly?'

'My conscience won't let me, sir. They say every man for himself: but, thank God, I'm not so mean as to lessen old fokes' chances by being earnest at my time o' life, and they so much nearer the need o't.'

'It's bad reasoning, Nat, I fear. Now, perhaps we had better sol-fa the tune. Eyes on your books, please. *Sol-sol! fa-fa! mi*——'

'I can't sing like that, not I!' said Sammy Blore, with condemnatory astonishment. 'I can sing genuine music, like F and G; but not anything so much out of the order of nater as that.'

'Perhaps you've brought the wrong book, sir?' chimed in Haymoss, kindly. 'I've knowed music early in life and late,—in short, ever since Luke Sneap broke his new fiddle-bow in the wedding psalm, when Pa'son Wilton brought home his bride (you can mind the time, Sammy?—when we sung "His wife, like a fair fertile vine, her lovely fruit shall bring," when the young woman turned as red as a rose, not knowing 'twas coming). I've knowed music ever since then, I say, sir, and never heard the like o' that. Every martel note had his name of A, B, C, at that time.'

'Yes, yes, men; but this is a more recent system!'

'Still, you can't alter a old-established note that's A or B by nater,' rejoined Haymoss, with yet deeper conviction that Mr. Torkingham was getting off his head. 'Now sound A, neighbour Sammy, and let's have a slap at Christen sojers again, and show the Pa'son the true way!'

Sammy produced a private tuning-fork, black and grimy, which, being about seventy years of age, and wrought before pianoforte builders had sent up the pitch to make their instruments brilliant, was nearly a note flatter than the parson's. While an argument as to the true pitch was in progress, there came a knocking without.

'Somebody's at the door!' said a little treble girl.

'Thought I heard a knock before!' said the relieved choir.

The latch was lifted, and a man asked from the darkness, 'Is Mr. Torkingham here?'

'Yes, Mills. What do you want?'

It was the parson's man.

'Oh, if you please,' said Mills, showing an advanced margin of himself round the door, 'Lady Constantine wants to see you very particular, sir, and could you call on her after dinner, if you ben't engaged with poor folks? She's just had a letter,—so they say,—and it's about that, I believe.'

Finding, on looking at his watch, that it was necessary to start at once if he meant to see her that night, the parson cut short the practising, and, naming another night for meeting, he withdrew. All the singers assisted him on to his cob, and watched him till he disappeared over the edge of the Bottom.

II

POEMS OF ENGLAND

PUCK'S SONG

SEE you the ferny ride that steals
    Into the oak-woods far?
    O that was whence they hewed the keels
That rolled to Trafalgar.

And mark you where the ivy clings
To Bayham's mouldering walls?
O there we cast the stout railings
That stand around St. Paul's.

See you the dimpled track that runs
All hollow through the wheat?
O that was where they hauled the guns
That smote King Philip's fleet.

(Out of the Weald, the secret Weald,
Men sent in ancient years
The horse-shoes red at Flodden Field,
The arrows at Poitiers!)

See you our little mill that clacks,
So busy by the brook?
She has ground her corn and paid her tax
Ever since Domesday Book.

See you our stilly woods of oak?
And the dread ditch beside?
O that was where the Saxons broke
On the day that Harold died.

See you the windy levels spread
About the gates of Rye?
O that was where the Northmen fled,
When Alfred's ships came by.

See you our pastures wide and lone,
Where the red oxen browse?
O there was a City thronged and known,
Ere London boasted a house.

And see you, after rain, the trace
Of mound and ditch and wall?
O that was a Legion's camping-place,
When Cæsar sailed from Gaul,

And see you marks that show and fade,
Like shadows on the Downs?
O they are the lines the Flint Men made,
To guard their wondrous towns.

Trackway and Camp and City lost,
Salt Marsh where now is corn;
Old Wars, old Peace, old Arts that cease,
And so was England born!

She is not any common Earth,
Water or wood or air,
But Merlin's Isle of Gramarye,
Where you and I will fare!

SUSSEX

God gave all men all earth to love,
 But since our hearts are small,
Ordained for each one spot should prove
 Belovèd over all;
That, as He watched Creation's birth,
 So we, in godlike mood,
May of our love create our earth
 And see that it is good.

So one shall Baltic pines content,
 As one some Surrey glade,
Or one the palm-grove's droned lament
 Before Levuka's Trade.
Each to his choice, and I rejoice
 The lot has fallen to me
In a fair ground—in a fair ground—
 Yea, Sussex by the sea!

No tender-hearted garden crowns,
 No bosomed woods adorn
Our blunt, bow-headed, whale-backed Downs,
 But gnarled and writhen thorn—

Bare slopes where chasing shadows skim,
  And through the gaps revealed
Belt upon belt, the wooded, dim
  Blue goodness of the Weald.

Clean of officious fence or hedge,
  Half-wild and wholly tame,
The wise turf cloaks the white cliff edge
  As when the Romans came.
What sign of those that fought and died
  At shift of sword and sword?
The barrow and the camp abide,
  The sunlight and the sward.

Here leaps ashore the full Sou'west
  All heavy-winged with brine,
Here lies above the folded crest
  The Channel's leaden line:
And here the sea-fogs lap and cling,
  And here, each warning each,
The sheep-bells and the ship-bells ring
  Along the hidden beach.

We have no waters to delight
  Our broad and brookless vales—
Only the dewpond on the height
  Unfed, that never fails,
Whereby no tattered herbage tells
  Which way the season flies—
Only our close-bit thyme that smells
  Like dawn in Paradise.

Here through the strong and shadeless days
  The tinkling silence thrills;
Or little, lost, Down churches praise
  The Lord Who made the hills:
But here the Old Gods guard their round,
  And, in her secret heart,
The heathen kingdom Wilfrid found
  Dreams, as she dwells, apart.

Though all the rest were all my share,
  With equal soul I'd see
Her nine-and-thirty sisters fair,
  Yet none more fair than she.
Choose ye your need from Thames to Tweed,
  And I will choose instead
Such lands as lie 'twixt Rake and Rye,
  Black Down and Beachy Head.

I will go out against the sun
  Where the rolled scarp retires,
And the Long Man of Wilmington
  Looks naked toward the shires;
And east till doubling Rother crawls
  To find the fickle tide,
By dry and sea-forgotten walls,
  Our ports of stranded pride.

I will go north about the shaws
  And the deep ghylls that breed
Huge oaks and old, the which we hold
  No more than Sussex weed;
Or south where windy Piddinghoe's
  Begilded dolphin veers,
And red beside wide-bankèd Ouse
  Lie down our Sussex steers.

So to the land our hearts we give
  Till the sure magic strike,
And Memory, Use, and Love make live
  Us and our fields alike—
That deeper than our speech and thought,
  Beyond our reason's sway,
Clay of the pit whence we were wrought
  Yearns to its fellow-clay.

God gives all men all earth to love,
  But since man's heart is small,
Ordains for each one spot shall prove
  Belovèd over all.

Each to his choice, and I rejoice
The lot has fallen to me
In a fair ground—in a fair ground—
Yea, Sussex by the sea!

THE ROMAN CENTURION'S SONG

Legate, I had the news last night. My cohort's ordered home
By ship to Portus Itius and thence by road to Rome.
I've marched the companies aboard, the arms are stowed below:
Now let another take my sword. Command me not to go!

I've served in Britain forty years, from Vectis to the Wall
I have none other home than this, nor any life at all.
Last night I did not understand, but, now the hour draws near
That calls me to my native land, I feel that land is here.

Here where men say my name was made, here where my work was done,
Here where my dearest dead are laid—my wife—my wife and son;
Here where time, custom, grief and toil, age, memory, service, love,
Have rooted me in British soil. Ah, how shall I remove?

For me this land, that sea, these airs, those folk and fields suffice.
What purple Southern pomp can match our changeful Northern skies,
Black with December snows unshed or pearled with August haze,
The clanging arch of steel-grey March, or June's long-lighted days?

You'll follow widening Rhodanus till vine and olive lean
Aslant before the sunny breeze that sweeps Nemausus clean
To Arelate's triple gate; but let me linger on,
Here where our stiff-necked British oaks confront Euroclydon!

You'll take the old Aurelian Road through shore-descending pines
Where, blue as any peacock's neck, the Tyrrhene Ocean shines.
You'll go where laurel crowns are won, but will you e'er forget
The scent of hawthorn in the sun, or bracken in the wet?

Let me work here for Britain's sake—at any task you will—
A marsh to drain, a road to make or native troops to drill;
Some Western camp (I know the Pict) or granite Border keep,
Mid seas of heather derelict, where our old messmates sleep.

Legate, I come to you in tears—My cohort ordered home!
I've served in Britain forty years. What should I do in Rome?
Here is my heart, my soul, my mind—the only life I know.—
I cannot leave it all behind. Command me not to go!

III

ST. CRISPIN'S DAY

*K*ING HENRY. By Jove, I am not covetous for gold,
  Nor care I who doth feed upon my cost;
  It yearns me not if men my garments wear;
Such outward things dwell not in my desires:
But if it be a sin to covet honour,
I am the most offending soul alive.
No, faith, my coz, wish not a man from England:
God's peace! I would not lose so great an honour

ST. CRISPIN'S DAY

As one man more, methinks, would share from me
For the best hope I have. O, do not wish one more!
Rather proclaim it, Westmoreland, through my host,
That he which hath no stomach to this fight,
Let him depart; his passport shall be made
And crowns for convoy put into his purse:
We would not die in that man's company
That fears his fellowship to die with us.
This day is called the feast of Crispian:
He that outlives this day, and comes safe home,
Will stand a tip-toe when this day is named,
And rouse him at the name of Crispian.
He that shall live this day, and see old age,
Will yearly on the vigil feast his neighbours,
And say 'To-morrow is Saint Crispian':
Then will he strip his sleeve and show his scars,
And say 'These wounds I had on Crispin's day.'
Old men forget; yet all shall be forgot,
But he'll remember with advantages
What feats he did that day: then shall our names,
Familiar in his mouth as household words,
Harry the king, Bedford and Exeter,
Warwick and Talbot, Salisbury and Gloucester,
Be in their flowing cups freshly remember'd.
This story shall the good man teach his son;
And Crispin Crispian shall ne'er go by,
From this day to the ending of the world,
But we in it shall be remembered;
We few, we happy few, we band of brothers;
For he to-day that sheds his blood with me
Shall be my brother; be he ne'er so vile,
This day shall gentle his condition;
And gentlemen in England now a-bed
Shall think themselves accursed they were not here,
And hold their manhoods cheap whiles any speaks
That fought with us upon Saint Crispin's day.

IV

ON BIRDS AND TROUTS

THE BIRDS

NAY more; the very birds of the air, those that be not Hawks, are both so many and so useful and pleasant to mankind, that I must not let them pass without some observations. They both feed and refresh him; feed him with their choice bodies, and refresh him with their heavenly voices. I will not undertake to mention the several kinds of Fowl by which this is done; and his curious palate pleased by day, and which with their very excrements afford him a soft lodging at night. These I will pass by, but not those little nimble musicians of the air, that warble forth their curious ditties, with which nature hath furnished them to the shame of art.

As first the Lark, when she means to rejoice, to cheer herself and those that hear her; she then quits the earth, and sings as she ascends higher into the air, and having ended her heavènly employment, grows then mute, and sad, to think she must descend to the dull earth, which she would not touch, but for necessity.

How do the Blackbird and Thrassel with their melodious voices bid welcome to the cheerful Spring, and in their fixed months warble forth such ditties as no art or instrument can reach to!

Nay, the smaller birds also do the like in their particular seasons, as namely the Laverock, the Tit-lark, the little Linnet, and the honest Robin that loves mankind both alive and dead.

But the Nightingale, another of my airy creatures, breathes such sweet loud music out of her little instrumental throat, that it might make mankind to think miracles are not ceased. He that at midnight, when the very labourer sleeps securely, should hear, as I have very often, the clear airs, the sweet descants, the natural rising and falling, the doubling and redoubling of her voice, might well be lifted above earth, and say, 'Lord, what music hast thou provided for the Saints in Heaven, when thou affordest bad men such music on Earth!'

And this makes me the less to wonder at the many Aviaries in Italy, or at the great charge of Varro his Aviary, the ruins of which are yet to be seen in Rome, and is still so famous there, that it is reckoned for one of those notables which men of foreign nations either record, or lay up in their memories when they return from travel.

This for the birds of pleasure, of which very much more might be said. My next shall be of birds of political use. I think 'tis not to be doubted that Swallows have been taught to carry letters betwixt two armies; but 'tis certain that when the Turks besieged Malta or Rhodes, I now remember not which 'twas, Pigeons are then related to carry and recarry letters. And Mr. G. Sandis, in his 'Travels' (fol. 269) relates it to be done betwixt Aleppo and Babylon. But if that be disbelieved, 'tis not to be doubted that the Dove was sent out of the ark by Noah, to give him notice of land, when to him all appeared to be sea; and the Dove proved a faithful and comfortable messenger. And for the sacrifices of the law, a pair of Turtle-doves, or young Pigeons, were as well accepted as costly Bulls and Rams. And when God would feed the Prophet Elijah (1 Kings xvii.), after a kind of miraculous manner, he did it by Ravens, who brought him meat morning and evening. Lastly, the Holy Ghost, when he descended visibly upon our Saviour, did it by assuming the shape of a Dove. And, to conclude this part of my discourse, pray remember these wonders were done by birds of the air, the element in which they, and I, take so much pleasure.

TROUT FISHING

Now you are to know, that it is observed, that usually the best Trouts are either red or yellow; though some (as the Fordidge Trout) be white and yet good; but that is not usual: and it is a note observable, that the female Trout hath usually a less head, and a deeper body than the male

Trout, and is usually the better meat. And note, that a hogback, and a little head to either Trout, Salmon, or any other fish, is a sign that that fish is in season.

But yet you are to note, that as you see some willows or palm-trees bud and blossom sooner than others do, so some Trouts be, in rivers, sooner in season: and as some hollies or oaks are longer before they cast their leaves, so are some Trouts, in rivers, longer before they go out of season.

And you are to note, that there are several kinds of Trouts, but these several kinds are not considered but by very few men, for they go under the general name of Trouts: just as pigeons do in most places; though it is certain, there are tame and wild pigeons: and of the tame, there be helmits and runts and carriers and cropers, and indeed too many to name. Nay, the Royal Society have found and published lately, that there be thirty and three kinds of spiders; and yet all, for aught I know, go under that one general name of Spider. And 'tis so with many kinds of fish, and of Trouts especially; which differ in their bigness and shape, and spots and colour. The great Kentish hens may be an instance, compared to other hens; and, doubtless, there is a kind of small Trout, which will never thrive to be big, that breeds very many more than others do, that be of a larger size; which you may rather believe, if you consider, that the little wren and titmouse will have twenty young ones at a time, when usually the noble hawk, or the musical thrassel or blackbird exceed not four or five.

And now you shall see me try my skill to catch a Trout; and at my next walking, either this evening or to-morrow morning, I will give you direction how you yourself shall fish for him.

VENATOR. Trust me, master, I see now it is a harder matter to catch a Trout than a Chub: for I have put on patience, and followed you these two hours, and not seen a fish stir, neither at your minnow nor your worm.

PISCATOR. Well, scholar, you must endure worse luck some time, or you will never make a good angler. But what say you now? there is a Trout now, and a good one too, if I can but hold him, and two or three turns more will tire him. Now you see he lies still, and the sleight is to land him: reach me that landing-net. So, Sir, now he is mine own: what say you now? is not this worth all my labour and your patience?

VENATOR. On my word, master, this is a gallant Trout; what shall we do with him?

PISCATOR. Marry, e'en eat him to supper: we'll go to my hostess from whence we came; she told me, as I was going out of door, that my brother Peter, a good angler and a cheerful companion, had sent word he would lodge there to-night, and bring a friend with him. My hostess has two beds, and I know you and I may have the best: we'll rejoice with my brother Peter and his friend, tell tales, or sing ballads, or make a catch, or find some harmless sport to content us, and pass away a little time without offence to God or man.

VENATOR. A match, good master, let's go to that house, for the linen looks white, and smells of lavender, and I long to lie in a pair of sheets that smell so. Let's be going, good master, for I am hungry again with fishing.

PISCATOR. Nay, stay a little, good scholar. I caught my last Trout with a worm; now I will put on a minnow, and try a quarter of an hour about yonder trees for another; and so walk towards our lodging. Look you, scholar, thereabout we shall have a bite presently, or not at all. Have with you, Sir! o' my word I have hold of him! Oh! it is a great logger-headed Chub; come, hang him upon that willow twig, and let's be going. But turn out of the way a little, good scholar, towards yonder high honeysuckle hedge; there we'll sit and sing, whilst this shower falls so gently upon the teeming earth, and gives yet a sweeter smell to the lovely flowers that adorn these verdant meadows.

Look! under that broad beech-tree I sat down, when I was last this way a-fishing; and the birds in the adjoining grove seemed to have a friendly contention with an echo, whose dead voice seemed to live in a hollow tree, near to the brow of that primrose-hill; there I sat viewing the silver streams glide silently towards their centre, the tempestuous sea; yet sometimes opposed by rugged roots, and pebble-stones, which broke their waves, and turned them into foam: and sometimes I beguiled time by viewing the harmless lambs; some leaping securely in the cool shade, whilst others sported themselves in the cheerful sun; and saw others craving comfort from the swollen udders of their bleating dams. As I thus sat, these and other sights had so fully possessed my soul with content, that I thought, as the poet has happily expressed it:—

> I was for that time lifted above earth;
> And possest joys not promis'd in my birth.

As I left this place, and entered into the next field, a second pleasure entertained me; 'twas a handsome milkmaid that had not yet attained so much age and wisdom as to load her mind with any fears of many things that will never be, as too many men too often do; but she cast away all care, and sung like a nightingale. Her voice was good, and the ditty fitted for it; 'twas that smooth song which was made by Kit Marlow, now at least fifty years ago: and the milkmaid's mother sung an answer to it, which was made by Sir Walter Raleigh in his younger days.

They were old-fashioned poetry, but choicely good, I think much better than the strong lines that are now in fashion in this critical age. Look yonder! on my word, yonder they both be a-milking again. I will give her the Chub, and persuade them to sing those two songs to us.

V

A GAME OF CRIBBAGE

WHILE these acts and deeds were in progress in and out of the office of Sampson Brass, Richard Swiveller, being often left alone therein, began to find the time hang heavy on his hands. For the better preservation of his cheerfulness therefore, and to prevent his faculties from rusting, he provided himself with a cribbage-board and pack of cards, and accustomed himself to play at cribbage with a dummy, for twenty, thirty, or sometimes even fifty thousand pounds a side, besides many hazardous bets to a considerable amount.

As these games were very silently conducted, notwithstanding the magnitude of the interests involved, Mr. Swiveller began to think that on those evenings when Mr. and Miss Brass were out (and they often went out now) he heard a kind of snorting or hardbreathing sound in the direction of the door which it occurred to him, after some reflection, must proceed from the small servant, who always had a cold from damp living. Looking intently that way one night, he plainly distinguished an eye gleaming and glistening at the keyhole; and having now no doubt that his suspicions were correct, he stole softly to the door, and pounced upon her before she was aware of his approach.

'Oh! I didn't mean any harm indeed, upon my word I didn't,' cried the small servant, struggling like a much larger one. 'It's so very dull, downstairs. Please don't you tell upon me, please don't.'

'Tell upon you!' said Dick. 'Do you mean to say you were looking through the keyhole for company?'

'Yes, upon my word I was,' replied the small servant.

'How long have you been cooling your eye there?' said Dick.

'Oh ever since you first began to play them cards, and long before.'

Vague recollections of several fantastic exercises with which he had refreshed himself after the fatigues of business, and to all of which, no doubt, the small servant was a party, rather disconcerted Mr. Swiveller; but he was not very sensitive on such points, and recovered himself speedily.

'Well,—come in'—he said, after a little consideration. 'Here—sit down, and I'll teach you how to play.'

'Oh! I durstn't do it,' rejoined the small servant; 'Miss Sally 'ud kill me, if she know'd I come up here.'

'Have you got a fire downstairs?' said Dick.

'A very little one,' replied the small servant.

'Miss Sally couldn't kill me if she know'd I went down there, so I'll come,' said Richard, putting the cards into his pocket. 'Why, how thin you are! What do you mean by it?'

'It an't my fault.'

'Could you eat any bread and meat?' said Dick, taking down his hat. 'Yes? Ah! I thought so. Did you ever taste beer?'

'I had a sip of it once,' said the small servant.

'Here's a state of things!' cried Mr. Swiveller, raising his eyes to the ceiling. 'She *never* tasted it—it can't be tasted in a sip! Why, how old are you?'

'I don't know.'

Mr. Swiveller opened his eyes very wide, and appeared thoughtful for a moment; then, bidding the child mind the door until he came back, vanished straightway.

Presently, he returned, followed by the boy from the public-house, who bore in one hand a plate of bread and beef, and in the other a great pot, filled with some very fragrant compound, which sent forth a grateful steam, and was indeed choice purl, made after a particular recipe which Mr. Swiveller had imparted to the landlord, at a period when he was deep in his books and desirous to conciliate his friendship. Relieving the boy of his burden at the door, and charging his little companion to fasten it to prevent surprise, Mr. Swiveller followed her into the kitchen.

'There!' said Richard, putting the plate before her. 'First of all clear that off, and then you'll see what's next.'

The small servant needed no second bidding, and the plate was soon empty.

'Next,' said Dick, handing the purl, 'take a pull at that; but moderate your transports, you know, for you're not used to it. Well, is it good?'

'Oh! isn't it?' said the small servant.

Mr. Swiveller appeared gratified beyond all expression by this reply, and took a long draught himself: steadfastly regarding his companion while he did so. These prelimin-

A GAME OF CRIBBAGE

aries disposed of, he applied himself to teaching her the game, which she soon learnt tolerably well, being both sharp-witted and cunning.

'Now,' said Mr. Swiveller, putting two sixpences into a saucer, and trimming the wretched candle, when the cards had been cut and dealt, 'those are the stakes. If you win, you get 'em all. If I win, I get 'em. To make it seem more real and pleasant, I shall call you the Marchioness, do you hear?'

The small servant nodded.

'Then, Marchioness,' said Mr. Swiveller, 'fire away!'

The Marchioness, holding her cards very tight in both hands, considered which to play, and Mr. Swiveller, assuming the gay and fashionable air which such society required, took another pull at the tankard, and waited for her lead.

Mr. Swiveller and his partner played several rubbers with varying success, until the loss of three sixpences, the gradual sinking of the purl, and the striking of ten o'clock, combined to render that gentleman mindful of the flight of Time, and the expediency of withdrawing before Mr. Sampson and Miss Sally Brass returned.

'With which object in view, Marchioness,' said Mr. Swiveller gravely, 'I shall ask your ladyship's permission to put the board in my pocket, and to retire from the presence when I have finished this tankard; merely observing, Marchioness, that since life like a river is flowing, I care not how fast it rolls on, ma'am, on, while such purl on the bank still is growing, and such eyes light the waves as they run. Marchioness, your health. You will excuse my wearing my hat, but the palace is damp, and the marble floor is—if I may be allowed the expression—sloppy.'

As a precaution against this latter inconvenience, Mr. Swiveller had been sitting for some time with his feet on the hob, in which attitude he now gave utterance to these apologetic observations, and slowly sipped the last choice drops of nectar.

'The Baron Sampsono Brasso and his fair sister are (you tell me) at the Play?' said Mr. Swiveller, leaning his left arm heavily upon the table, and raising his voice and his right leg after the manner of a theatrical bandit.

The Marchioness nodded.

'Ha!' said Mr. Swiveller, with a portentous frown. ''Tis well. Marchioness!—but no matter. Some wine there. Ho!' He illustrated these melodramatic morsels, by handing the tankard to himself with great humility, receiving it haughtily, drinking from it thirstily, and smacking his lips fiercely.

The small servant, who was not so well acquainted with theatrical conventionalities as Mr. Swiveller (having indeed never seen a play, or heard one spoken of, except by chance through chinks of doors and in other forbidden places), was rather alarmed by demonstrations so novel in their nature, and showed her concern so plainly in her looks, that Mr. Swiveller felt it necessary to discharge his brigand manner for one more suitable to private life, as he asked,

'Do they often go where glory waits 'em, and leave you here?'

'Oh, yes; I believe you they do,' returned the small servant. 'Miss Sally's such a one-er for that, she is.'

'Such a what?' said Dick.

'Such a one-er,' returned the Marchioness.

After a moment's reflection, Mr. Swiveller determined to forgo his responsible duty of setting her right, and to suffer her to talk on; as it was evident that her tongue was loosened by the purl, and her opportunities for conversation were not so frequent as to render a momentary check of little consequence.

'They sometimes go to see Mr. Quilp,' said the small servant with a shrewd look; 'they go to a many places, bless you!'

'Is Mr. Brass a wunner?' said Dick.

'Not half what Miss Sally is, he isn't,' replied the small servant, shaking her head. 'Bless you, he'd never do anything without her.'

'Oh! He wouldn't, wouldn't he?' said Dick.

'Miss Sally keeps him in such order,' said the small servant; 'he always asks her advice, he does; and he catches it sometimes. Bless you, you wouldn't believe how much he catches it.'

'I suppose,' said Dick, 'that they consult together a good deal, and talk about a great many people—about me for instance, sometimes, eh, Marchioness?'

The Marchioness nodded amazingly.

'Complimentary?' said Mr. Swiveller.

The Marchioness changed the motion of her head, which had not yet left off nodding, and suddenly began to shake it from side to side, with a vehemence which threatened to dislocate her neck.

'Humph!' Dick muttered. 'Would it be any breach of confidence, Marchioness, to relate what they say of the humble individual who has now the honour to——?'

'Miss Sally says you're a funny chap,' replied his friend.

'Well, Marchioness,' said Mr. Swiveller, 'that's not uncomplimentary. Merriment, Marchioness, is not a bad or a degrading quality. Old King Cole was himself a merry old soul, if we may put any faith in the pages of history.'

'But she says,' pursued his companion, 'that you an't to be trusted.'

'Why, really, Marchioness,' said Mr. Swiveller, thoughtfully; 'several ladies and gentlemen—not exactly professional persons, but tradespeople, ma'am, tradespeople—have made the same remark. The obscure citizen who keeps the hotel over the way, inclined strongly to that opinion to-night when I ordered him to prepare the banquet. It's a popular prejudice, Marchioness; and yet I am sure I don't know why, for I have been trusted in my time to a considerable amount, and I can safely say that I never forsook my trust until it deserted me—never. Mr. Brass is of the same opinion, I suppose?'

His friend nodded again, with a cunning look which seemed to hint that Mr. Brass held stronger opinions on the subject than his sister; and seeming to recollect herself, added imploringly, 'But don't you ever tell upon me, or I shall be beat to death.'

'Marchioness,' said Mr. Swiveller, rising, 'the word of a gentleman is as good as his bond—sometimes better, as in the present case, where his bond might prove but a doubtful sort of security. I am your friend, and I hope we shall play many more rubbers together in this same saloon. But, Marchioness,' added Richard, stopping in his way to the door, and wheeling slowly round upon the small servant, who was following with the candle; 'it occurs to me that you must be in the constant habit of airing your eye at keyholes, to know all this.'

'I only wanted,' replied the trembling Marchioness, 'to know where the key of the safe was hid; that was all; and I wouldn't have taken much, if I had found it—only enough to squench my hunger.'

'You didn't find it then?' said Dick. 'But of course you didn't, or you'd be plumper. Good night, Marchioness. Fare thee well, and if for ever, then for ever fare thee well —and put up the chain, Marchioness, in case of accidents.'

VI

ENGLAND AT WAR

ATTEND, all ye who list to hear our noble England's praise;
   I tell of the thrice famous deeds she wrought in ancient days,
When that great fleet invincible against her bore in vain
The richest spoils of Mexico, the stoutest hearts of Spain.

It was about the lovely close of a warm summer day,
There came a gallant merchant-ship full sail to Plymouth Bay;
Her crew hath seen Castile's black fleet, beyond Aurigny's isle,
At earliest twilight, on the waves lie heaving many a mile.

At sunrise she escaped their van, by God's especial grace;
And the tall Pinta, till the noon, had held her close in chase.
Forthwith a guard at every gun was placed along the wall;
The beacon blazed upon the roof of Edgecumbe's lofty hall:
Many a light fishing-bark put out to pry along the coast,
And with loose rein and bloody spur rode inland many a post.
With his white hair unbonneted, the stout old sheriff comes;
Behind him march the halberdiers; before him sound the drums;
His yeomen round the market cross make clear an ample space;
For there behoves him to set up the standard of Her Grace.
And haughtily the trumpets peal, and gaily dance the bells,
As slow upon the labouring wind the royal blazon swells.
Look how the Lion of the sea lifts up his ancient crown,
And underneath his deadly paw treads the gay lilies down.
So stalked he when he turned to flight, on that famed Picard field,
Bohemia's plume, and Genoa's bow, and Cæsar's eagle shield.
So glared he when at Agincourt in wrath he turned to bay,
And crushed and torn beneath his claws the princely hunters lay.
Ho! strike the flagstaff deep, Sir Knight: ho! scatter flowers, fair maids:
Ho! gunners, fire a loud salute: ho! gallants, draw your blades:
Thou sun, shine on her joyously; ye breezes, waft her wide;
Our glorious SEMPER EADEM, the banner of our pride.

The freshening breeze of eve unfurled that banner's massy fold;
The parting gleam of sunshine kissed that haughty scroll of gold;
Night sank upon the dusky beach, and on the purple sea,
Such night in England ne'er had been, nor e'er again shall be.
From Eddystone to Berwick bounds, from Lynn to Milford Bay,
That time of slumber was as bright and busy as the day;

For swift to east and swift to west the ghastly war-flame spread,
High on St. Michael's Mount it shone: it shone on Beachy Head.
Far on the deep the Spaniard saw, along each southern shire,
Cape beyond cape, in endless range, those twinkling points of fire.
The fisher left his skiff to rock on Tamar's glittering waves:
The rugged miners poured to war from Mendip's sunless caves:
O'er Longleat's towers, o'er Cranbourne's oaks, the fiery herald flew:
He roused the shepherds of Stonehenge, the rangers of Beaulieu.
Right sharp and quick the bells all night rang out from Bristol town,
And ere the day three hundred horse had met on Clifton down;
The sentinel on Whitehall gate looked forth into the night,
And saw o'erhanging Richmond Hill the streak of blood-red light.
Then bugle's note and cannon's roar the deathlike silence broke,
And with one start, and with one cry, the royal city woke.
At once on all her stately gates arose the answering fires;
At once the wild alarum clashed from all her reeling spires;
From all the batteries of the Tower pealed loud the voice of fear;
And all the thousand masts of Thames sent back a louder cheer:
And from the furthest wards was heard the rush of hurrying feet,
And the broad streams of pikes and flags rushed down each roaring street;
And broader still became the blaze, and louder still the din,
As fast from every village round the horse came spurring in:

And eastward straight from wild Blackheath the warlike errand went,
And roused in many an ancient hall the gallant squires of Kent.
Southward from Surrey's pleasant hills flew those bright couriers forth;
High on bleak Hampstead's swarthy moor they started for the north;
And on, and on, without a pause, untired they bounded still:
All night from tower to tower they sprang; they sprang from hill to hill:
Till the proud peak unfurled the flag o'er Darwin's rocky dales,
Till like volcanoes flared to heaven the stormy hills of Wales,
Till twelve fair counties saw the blaze on Malvern's lonely height,
Till streamed in crimson on the wind the Wrekin's crest of light,
Till broad and fierce the star came forth on Ely's stately fane,
And tower and hamlet rose in arms o'er all the boundless plain;
Till Belvoir's lordly terraces the sign to Lincoln sent,
And Lincoln sped the message on o'er the wide vale of Trent;
Till Skiddaw saw the fire that burned on Gaunt's embattled pile,
And the red glare on Skiddaw roused the burghers of Carlisle

VII

DAVID HARRIS, CRICKETER

DAVID HARRIS was, I believe, born, at all events he lived, at Odiham, in Hampshire; he was by trade a potter. He was a muscular, bony man, standing about five feet nine and a half inches. His features were not regularly handsome, but a remarkably kind and gentle expression amply compensated the defect of mere linear beauty. The fair qualities of his heart shone through his honest face, and I can call to mind no worthier, or, in the active sense of the word, not a more '*good* man' than David Harris. He was one of the rare species that link man to man in bonds of fellowship by good works; that inspire confidence, and prevent the structure of society from becoming disjointed, and, 'as it were, a bowing wall, or a tottering fence.' He was a man of so strict a principle, and such high honour, that I believe his moral character was never impeached. I never heard even a suspicion breathed against his integrity, and I knew him long and intimately. I do not mean that he was a *canter*.—Oh, no —no one thought of standing on guard and buttoning up his pockets in Harris's company. I never busied myself about his mode of faith, or the peculiarity of his creed; that was his own affair, not mine, or any other being's on earth: all I know is, that he was an '*honest man*,' and the poet has assigned the rank of such a one in creation.

It would be difficult, perhaps impossible, to convey in writing an accurate idea of the grand effect of Harris's bowling; they only who have played against him can fully appreciate it. His attitude when preparing for his run previously to delivering the ball would have made a beautiful study for the sculptor. Phidias would certainly have taken him for a model. First of all, he stood erect like a soldier at drill; then, with a graceful curve of the arm, he raised the ball to his forehead, and drawing back his right foot, started off with his left. The calm look and general air of the man were uncommonly striking, and from this series of preparations he never deviated. I am sure that from this simple account of his manner, all my countrymen who were acquainted with his play will recall him to their minds. His mode of delivering the ball was very singular. He would bring it from under the arm by a twist, and nearly as high as his arm-pit, and with this action *push* it, as it were, from him. How it was that the balls acquired the velocity they did by this mode of delivery I never could comprehend.

When first he joined the Hambledon Club, he was quite a

raw countryman at cricket, and had very little to recommend him but his noble delivery. He was also very apt to give tosses. I have seen old Nyren scratch his head, and say—'Harris would make the best bowler in England if he did not toss.' By continual practice, however, and following the advice of the old Hambledon players, he became as steady as could be wished; and in the prime of his playing very rarely indeed gave a toss, although his balls were pitched the full length. In bowling, he never stooped in the least in his delivery, but kept himself upright all the time. His balls were very little beholden to the ground when pitched; it was but a touch, and up again; and woe be to the man who did not get in to block them, for they had such a peculiar curl, that they would grind his fingers against the bat: many a time have I seen the blood drawn in this way from a batter who was not up to the trick; old Tom Walker was the only exception—I have before classed him among the bloodless animals.

Harris's bowling was the finest of all tests for a hitter, and hence the great beauty, as I observed before, of seeing Beldham in, with this man against him; for unless a batter were of the very first class, and accustomed to the best style of stopping, he could do little or nothing with Harris. If the thing had been possible, I should have liked to have seen such a player as Budd (fine hitter as he was) standing against him. My own opinion is that he could not have stopped his balls, and this will be a criterion, by which those who have seen some of that gentleman's brilliant hits may judge of the extraordinary merit of this man's bowling. He was considerably faster than Lambert, and so superior in style and finish that I can draw no comparison between them. Lord Frederick Beauclerc has been heard to say that Harris's bowling was one of the grandest things of the kind he had ever seen; but his lordship could not have known him in his prime; he never saw him play till after he had had many fits of the gout, and had become slow and feeble.

To Harris's fine bowling I attribute the great improvement that was made in hitting, and above all in stopping; for it was utterly impossible to remain at the crease, when the ball was tossed to a fine length; you were obliged to get in, or it would be about your hands, or the handle of your bat; and every player knows where its next place would be.

Some years after Harris had played with the Hambledon Club, he became so well acquainted with the science of the game of cricket that he could take a very great advantage in pitching the wickets. And not only would he pitch a good wicket for himself, but he would also consider those who had to bowl with him. The writer of this has often walked with him up to Windmill-down at six o'clock in the morning of the day that a match was to be played, and has with pleasure noticed the pains he has taken in choosing the ground for his fellow-bowler as well as himself. The most eminent men in every walk of life have at all times been the most painstaking;—slabberdash work and indifference may accompany genius, and it does so too frequently; such geniuses, however, throw away more than half their chance. There are more brilliant talents in this world than people give the world credit for; and that their lustre does not exhibit to the best advantage, commonly depends upon the owners of them. Ill luck, and the preference that frequently attends industrious mediocrity, are the only anodynes that wounded self-love or indolence can administer to misapplied or unused ability. In his walk, Harris was a man of genius, and he let slip no opportunity to maintain his pre-eminence. Although unwilling to detract from the fame of old Lumpy, I must here observe upon the difference in these two men with regard to pitching their wickets. Lumpy would uniformly select a point where the ball was likely to shoot, that is, over the brow of a little hill; and when by this forethought and contrivance the old man would prove successful in bowling his men out, he would turn round to his party with a little grin of triumph; nothing gratified him like this reward of his knowingness. Lumpy, however, thought only of himself in choosing his ground; his fellow-bowler might take his chance; this was neither wise nor liberal. Harris, on the contrary, as I have already observed, considered his partner; and, in so doing, the main chance of the game. Unlike Lumpy, too, he would choose a rising ground to pitch the ball against, and he who is well acquainted with the game of cricket will at once perceive the advantage that must arise from a wicket pitched in this way to such a tremendous bowler as Harris was. If I were urged to draw a comparison between these two great players, the greatest certainly in their department I ever saw, I could do it in no other way than the following:—Lumpy's ball was always pitched to the length, but delivered lower than Harris's, and never got up so high; he was also slower than Harris, and lost his advantage by the way in which he persisted in pitching his wicket; yet I think he would bowl more wickets down than the other, for the latter never pitched his wicket with this end in view; almost all his balls, therefore, rose over the wicket; consequently, more players would be caught out from Harris than Lumpy, and not half the number of runs got from his bowling. I passed a very pleasant time with Harris when he came to my father's house at Hambledon, by invitation, after an illness, and for the benefit of the change of air. Being always his companion in his walks about the neighbourhood, I had full opportunity of observing the sweetness of his disposition; this, with his manly contempt of every action that bore the character of meanness, gained him the admiration of every cricketer in Hambledon.

In concluding my recollections of Harris, I had wellnigh omitted to say something of his skill in the other departments of the game. The fact is, the extraordinary merit of his bowling would have thrown any other fair accomplishments he might possess into the shade; but, indeed, as a batter, I considered him rather an indifferent hand; I never recollect his getting more than ten runs, and those very rarely. Neither was his fielding remarkable. But he was game to the backbone, and never suffered a ball to pass him without putting his body in the way of it.

VIII

PARTRIDGE AT THE PLAY

IN the first row then of the first gallery did Mr. Jones, Mrs. Miller, her youngest daughter, and Partridge, take their places. Partridge immediately declared it was the finest place he had ever been in. When the first music was played, he said, 'It was a wonder how so many fiddlers could play at one time, without putting one another out.' While the fellow was lighting the upper candles, he cried out to Mrs. Miller, 'Look, look, madam, the very picture of the man in the end of the common-prayer book before the gunpowder-treason service.' Nor could he help observing, with a sigh, when all the candles were lighted, 'That here were candles enough burnt in one night to keep an honest poor family for a whole twelvemonth.'

As soon as the play, which was Hamlet, Prince of Denmark, began, Partridge was all attention, nor did he break silence till the entrance of the ghost; upon which he asked Jones, 'What man that was in the strange dress; something,' said he, 'like what I have seen in the picture. Sure it is not armour, is it?' Jones answered, 'That is the ghost.' To which Partridge replied with a smile, 'Persuade me to that, sir, if you can. Though I can't say I ever actually saw a ghost in my life, yet I am certain I should know one, if I saw him, better than that comes to. No, no, sir, ghosts don't appear in such dresses as that, neither.' In this mistake, which caused much laughter in the neighbourhood of Partridge, he was suffered to continue, till the scene between the ghost and Hamlet, when Partridge gave that credit to Mr. Garrick, which he had denied to Jones, and fell into so violent a trembling that his knees knocked against each other. Jones asked him what was the matter, and whether he was afraid of the warrior upon the stage? 'O la! sir,' said he, 'I perceive now it is what you told me. I am not afraid of anything; for I know it is but a play. And if it was really a ghost, it could do one no harm at such a distance, and in so much company; and yet if I was frightened, I am not the only person.' 'Why, who,' cries Jones, 'dost thou take to be such a coward here besides thyself?' 'Nay, you may call me coward if you will; but if that little man there upon the stage is not frightened, I never saw any man frightened in my life. Ay, ay: go along with you! Ay, to be sure! Who's fool then? Will you? Lud have mercy upon such fool-hardiness? Whatever happens, it is good enough for you. Follow you? I'd follow the devil as soon. Nay, perhaps it is the devil—for they say, he can put on what likeness he pleases. Oh! here he is again. No farther! No, you have gone far enough already; farther than I'd have gone for all the king's dominions.' Jones offered to speak, but Partridge cried, 'Hush! hush! dear sir, don't you hear him?' And during the whole speech of the ghost, he sat with his eyes fixed partly on the ghost and partly on Hamlet, and with his mouth open; the same passions which succeeded each other in Hamlet, succeeding likewise in him.

When the scene was over Jones said, 'Why, Partridge, you exceed my expectations. You enjoy the play more than I conceived possible.' 'Nay, sir,' answered Partridge, 'if you are not afraid of the devil, I can't help it; but to be sure, it is natural to be surprised at such things, though I know there is nothing in them: not that it was the ghost that surprised me, neither; for I should have known that to have been only a man in a strange dress; but when I saw the little man so frightened himself, it was that which took hold of me.' 'And dost thou imagine, then, Partridge,' cries Jones, 'that he was really frightened?' 'Nay, sir,' said Partridge, 'did not you yourself observe afterwards, when he found it was his own father's spirit, and how he was murdered in the garden, how his fear forsook him by degrees, and he was struck dumb with sorrow, as it were, just as I should have been, had it been my own case? But hush! O la! what noise is that? There he is again. Well, to be certain, though I know there is nothing at all in it, I am glad I am not down yonder, where those men are.' Then turning his eyes again upon Hamlet, 'Ay, you may draw your sword; what signifies a sword against the power of the devil?'

During the second act Partridge made very few remarks. He greatly admired the fineness of the dresses; nor could he help observing upon the king's countenance. 'Well,' said he, 'how people may be deceived by faces! *Nulla fides fronti* is, I find, a true saying. Who would think, by looking in the king's face, that he had ever committed a murder?' He then inquired after the ghost; but Jones, who intended he should be surprised, gave him no other satisfaction than, 'that he might possibly see him again soon, and in a flash of fire.'

Partridge sat in fearful expectation of this; and now, when the ghost made his next appearance Partridge cried out, 'There, sir, now; what say you now? is he frightened now or no? As much frightened as you think me, and, to be sure, nobody can help some fears. I would not be in so bad a condition as what's his name, squire Hamlet, is there, for all the world. Bless me! what's become of the spirit? As I am a living soul, I thought I saw him sink into the earth.' 'Indeed, you saw right,' answered Jones. 'Well, well,' cries Partridge, 'I know it is only a play; and besides, if there was anything in all this, Madam Miller would not laugh so; for as to you, sir, you would not be afraid, I believe, if the devil was here in person. There, there—Ay, no wonder you are in such a passion, shake the vile wicked wretch to pieces. If she was my own mother, I would serve her so. To be sure all duty to a mother is forfeited by such wicked doings—Ay, go about your business, I hate the sight of you.'

Our critic was now pretty silent till the play which Hamlet introduces before the king. This he did not at first understand, till Jones explained it to him; but he no sooner entered into the spirit of it, than he began to bless himself that he had never committed murder. Then turning to Mrs. Miller, he asked her, 'If she did not imagine the king looked as if he was touched; though he is,' said he, 'a good actor, and doth all he can to hide it. Well, I would not have so much to answer for, as that wicked man there hath, to sit upon a much higher chair than he sits upon. No wonder he run away; for your sake I'll never trust an innocent face again.'

The grave-digging scene next engaged the attention of Partridge, who expressed much surprise at the number of skulls thrown upon the stage. To which Jones answered, 'That it was one of the most famous burial-places about town.' 'No wonder then,' cries Partridge, 'that the place is haunted. But I never saw in my life a worse gravedigger. I had a sexton, when I was clerk, that should have dug three graves while he is digging one. The fellow handles a spade as if it was the first time he had ever had one in his hand. Ay, ay, you may sing. You had rather sing than work, I believe.' Upon Hamlet's taking up the skull, he cried out, 'Well! it is strange to see how fearless some men are: I never could bring myself to touch anything belonging to a dead man, on any account. He seemed frightened enough too at the ghost, I thought. *Nemo omnibus horis sapit.*'

Little more worth remembering occurred during the play, at the end of which Jones asked him, 'Which of the players he had liked best?' To this he answered, with some appearance of indignation at the question, 'The king, without doubt.' 'Indeed, Mr. Partridge,' says Mrs. Miller, 'you are not of the same opinion with the town; for they are all agreed that Hamlet is acted by the best player who ever was on the stage.' 'He the best player!' cries Partridge, with a contemptuous sneer, 'why, I could act as well as he myself. I am sure, if I had seen a ghost, I should have looked in the very same manner, and done just as he did. And then, to be sure, in that scene, as you called it, between him and his mother, where you told me he acted so fine, why, Lord help me, any man, that is, any good man, that had such a mother, would have done exactly the same. I know you are only joking with me; but indeed, madam, though I was never to a play in London, yet I have seen acting before in the country; and the king for my money; he speaks all his words distinctly, half as loud again as the other. Anybody may see he is an actor.'

IX

THE LAST FIGHT OF THE 'REVENGE'

THE names of Her Majesty's ships were these as followeth: the *Defiance*, which was admiral; the *Revenge*, vice-admiral; the *Bonaventure*, commanded by Captain Cross; the *Lion*, by George Fenner; the *Foresight*, by Master Thomas Vavisour; and the *Crane*, by Duffeild. The *Foresight* and the *Crane* being but small ships; only the other were of the middle size; the rest, besides the barque *Ralegh*, commanded by Captain Thin, were victuallers, and of small force or none. The Spanish fleet having shrouded their approach by reason of the island, were now so soon at hand as our ships had scarce time to weigh their anchors, but some of them were driven to let slip their cables, and set sail. Sir Richard Grinvile was the last weighed, to recover the men that were upon the island, which otherwise had been lost. The Lord Thomas with the rest very hardly recovered the wind, which Sir Richard Grinvile not being able to do, was persuaded by the Master and others to cut his mainsail and cast about, and to trust to the sailing of his ship: for the squadron of Sivil were on his weather-bow.

But Sir Richard utterly refused to turn from the enemy, alleging that he would rather choose to die than to dishonour himself, his country, and her Majesty's ship, persuading his company that he would pass through the two squadrons, in despite of them, and enforce those of Sivil to give him way. Which he performed upon divers of the foremost, who, as the mariners term it, sprang their luff, and fell under the lee of the *Revenge*. But the other course had been the better, and might right well have been answered in so great an impossibility of prevailing. Notwithstanding, out of the greatness of his mind, he could not be persuaded. In the meanwhile as he attended those which were nearest him, the great *San Philip* being in the wind of him, and coming towards him, becalmed his sails in such sort, as the ship could neither weigh nor feel the helm: so huge and high cargued was the Spanish ship, being of a thousand and five hundred tons. Who after laid the *Revenge* aboard. When he was thus bereft of his sails, the ships that were under his lee luffing up, also laid him aboard: of which the next was the Admiral of the *Biscaines*, a very mighty and puissant ship commanded by Brittan Dona. The said *Philip* carried three tier of ordnance on a side, and eleven pieces in every tier. She shot eight forth right out of her chase, besides those of her stern ports.

After the *Revenge* was intangled with this *Philip*, four other boarded her: two on her larboard, and two on her starboard. The fight, thus beginning at three of the clock in the afternoon, continued very terrible all that evening. But the great *San Philip* having received the lower tier of the *Revenge*, discharged with crossbarshot, shifted herself with all diligence from her sides, utterly misliking her first entertainment. Some say that the ship foundered, but we cannot report it for truth, unless we were assured. The Spanish ships were filled with companies of soldiers, in some two hundred besides the mariners; in some five, in others eight hundred. In ours there were none at all, beside the mariners, but the servants of the commanders and some few voluntary gentlemen only. After many interchanged volleys of great ordnance and small shot, the Spaniards deliberated to enter the *Revenge*, and made divers attempts, hoping to force her by the multitudes of their armed soldiers and musketeers, but were still repulsed again and again, and at all times beaten back, into their own ships, or into the seas. In the beginning of the fight, the *George Noble* of London, having received some shot through her by the Armadoes, fell under the lee of the *Revenge*, and asked Sir Richard what he would command him, being but one of the victuallers and of small force: Sir Richard bid him save himself, and leave him to his fortune.

After the fight had thus without intermission continued while the day lasted and some hours of the night, many of our men were slain and hurt, and one of the great galleons of the Armada, and the admiral of the Hulks both sunk, and in many other of the Spanish ships great slaughter was made. Some write that Sir Richard was very dangerously hurt almost in the beginning of the fight, and lay speechless for a time ere he recovered. But two of the *Revenge's* own company brought home in a ship of Lime from the Islands, examined by some of the Lords and others, affirmed that he was never so wounded as that he forsook the upper deck, till an hour before midnight; and then being shot into the body with a musket as he was a-dressing, was again shot into the head, and withal his Chirurgeon wounded to death. This agreeth also with an examination taken by Sir Frances Godolphin, of four other mariners of the same ship being returned, which examination the said Sir Frances sent unto Mr. William Killigrue, of her Majesty's Privy Chamber.

But to return to the fight: the Spanish ships which attempted to board the *Revenge*, as they were wounded and beaten off, so always others came in their places, she having never less than two mighty galleons by her sides, and aboard her. So that ere the morning from three of the clock the day before, there had fifteen several Armadoes assailed her; and all so ill approved their entertainment, as they were by the break of day far more willing to hearken to a composition than hastily to make any more assaults or entries. But as the day increased, so our men decreased: and as the light grew more and more, by so much more grew our discomforts. For none appeared in sight but enemies, saving one small ship called the *Pilgrim*, commanded by Jacob Whiddon, who hovered all night to see the success: but, in the morning bearing with the *Revenge*, was hunted like a hare amongst many ravenous hounds, but escaped.

All the powder of the *Revenge* to the last barrel was now spent, all her pikes broken, forty of her best men slain, and the most part of the rest hurt. In the beginning of the fight she had but one hundred free from sickness, and fourscore and ten sick, laid in hold upon the ballast. A small troop to man such a ship, and a weak garrison to resist so mighty an army. By those hundred all was sustained, the volleys, boardings, and enterings of fifteen ships of war, besides those which beat her at large. On the contrary, the Spanish were always supplied with soldiers brought from every squadron: all manner of arms and powder at will. Unto ours there remained no comfort at all, no hope, no supply either of ships, men, or weapons; the masts all beaten overboard, all her tackle cut asunder, her upper work altogether rased, and in effect evened she was with the water, but the very foundation or bottom of a ship, nothing being left overhead either for flight or defence.

Sir Richard finding himself in this distress, and unable any longer to make resistance, having endured in this fifteen hours' fight the assault of fifteen several Armadoes, all by turns aboard him, and by estimation eight hundred shot of great artillery, besides many assaults and entries; and that himself and the ship must needs be possessed by the enemy, who were now all cast in a ring round about him; the *Revenge* not able to move one way or other, but as she was moved with the waves and billow of the sea: commanded the Master-Gunner, whom he knew to be a most resolute man, to split and sink the ship; that thereby nothing might remain of glory or victory to the Spaniards, seeing in so many hours' fight, and with so great a navy they were not able to take her, having had fifteen hours' time, fifteen thousand men, and fifty and three sail of men-of-war to perform it withal: and persuaded the company, or as many as he could induce, to yield themselves unto God, and to the mercy of none else.

X

THE WINCHESTER COUNTRY

BURGHCLERE, MONDAY MORNING,
31st October, 1825.

WE had, or I had, resolved not to breakfast at Winchester yesterday: and yet we were detained till nearly noon. But, at last off we came, *fasting*. The turnpike road from Winchester to this place comes through a village, called Sutton Scotney, and then through Whitchurch, which lies on the Andover and London road, through Basingstoke. We did not take the cross-turnpike till we came to Whitchurch. We went to King's Worthy; that is, about two miles on the road from Winchester to London; and then, turning short to our left, came up upon the downs to the north of Winchester race-course. Here, looking back at the city and at the fine valley above and below it, and at the many smaller valleys that run down from the high ridges into that great and fertile valley, I could not help admiring the taste of the ancient kings, who made this city (which once covered all the hill round about, and which contained 92 churches and chapels) a chief place of their residence. There are not many finer spots in England; and if I were to take in a circle of eight or ten miles of semi-diameter, I should say that I believe there is not one so fine. Here are hill, dell, water, meadows, woods, corn-fields, downs: and all of them very fine and very beautifully disposed. This country does not present to us that sort of beauties which we see about Guildford and Godalming, and round the skirts of Hindhead and Blackdown, where the ground lies in the form that the surface-water in a boiling copper would be in, if you could, by word of command, *make it be still*, the variously-shaped bubbles all sticking up; and really, to look at the face of the earth, who can help imagining, that some such process has produced its present form? Leaving this matter to be solved by those who laugh at mysteries, I repeat, that the country round Winchester does not present to us beauties of *this sort*; but of a sort which I like a great deal better. Arthur Young calls the vale between Farnham and Alton *the finest ten miles* in England. Here is a river with fine meadows on each side of it, and with rising grounds on each outside of the meadows, those grounds having some hop-gardens and some pretty woods. But, though I was born in this vale, I must confess, that the ten miles between Maidstone and Tunbridge (which the Kentish folks call the *Garden of Eden*) is a great deal finer; for here, with a river three times as big, and a vale three times as broad, there are, on rising grounds six times as broad, not only hop-gardens and beautiful woods, but immense orchards of apples, pears, plums, cherries and filberts, and these, in many cases, with gooseberries and currants and raspberries beneath; and, all taken together, the vale is really worthy of the appellation which it bears. But, even this spot, which I believe to be the very finest, as to fertility and diminutive beauty, in this whole world, I, for my part, do not like so well; nay, as a spot to *live on* I think nothing at all of it, compared with a country where high downs prevail, with here and there a large wood on the top or the side of a hill, and where you see, in the deep dells, here and there a farm-house, and here and there a village, the buildings sheltered by a group of lofty trees.

This is my taste, and here, in the north of Hampshire, it has its full gratification. I like to look at the winding side of a great down, with two or three numerous flocks of sheep on it, belonging to different farms; and to see, lower down, the folds, in the fields, ready to receive them for the night. We had, when we got upon the downs, after leaving Winchester, this sort of country all the way to Whitchurch. Our point of destination was this village of Burghclere, which lies close under the north side of the lofty hill at Highclere, which is called Beacon-hill, and on the top of which there are still the marks of a Roman encampment. We saw this hill as soon as we got on Winchester downs; and without any regard to *roads*, we *steered* for it, as sailors do for a land-mark. Of these 13 miles (from Winchester to Whitchurch) we rode about eight or nine upon the *greensward*, or over fields equally smooth. And, here is one great pleasure of living in countries of this sort: no sloughs, no ditches, no nasty dirty lanes, and the hedges, where there are any, are more for boundary marks than for fences. Fine for hunting and coursing: no impediments; no gates to open; nothing to impede the dogs, the horses, or the view. The water is not *seen running*; but the great bed of chalk *holds it*, and the sun draws it up for the benefit of the grass and the corn; and, whatever inconvenience is experienced from the necessity of deep wells, and of driving sheep and cattle far to water, is amply made up for by the goodness of the water, and by the complete absence of floods, of drains, of ditches and of water-furrows. As *things now are*, however, these countries have one great drawback: the poor day-labourers suffer from the want of fuel, and they have nothing but their *bare pay*. For these reasons they are greatly worse off than those of the *woodland countries*; and it is really surprising what a difference there is between the faces that you see here, and the round, red faces that you see in the *wealds* and the *forests*, particularly in Sussex, where the labourers *will* have a *meat-pudding* of some sort or other; and where they *will* have *a fire* to sit by in the winter.

After steering for some time, we came down to a very fine farm-house, which we stopped a little to admire; and I asked Richard whether *that* was not a place to be happy in. The village, which we found to be Stoke-Charity, was about a mile lower down this little vale. Before we got to it, we overtook the owner of the farm, who knew me, though I did not know him; but, when I found it was Mr. Hinton Bailey, of whom and whose farm I had heard so much, I was not at all surprised at the fineness of what I had just seen. I told him that the word *charity*, making, as it did, part of the name of this place, had nearly inspired me with boldness enough to go to the farm-house, in the ancient style, and ask for something to eat; for, that we had not yet breakfasted. He asked us to go back; but, at Burghclere we were *resolved to dine*. After, however, crossing the village, and beginning again to ascend the downs, we came to a labourer's (*once a farm-house*), where I asked the man, whether he had any *bread and cheese*, and was not a little pleased to hear him say '*Yes*.' Then I asked him to give us a bit, protesting that we had not yet broken our fast. He answered in the affirmative, at once, though I did not talk of payment. His wife brought out the cut loaf, and a piece of Wiltshire cheese, and I took them in hand, gave Richard a good hunch, and took another for myself. I verily believe, that all the pleasure of eating enjoyed by all the feeders in London in a whole year, does not equal that which we enjoyed in gnawing this bread and cheese, as we rode over this cold down, whip and bridle-reins in one hand, and the hunch in the other. Richard, who was purse bearer, gave the woman, by my direction, about enough to buy two quartern loaves: for she told me, that they had to buy their bread at *the mill*, not being able to bake themselves for *want of fuel*; and this, as I said before, is one of the draw-backs in this sort of country. I wish every one of these people had an *American fire-place*. Here they might, then, even in these bare countries have comfortable warmth. Rubbish of any sort would, by this means, give them warmth. I am now, at six o'clock in the morning, sitting in a room, where one of these fire-places, with very light *turf* in it, gives as good and steady a warmth as it is possible to feel, and which room has, too, been *cured of smoking* by this fire-place.

Before we got this supply of bread and cheese, we, though in ordinary times a couple of singularly jovial companions, and seldom going a hundred yards (except going very fast) without one or the other speaking, began to grow *dull*, or rather *glum*. The way seemed long; and, when I had to speak in answer to Richard, the speaking was as brief as might be. Unfortunately, just as this critical period, one of the loops that held the straps of Richard's little portmanteau broke; and it became necessary (just before we overtook Mr. Bailey) for me to fasten the portmanteau on before me, upon my saddle. This, which was not the work of more than five minutes, would, had I had *a breakfast*, have been nothing at all, and, indeed, matter of laughter. But, *now*, it was *something*. It was his *'fault'* for capering and jerking about '*so*.' I jumped off, saying, '*Here!* I'll carry it *myself*.' And then I began to take off the remaining strap, pulling, with great violence and in great haste. Just at this time, my eyes met his, in which I saw *great surprise*; and, feeling the just rebuke, feeling heartily ashamed of myself, I instantly changed my tone and manner, cast the blame upon the saddler, and talked of the effectual means which we would take to prevent the like in future.

Now, if such was the effect produced upon me by the want of food for only two or three hours; me, who had dined well the day before and eaten toast and butter the over-night; if the missing of only one breakfast, and that, too, from my own whim, while I had money in my pocket, to get one at any public-house, and while I could get one only for asking for at any farm-house; if the not having breakfasted could, and under such circumstances, make me what you may call '*cross*' to a child like this, whom I must necessarily love so much, and to whom I never speak but in the very kindest manner; if this mere absence of a breakfast could thus put me *out of temper*, how great are the allowances that we ought to make for the poor creatures, who, in this once happy and now miserable country, are doomed to lead a life of constant labour and of half-starvation. I suppose, that, as we rode away from the cottage, we gnawed up, between us, a pound of bread and a quarter of a pound of cheese. Here was about *five-pence* worth at present prices. Even this, which was only a mere *snap*, a mere *stay-stomach*, for us, would, for us two, come to 3s. a week all but a penny. How, then, gracious God! is a labouring man, his wife, and, perhaps, four or five small children, to exist upon 8s. or 9s. a week! Aye, and to find house-rent, clothing, bedding and fuel out of it? Richard and I ate here, at this snap, more, and much more, than the average of labourers, their wives and children, have to eat in a whole day, and that the labourer has to *work* on too!

XI

NINE SONGS FROM SHAKESPEARE

I

O MISTRESS mine, where are you roaming?
    O stay and hear! your true-love's coming
        That can sing both high and low;
Trip no further, pretty sweeting,
Journeys end in lovers' meeting—
    Every wise man's son doth know.

What is love? 'tis not hereafter;
Present mirth hath present laughter;
    What's to come is still unsure:
In delay there lies no plenty,—
Then come kiss me, Sweet-and-twenty,
    Youth's a stuff will not endure.

II

Under the greenwood tree
Who loves to lie with me,
And tune his merry note
Unto the sweet bird's throat—
Come hither, come hither, come hither!
    Here shall he see
    No enemy
But winter and rough weather.

Who doth ambition shun
And loves to live i' the sun,
Seeking the food he eats
And pleased with what he gets—
Come hither, come hither, come hither!
    Here shall he see
    No enemy
But winter and rough weather.

III

Orpheus with his lute made trees,
And the mountain tops that freeze,
   Bow themselves when he did sing:
To his music plants and flowers
Ever sprung, as sun and showers
   There had made a lasting spring.

Every thing that heard him play,
Even the billows of the sea,
   Hung their heads, and then lay by.
In sweet music is such art,
Killing care and grief of heart
   Fall asleep, or hearing die.

IV

Come away, come away, Death,
And in sad cypress let me be laid;
   Fly away, fly away, breath;
I am slain by a fair cruel maid.
My shroud of white, stuck all with yew,
      O prepare it!
My part of death, no one so true
      Did share it.

Not a flower, not a flower sweet
On my black coffin let there be strown;
   Not a friend, not a friend greet
My poor corpse, where my bones shall be thrown:
A thousand thousand sighs to save,
      Lay me, O where
Sad true lover never find my grave
      To weep there.

V

When that I was and a little tiny boy,
   With hey, ho, the wind and the rain,
A foolish thing was but a toy,
   For the rain it raineth every day.

But when I came to man's estate,
  With hey, ho, the wind and the rain,
'Gainst knaves and thieves men shut their gate,
  For the rain it raineth every day.

But when I came, alas! to wive,
  With hey, ho, the wind and the rain,
By swaggering could I never thrive,
  For the rain it raineth every day.

A great while ago the world begun,
  With hey, ho, the wind and the rain,
But that's all one, our play is done,
  And we'll strive to please you every day.

VI

It was a lover and his lass
  With a hey and a ho, and a hey-nonino!
That o'er the green cornfield did pass
In the spring time, the only pretty ring time,
When birds do sing hey ding a ding ding:
  Sweet lovers love the Spring.

Between the acres of the rye
These pretty country folks would lie:
This carol they began that hour,
How that life was but a flower:

And therefore take the present time
  With a hey and a ho, and a hey-nonino!
For love is crownéd with the prime
In spring time, the only pretty ring time,
When birds do sing hey ding a ding ding:
  Sweet lovers love the Spring.

VII

When icicles hang by the wall
  And Dick the shepherd blows his nail,
  And Tom bears logs into the hall,
    And milk comes frozen home in pail;

When blood is nipt, and ways be foul,
Then nightly sings the staring owl
      Tuwhoo!
Tuwhit! tuwhoo! A merry note!
While greasy Joan doth keel the pot.

When all around the wind doth blow
   And coughing drowns the parson's saw,
And birds sit brooding in the snow,
   And Marian's nose looks red and raw;
When roasted crabs hiss in the bowl—
Then nightly sings the staring owl
        Tuwhoo!
Tuwhit! tuwhoo! A merry note!
While greasy Joan doth keel the pot.

VIII

Blow, blow, thou winter wind,
Thou art not so unkind
As man's ingratitude:
Thy tooth is not so keen
Because thou art not seen,
Although thy breath be rude.
Heigh ho! sing heigh ho! unto the green holly:
Most friendship is feigning, most loving mere folly:
   Then heigh ho! the holly!
   This life is most jolly.

Freeze, freeze, thou bitter sky,
Thou dost not bite so nigh
As benefits forgot:
Though thou the waters warp,
Thy sting is not so sharp
As friend remember'd not.
Heigh ho! sing heigh ho! unto the green holly:
Most friendship is feigning, most loving mere folly:
   Then heigh ho! the holly!
   This life is most jolly.

IX

Fear no more the heat o' the sun
    Nor the furious winter's rages;
Thou thy worldly task hast done,
    Home art gone and ta'en thy wages:
Golden lads and girls all must,
As chimney-sweepers, come to dust.

Fear no more the frown o' the great,
    Thou art past the tyrant's stroke;
Care no more to clothe and eat;
    To thee the reed is as the oak:
The sceptre, learning, physic, must
All follow this, and come to dust.

Fear no more the lightning-flash
    Nor the all-dreaded thunder-stone;
Fear not slander, censure rash;
    Thou hast finish'd joy and moan:
All lovers young, all lovers must
Consign to thee, and come to dust.

XII

MR. MICAWBER'S TRANSACTIONS

'WELL, Mr. and Mrs. Micawber,' was my aunt's first salutation after we were seated. 'Pray, have you thought about that emigration proposal of mine?'

'My dear madam,' returned Mr. Micawber, 'perhaps I cannot better express the conclusion at which Mrs. Micawber, your humble servant, and I may add our children, have jointly and severally arrived, than by borrowing the language of an illustrious poet, to reply that our Boat is on the shore, and our Bark is on the sea.'

'That's right,' said my aunt. 'I augur all sorts of good from your sensible decision.'

'Madam, you do us a great deal of honour,' he rejoined. He then referred to a memorandum. 'With respect to the pecuniary assistance enabling us to launch our frail canoe on the ocean of enterprise, I have reconsidered that important business point; and would beg to propose my notes of hand—drawn, it is needless to stipulate, on stamps of the amounts respectively required by the various Acts of Parliament applying to such securities—at eighteen, twenty-four, and thirty months. The proposition I originally submitted, was twelve, eighteen, and twenty-four; but I am apprehensive that such an arrangement might not allow sufficient time for the requisite amount of—Something—to turn up. We might not,' said Mr. Micawber, looking round the room as if it represented several hundred acres of highly cultivated land, 'on the first responsibility becoming due, have been successful in our harvest, or we might not have got our harvest in. Labour, I believe, is sometimes difficult to obtain in that portion of our colonial possessions where it will be our lot to combat with the teeming soil.'

'Arrange it in any way you please, sir,' said my aunt.

'Madam,' he replied, 'Mrs. Micawber and myself are deeply sensible of the very considerate kindness of our friends and patrons. What I wish is, to be perfectly business-like, and perfectly punctual. Turning over, as we are about to turn over, an entirely new leaf, and falling back, as we are now in the act of falling back, for a Spring of no common magnitude; it is important to my sense of self-respect, besides being an example to my son, that these arrangements should be concluded as between man and man.'

I don't know that Mr. Micawber attached any meaning to this last phrase; I don't know that anybody ever does, or did; but he appeared to relish it uncommonly, and repeated, with an impressive cough, 'as between man and man.'

'I propose,' said Mr. Micawber, 'Bills—a convenience to the mercantile world, for which, I believe, we are originally indebted to the Jews, who appear to me to have had a devilish deal too much to do with them ever since—because they are negotiable. But if a Bond, or any other description of security, would be preferred, I should be happy to execute any such instrument. As between man and man.'

My aunt observed, that in a case where both parties were willing to agree to anything, she took it for granted there would be no difficulty in settling this point. Mr. Micawber was of her opinion.

'In reference to our domestic preparations, madam,' said Mr. Micawber, with some pride, 'for meeting the destiny to which we are now understood to be self-devoted, I beg to report them. My eldest daughter attends at five every morning in a neighbouring establishment, to acquire the process—if process it may be called—of milking cows. My younger children are instructed to observe, as closely as circumstances will permit, the habits of the pigs and poultry maintained in the poorer parts of this city: a pursuit from which they have, on two occasions, been brought home within an inch of being run over. I have myself directed some attention, during the past week, to the art of baking: and my son Wilkins has issued forth with a walking-stick and driven cattle, when permitted, by the rugged hirelings who had them in charge, to render any voluntary service in that direction—which I regret to say, for the credit of our nature, was not often; he being generally warned, with imprecations, to desist.'

'All very right indeed,' said my aunt, encouragingly. 'Mrs. Micawber has been busy, too, I have no doubt.'

'My dear madam,' returned Mrs. Micawber, with her business-like air, 'I am free to confess, that I have not been actively engaged in pursuits immediately connected with cultivation or with stock, though well aware that both will claim my attention on a foreign shore. Such opportunities as I have been enabled to alienate from my domestic duties, I have devoted to corresponding at some length with my family. For I own it seems to me, my dear Mr. Copperfield,' said Mrs. Micawber, who always fell back on me (I suppose from old habit) to whomsoever else she might address her discourse at starting, 'that the time is come when the past should be buried in oblivion; when my family should take Mr. Micawber by the hand, and Mr. Micawber should take my family by the hand; when the lion should lie down with the lamb, and my family be on terms with Mr. Micawber.'

I said I thought so too.

'This, at least, is the light, my dear Mr. Copperfield,' pursued Mrs. Micawber, 'in which *I* view the subject. When I lived at home with my papa and mama, my papa was accustomed to ask, when any point was under discussion in our limited circle, "In what light does my Emma view the subject?" That my papa was too partial, I know; still, on such a point as the frigid coldness which has ever subsisted between Mr. Micawber and my family, I necessarily have formed an opinion, delusive though it may be.'

'No doubt. Of course you have, ma'am,' said my aunt.

'Precisely so,' assented Mrs. Micawber. 'Now, I may be wrong in my conclusions; it is very likely that I am; but my individual impression is, that the gulf between my family and Mr. Micawber may be traced to an apprehension, on the part of my family, that Mr. Micawber would require pecuniary accommodation. I cannot help thinking,' said Mrs. Micawber, with an air of deep sagacity, 'that there are members of my family who have been apprehensive that Mr. Micawber would solicit them for their names.—I do not mean to be conferred in Baptism upon our children, but to be inscribed on Bills of Exchange, and negotiated in the Money Market.'

The look of penetration with which Mrs. Micawber announced this discovery, as if no one had ever thought of it before, seemed rather to astonish my aunt; who abruptly replied, 'Well, ma'am, upon the whole, I shouldn't wonder if you were right!'

'Mr. Micawber being now on the eve of casting off the pecuniary shackles that have so long enthralled him,' said Mrs. Micawber, 'and of commencing a new career in a country where there is sufficient range for his abilities,—

which, in my opinion, is exceedingly important; Mr. Micawber's abilities peculiarly requiring space,—it seems to me that my family should signalize the occasion by coming forward. What I could wish to see, would be a meeting between Mr. Micawber and my family at a festive entertainment, to be given at my family's expense; where Mr. Micawber's health and prosperity being proposed, by some leading member of my family, Mr. Micawber might have an opportunity of developing his views.'

'My dear,' said Mr. Micawber, with some heat, 'it may be better for me to state distinctly, at once, that if I were to develop my views to that assembled group, they would possibly be found of an offensive nature; my impression being that your family are, in the aggregate, impertinent Snobs; and, in detail, unmitigated Ruffians.'

'Micawber,' said Mrs. Micawber, shaking her head, 'no! You have never understood them, and they have never understood you.'

Mr. Micawber coughed.

'They have never understood you, Micawber,' said his wife. 'They may be incapable of it. If so, that is their misfortune. I can pity their misfortune.'

'I am extremely sorry, my dear Emma,' said Mr. Micawber, relenting, 'to have been betrayed into any expressions that might, even remotely, have the appearance of being strong expressions. All I would say, is, that I can go abroad without your family coming forward to favour me,—in short, with a parting Shove of their cold shoulders; and that, upon the whole, I would rather leave England with such impetus as I possess, than derive any acceleration of it from that quarter. At the same time, my dear, if they should condescend to reply to your communications—which our joint experience renders most improbable—far be it from me to be a barrier to your wishes.'

The matter being thus amicably settled, Mr. Micawber gave Mrs. Micawber his arm, and glancing at the heap of books and papers lying before Traddles on the table, said they would leave us to ourselves; which they ceremoniously did.

XIII

JOHN CAVANAGH, THE FIVES-PLAYER

DIED at his house in Burbage Street, St. Giles's, John Cavanagh, the famous hand fives-player. When a person dies, who does any one thing better than any one else in the world, which so many others are trying to do well, it leaves a gap in society. It is not likely that any one will now see the game of fives played in its perfection for many years to come—for Cavanagh is dead, and has not left his peer behind him. It may be said that there are things of more importance than striking a ball against a wall—there are things indeed which make more noise and do as little good, such as making war and peace, making speeches and answering them, making verses and blotting them; making money and throwing it away. But the game of fives is what no one despises who has ever played at it. It is the finest exercise for the body, and the best relaxation for the mind. The Roman poet said that 'Care mounted behind the horseman and stuck to his skirts.' But this remark would not have applied to the fives-player. He who takes to playing at fives is twice young. He feels neither the past nor future 'in the instant.' Debts, taxes, 'domestic treason, foreign levy, nothing can touch him further.' He has no other wish, no other thought, from the moment the game begins, but that of striking the ball, of placing it, of *making* it! This Cavanagh was sure to do. Whenever he touched the ball, there was an end of the chase. His eye was certain, his hand fatal, his presence of mind complete. He could do what he pleased, and he always knew exactly what to do. He saw the whole game, and played it; took instant advantage of his adversary's weakness, and recovered balls, as if by a miracle and from sudden thought, that every one gave for lost. He had equal power and skill, quickness, and judgment. He could either outwit his antagonist by finesse, or beat him by main strength. Sometimes, when he seemed preparing to send the ball with the full swing of his arm, he would by a slight turn of his wrist drop it within an inch of the line. In general, the ball came from his hand, as if from a racket, in a straight horizontal line; so that it was in vain to attempt to overtake or stop it. As it was said of a great orator that he never was at a loss for a word, and for the properest word, so Cavanagh always could tell the degree of force necessary to be given to a ball, and the precise direction in which it should be sent. He did his work with the greatest ease; never took more pains than was necessary; and while others were fagging themselves to death, was as cool and collected as if he had just entered the court. His style of play was as remarkable as his power of execution. He had no affectation, no trifling. He did not throw away the game to show off an attitude, or try an experiment. He was a fine, sensible, manly player, who did what he could, but that was more than any one else could even affect to do. His blows were not undecided and ineffectual—lumbering like Mr. Wordsworth's epic poetry, nor wavering like Mr. Coleridge's lyric prose, nor short of the mark like Mr. Brougham's speeches, nor wide of it like Mr. Canning's wit, nor foul like the *Quarterly*, nor *let* balls like the *Edinburgh Review*. Cobbett and Junius together would have made a Cavanagh. He was the best *up-hill* player in the world; even when his adversary was fourteen, he would play on the same or better, and as he never flung away the game through carelessness and conceit, he never gave it up through laziness or want of heart. The only peculiarity of his play was that he never *volleyed*, but let the balls hop; but if they rose an inch from the ground, he never missed having them. There was not only nobody equal, but nobody second to him. It is supposed that he could give any other player half the game, or beat him with his left hand. His service was tremendous. He once played Woodward and Meredith together (two of the best players in England) in the Fives-court, St. Martin's Street, and made seven and twenty aces following by services alone—a thing unheard of. He another time played Peru, who was considered a first-rate fives-player, a match of the best out of five games, and in the three first games, which of course decided the match, Peru got only one ace.

Cavanagh was an Irishman by birth, and a house-painter by profession. He had once laid aside his working-dress, and walked up, in his smartest clothes, to the Rosemary Branch to have an afternoon's pleasure. A person accosted him, and asked him if he would have a game. So they agreed to play for half-a-crown a game, and a bottle of cider. The first game began—it was seven, eight, ten, thirteen, fourteen all. Cavanagh won it. The next was the same. They played on, and each game was hardly contested. 'There,' said the unconscious fives-player, 'there was a stroke that Cavanagh could not take: I never played better in my life, and yet I can't win a game. I don't know how it is.' However, they played on, Cavanagh winning every game, and the by-standers drinking the cider, and laughing all the time. In the twelfth game, when Cavanagh was only four, and the stranger thirteen, a person came in, and said, 'What! are you here, Cavanagh?' The words were no sooner pronounced than the astonished player let the ball drop from his hand, and saying, 'What! have I been breaking my heart all this time to beat Cavanagh?' refused to make another effort. 'And yet, I give you my word,' said Cavanagh, telling the story with some triumph, 'I played all the while with my clenched fist.' He used frequently to play matches at Copenhagen-house for wagers and dinners. The wall against which they play is the same that supports the kitchen-chimney, and when the wall resounded louder than usual, the cooks exclaimed, 'Those are the Irishman's balls,' and the joints trembled on the spit! Goldsmith consoled himself that there were places where he was too admired; and Cavanagh was the admiration of all the fives-courts, where he ever played. Mr. Powell, when he played matches in the Court in St. Martin's Street, used to fill his gallery at half-a-crown a head, with amateurs and admirers of talent in whatever department it is shown. He could not have shown himself in any ground in England, but he would have been immediately surrounded with inquisitive gazers, trying to find out in what part of his frame his unrivalled skill lay, as politicians wonder to see the balance of Europe suspended in Lord Castlereagh's face, and admire the trophies of the British Navy lurking under Mr. Croker's hanging brow. Now Cavanagh was as good-looking a man as the noble lord, and much better looking than the right hon. secretary. He had a clear, open countenance, and did not look sideways or down, like Mr. Murray the bookseller. He was a young fellow of sense, humour, and courage. He once had a quarrel with a waterman at Hungerford-stairs, and, they say, served him out in great style.

In a word, there are hundreds at this day, who cannot mention his name without admiration, as the best fives-player that perhaps ever lived (the greatest excellence of which they have any notion)—and the noisy shout of the ring happily stood him in stead of the unheard voice of posterity! The only person who seems to have excelled as much in another way as Cavanagh did in his, was the late John Davies, the racket-player. It was remarked of him that he did not seem to follow the ball, but the ball seemed to follow him. Give him a foot of wall, and he was sure to make the ball. The four best racket-players of that day were Jack Spines, Jem Harding, Armitage, and Church. Davies could give any one of these two hands a time—that is, half the game—and each of these, at their best, could give the best player now in London the same odds. Such are the gradations in all exertions of human skill and art. He once played four capital players together, and beat them. He was also a first-rate tennis-player, and an excellent fives-player. In the Fleet or King's Bench, he would have stood against Powell, who was reckoned the best open-ground player of his time. This last-mentioned player is at present the keeper of the Fives Court, and we might recommend to him for a motto over his door, 'Who enters here, forgets himself, his country, and his friends.' And the best of it is, that by the calculation of the odds, none of the three are worth remembering! Cavanagh died from the bursting of a blood-vessel, which prevented him from playing for the last two or three years. This, he was often heard to say, he thought hard upon him. He was fast recovering, however, when he was suddenly carried off, to the regret of all who knew him. As Mr. Peel made it a qualification of the present Speaker, Mr. Manners Sutton, that he was an excellent moral character, so Jack Cavanagh was a zealous Catholic, and could not be persuaded to eat meat on a Friday, the day on which he died. We have paid this willing tribute to his memory.

> 'Let no rude hand deface it,
> And his forlorn *"Hic jacet."* '

XIV

THE MEN IN BUCKRAM

Poins. Welcome, Jack; where hast thou been?

Falstaff. A plague of all cowards, I say, and a vengeance too! marry, and amen! Give me a cup of sack, boy. Ere I lead this life long, I'll sew nether stocks and mend them and foot them too. A plague of all cowards! Give me a cup of sack, rogue. Is there no virtue extant?

[*He drinks.*

Prince. Didst thou never see Titan kiss a dish of butter? pitiful-hearted Titan, that melted at the sweet tale of the sun's! if thou didst, then behold that compound.

Fal. You rogue, here's lime in this sack, too: there is nothing but roguery to be found in villanous man: yet a coward is worse than a cup of sack with lime in it. A villanous coward! Go thy ways, old Jack; die when thou wilt, if manhood, good manhood, be not forgot upon the face of the earth, then am I a shotten herring. There lives not three good men unhanged in England; and one of them is fat and grows old: God help the while! a bad world, I say. I would I were a weaver; I could sing psalms or any thing. A plague of all cowards, I say still.

Prince. How now, wool-sack! what mutter you?

Fal. A king's son! If I do not beat thee out of thy

kingdom with a dagger of lath, and drive all thy subjects afore thee like a flock of wild-geese, I'll never wear hair on my face more. You Prince of Wales!

Prince. Why, you whoreson round man, what's the matter?

Fal. Are not you a coward? answer me to that: and Poins there?

Poins. 'Zounds, ye fat paunch, an ye call me coward, by the Lord, I'll stab thee.

Fal. I call thee coward! I'll see thee damned ere I call thee coward: but I would give a thousand pound I could run as fast as thou canst. You are straight enough in the shoulders, you care not who sees your back: call you that backing of your friends? A plague upon such backing! give me them that will face me. Give me a cup of sack: I am a rogue, if I drunk to-day.

Prince. O villain! thy lips are scarce wiped since thou drunkest last.

Fal. All's one for that. [*He drinks.*] A plague of all cowards, still say I.

Prince. What's the matter?

Fal. What's the matter! there be four of us here have ta'en a thousand pound this day morning.

Prince. Where is it, Jack? where is it?

Fal. Where is it! taken from us it is: a hundred upon poor four of us.

Prince. What, a hundred, man?

Fal. I am a rogue, if I were not at half-sword with a dozen of them two hours together. I have 'scaped by miracle. I am eight times thrust through the doublet, four through the hose; my buckler cut through and through; my sword hacked like a hand-saw—ecce signum! I never dealt better since I was a man: all would not do. A plague of all cowards! Let them speak: if they speak more or less than truth, they are villains and the sons of darkness.

Prince. Speak, sirs; how was it?

Gads. We four set upon some dozen——

Fal. Sixteen at least, my Lord.

Gads. And bound them.

Peto. No, no, they were not bound.

Fal. You rogue, they were bound, every man of them; or I am a Jew else, an Ebrew Jew.

Gads. As we were sharing, some six or seven fresh men set upon us——

Fal. And unbound the rest, and then come in the other.

Prince. What, fought you with them all?

Fal. All! I know not what you call all; but if I fought not with fifty of them, I am a bunch of radish: if there were not two or three and fifty upon poor old Jack, then am I no two-legged creature.

Prince. Pray God you have not murdered some of them.

Fal. Nay, that's past praying for: I have peppered two of them; two I am sure I have paid, two rogues in buckram suits. I tell thee what, Hal, if I tell thee a lie, spit in my face, call me horse. Thou knowest my old ward; here I lay, and thus I bore my point. Four rogues in buckram let drive at me——

Prince. What, four? thou saidst but two even now.

Fal. Four, Hal; I told thee four.

Poins. Ay, ay, he said four.

Fal. These four came all a-front, and mainly thrust at me. I made me no more ado but took all their seven points in my target, thus.

Prince. Seven? why, there were but four even now.

Fal. In buckram?

Poins. Ay, four, in buckram suits.

Fal. Seven, by these hilts, or I am a villain else.

Prince. Prithee, let him alone; we shall have more anon.

Fal. Dost thou hear me, Hal?

Prince. Ay, and mark thee too, Jack.

Fal. Do so, for it is worth the listening to. These nine in buckram that I told thee of,——

Prince. So, two more already.

Fal. Their points being broken,——

Poins. Down fell their hose.

Fal. Began to give me ground: but I followed me close,

came in foot and hand; and with a thought seven of the eleven I paid.

Prince. O monstrous! eleven buckram men grown out of two!

Fal. But, as the devil would have it, three misbegotten knaves in Kendal green came at my back and let drive at me; for it was so dark, Hal, that thou couldst not see thy hand.

Prince. These lies are like their father that begets them; gross as a mountain, open, palpable. Why, thou clay-brained guts, thou knotty-pated fool, thou whoreson, obscene, greasy tallow-catch,——

Fal. What, art thou mad? art thou mad? is not the truth the truth?

Prince. Why, how couldst thou know these men in Kendal Green, when it was so dark thou couldst not see thy hand? come, tell us your reason: what sayest thou to this?

Poins. Come, your reason, Jack, your reason.

Fal. What, upon compulsion? 'Zounds, an I were at the strappado, or all the racks in the world, I would not tell you on compulsion. Give you a reason on compulsion! if reasons were as plentiful as blackberries, I would give no man a reason upon compulsion, I.

Prince. I'll be no longer guilty of this sin; this sanguine coward, this bed-presser, this horse-back-breaker, this huge hill of flesh,——

Fal. 'Sblood, you starveling, you elf-skin, you dried neat's tongue, you bull's pizzle, you stock-fish! O for breath to utter what is like thee! you tailor's-yard, you sheath, you bow-case, you vile standing-tuck,——

Prince. Well, breathe a while, and then to it again: and when thou hast tired thyself in base comparisons, hear me speak but this.

Poins. Mark, Jack.

Prince. We two saw you four set on four and bound them, and were masters of their wealth. Mark now, how a plain tale shall put you down. Then did we two set on you four; and, with a word, out-faced you from your prize and have it; yea, and can show it you here in the house: and,

Falstaff, you carried your guts away as nimbly, with as quick dexterity, and roared for mercy, and still run and roared, as ever I heard bull-calf. What a slave art thou, to hack thy sword as thou hast done, and then say it was in fight! What trick, what device, what starting-hole, canst thou now find out to hide thee from this open and apparent shame?

Poins. Come, let's hear, Jack; what trick hast thou now?

Fal. By the Lord, I knew ye as well as he that made ye. Why, hear you, my masters: was it for me to kill the heir-apparent? should I turn upon the true prince? why, thou knowest I am as valiant as Hercules: but beware instinct; the lion will not touch the true prince. Instinct is a great matter; I was now a coward on instinct. I shall think the better of myself and thee during my life; I for a valiant lion, and thou for a true prince. But, by the Lord, lads, I am glad you have the money. Hostess, clap to the doors: watch to-night, pray to-morrow. Gallants, lads, boys, hearts of gold, all the titles of good fellowship come to you! What, shall we be merry? shall we have a play extempore?

Prince. Content; and the argument shall be thy running away.

Fal. Ah, no more of that, Hal, an thou lovest me!

XV

TWO LETTERS OF CHARLES LAMB

TO WORDSWORTH

January 30, 1801.

I OUGHT before this to have replied to your very kind invitation into Cumberland. With you and your sister I could gang anywhere; but I am afraid whether I shall ever be able to afford so desperate a journey. Separate from the pleasure of your company, I don't much care if I never see a mountain in my life. I have passed all my days in London, until I have formed as many and intense local attachments as any of you mountaineers can have done with dead Nature. The lighted shops of the Strand and Fleet Street; the innumerable trades, tradesmen, and customers, coaches, waggons, playhouses; all the bustle and wickedness round about Covent Garden; the very women of the Town; the watchmen, drunken scenes, rattles; life awake, if you awake, at all hours of the night; the impossibility of being dull in Fleet Street; the crowds, the very dirt and mud, the sun shining upon houses and pavements, the print shops, the old bookstalls, parsons cheapening books, coffee-houses, steams of soups from kitchens, the pantomimes—London itself a pantomime and a masquerade—all these things work themselves into my mind, and feed me, without a power of satiating me. The wonder of these sights impels me into night-walks about her crowded streets, and I often shed tears in the motley Strand from fulness of joy at so much life. All these emotions must be strange to you; so are your rural emotions to me. But consider, what must I have been doing all my life, not to have lent great portions of my heart with usury to such scenes?

My attachments are all local, purely local. I have no passion (or have had none since I was in love, and then it was the spurious engendering of poetry and books) for groves and valleys. The rooms where I was born, the furniture which has been before my eyes all my life, a book-case which has followed me about like a faithful dog (only exceeding him in knowledge), wherever I have moved, old chairs, old tables, streets, squares, where I have sunned myself, my old school,—these are my mistresses. Have I not enough, without your mountains? I do not envy you. I should pity you, did I not know that the mind will make friends of anything. Your sun, and moon, and skies, and hills, and lakes, affect me no more, or scarcely come to me in more venerable characters, than as a gilded room with tapestry and tapers, where I might live with handsome visible objects. I consider the clouds above me but as a roof beautifully painted, but unable to satisfy the mind; and at last, like the pictures of the apartment of a connoisseur, unable to afford him any longer a pleasure. So fading upon me, from disuse, have been the beauties of Nature, as they have been confinedly called; so ever fresh, and green, and warm are all the inventions of men, and assemblies of men in this great city. I should certainly have laughed with dear Joanna.

Give my kindest love, and my sister's, to D. and yourself; and a kiss from me to little Barbara Lewthwaite. Thank you for liking my play.

C. L.

TO COLERIDGE

March 9, 1822.

DEAR COLERIDGE—

It gives me great satisfaction to hear that the pig turned out so well: they are interesting creatures at a certain age. What a pity such buds should blow out into the maturity of rank bacon! You had all some of the crackling and brain sauce. Did you remember to rub it with butter, and gently dredge it a little, just before the crisis? Did the eyes come away kindly with no Œdipean avulsion? Was the crackling the colour of the ripe pomegranate? Had you no complement of boiled neck of mutton before it, to blunt the edge of delicate desire? Did you flesh maiden teeth in it? Not that *I* sent the pig, or can form the remotest guess what part Owen could play in the business. I never knew him give anything away in my life. He would not begin with strangers. I suspect the pig, after all, was meant for me; but at the unlucky juncture of time being absent, the present somehow went round to Highgate.

To confess an honest truth, a pig is one of those things which I could never think of sending away. Teal, widgeon, snipes, barn-door fowls, ducks, geese—your tame villatic things—Welsh mutton, collars of brawn, sturgeon, fresh or pickled, your potted char, Swiss cheeses, French pies, early grapes, muscadines, I impart as freely unto my friends as to myself. They are but self-extended; but pardon me if I stop somewhere. Where the fine feeling of benevolence giveth a higher smack than the sensual rarity, there my friends (or any good man) may command me; but pigs are pigs, and I myself therein am nearest to myself. Nay, I should think it an affront, an under-valuing done to Nature who bestowed such a boon upon me, if in a churlish mood I parted with the precious gift. One of the bitterest pangs of remorse I ever felt was when a child—when my kind old aunt had strained her pocket-strings to bestow a sixpenny whole plum-cake upon me. In my way home through the Borough I met a venerable old man, not a mendicant, but thereabouts; a look-beggar, not a verbal petitionist; and in the coxcombry of taught charity I gave away the cake to him. I walked on a little in all the pride of an Evangelical peacock, when of a sudden my old aunt's kindness crossed me; the sum it was to her; the pleasure she had a right to expect that I—not the old impostor—should take in eating her cake; the ingratitude by which, under the colour of a Christian virtue, I had frustrated her cherished purpose. I sobbed, wept, and took it to heart so grievously, that I think I never suffered the like; and I was right. It was a piece of unfeeling hypocrisy, and it proved a lesson to me ever after. The cake has long been masticated, consigned to the dunghill with the ashes of that unseasonable pauper.

But when Providence, who is better to us all than our aunts, gives me a pig, remembering my temptation and my fall, I shall endeavour to act towards it more in the spirit of the donor's purpose.

Yours (short of pig) to command in everything.

C. L.

XVI

DAVID AND GOLIATH

NOW the Philistines gathered together their armies to battle, and were gathered together at Shochoh which belongeth to Judah, and pitched between Shochoh and Azekah, in Ephes-dammim. And Saul and the men of Israel were gathered together, and pitched by the valley of Elah, and set the battle in array against the

Philistines. And the Philistines stood on a mountain on the one side, and Israel stood on a mountain on the other side: and there was a valley between them. And there went out a champion out of the camp of the Philistines, named Goliath, of Gath, whose height was six cubits and a span. And he had an helmet of brass upon his head, and he was armed with a coat of mail; and the weight of the coat was five thousand shekels of brass. And he had greaves of brass upon his legs, and a target of brass between his shoulders. And the staff of his spear was like a weaver's beam; and his spear's head weighed six hundred shekels of iron: and one bearing a shield went before him. And he stood and cried unto the armies of Israel, and said unto them, Why are ye come out to set your battle in array? am not I a Philistine, and ye servants to Saul? choose you a man for you, and let him come down to me. If he be able to fight with me, and to kill me, then will we be your servants: but if I prevail against him, and kill him, then shall ye be our servants, and serve us. And the Philistine said, I defy the armies of Israel this day; give me a man, that we may fight together. When Saul and all Israel heard those words of the Philistine, they were dismayed, and greatly afraid.

Now David was the son of that Ephrathite of Beth-lehem-judah, whose name was Jesse; and he had eight sons: and the man went among men for an old man in the days of Saul. And the three eldest sons of Jesse went and followed Saul to the battle: and the names of his three sons that went to the battle were Eliab the first-born; and next unto him, Abinadab; and the third, Shammah. And David was the youngest; and the three eldest followed Saul. But David went and returned from Saul to feed his father's sheep at Bethlehem. And the Philistine drew near morning and evening, and presented himself forty days. And Jesse said unto David his son, Take now for thy brethren an ephah of this parched corn, and these ten loaves, and run to the camp to thy brethren; and carry these ten cheeses unto the captain of their thousand, and look how thy brethren fare, and take their pledge. Now Saul, and they, and all the men of Israel, were in the valley of Elah, fighting with the Philistines.

And David rose up early in the morning, and left the sheep with a keeper, and took, and went, as Jesse had commanded him; and he came to the trench, as the host was going forth to the fight, and shouted for the battle. For Israel and the Philistines had put the battle in array, army against army. And David left his carriage in the hand of the keeper of the carriage, and ran into the army, and came and saluted his brethren. And as he talked with them, behold, there came up the champion (the Philistine of Gath, Goliath by name) out of the armies of the Philistines, and spake according to the same words: and David heard them. And all the men of Israel, when they saw the man, fled from him, and were sore afraid. And the men of Israel said, Have ye seen this man that is come up? surely to defy Israel is he come up: and it shall be, that the man who killeth him, the king will enrich him with great riches, and will give him his daughter, and make his father's house free in Israel. And David spake to the men that stood by him, saying, What shall be done to the man that killeth this Philistine, and taketh away the reproach from Israel? for who is this uncircumcized Philistine, that he should defy the armies of the living God? And the people answered him after this manner, saying, So shall it be done to the man that killeth him. And Eliab his eldest brother heard when he spake unto the men: and Eliab's anger was kindled against David, and he said, Why camest thou down hither? and with whom hast thou left those few sheep in the wilderness? I know thy pride, and the naughtiness of thine heart; for thou art come down that thou mightest see the battle. And David said, What have I now done? Is there not a cause? And he turned from him toward another, and spake after the same manner: and the people answered him again after the former manner.

And when the words were heard which David spake, they rehearsed them before Saul; and he sent for him. And David said to Saul, Let no man's heart fail because of him;

thy servant will go and fight with this Philistine. And Saul said to David, Thou art not able to go against this Philistine to fight with him: for thou art but a youth, and he a man of war from his youth. And David said unto Saul, Thy servant kept his father's sheep, and there came a lion and a bear and took a lamb out of the flock; and I went out after him, and smote him, and delivered it out of his mouth, and when he arose against me, I caught him by his beard, and smote him, and slew him. Thy servant slew both the lion and the bear; and this uncircumcized Philistine shall be as one of them, seeing he hath defied the armies of the living God. David said moreover, The Lord that delivered me out of the paw of the lion, and out of the paw of the bear, he will deliver me out of the hand of this Philistine. And Saul said unto David, Go, and the Lord be with thee.

And Saul armed David with his armour, and he put an helmet of brass upon his head; also he armed him with a coat of mail. And David girded his sword upon his armour, and he assayed to go; for he had not proved it. And David said unto Saul, I cannot go with these; for I have not proved them. And David put them off him. And he took his staff in his hand, and chose him five smooth stones out of the brook, and put them in a shepherd's bag which he had, even in a scrip; and his sling was in his hand: and he drew near to the Philistine. And the Philistine came on and drew near unto David; and the man that bare the shield went before him. And when the Philistine looked about, and saw David, he disdained him; for he was but a youth, and ruddy, and of a fair countenance. And the Philistine said unto David, Am I a dog, that thou comest to me with staves? And the Philistine cursed David by his gods. And the Philistine said to David, Come to me, and I will give thy flesh unto the fowls of the air, and to the beasts of the field. Then said David to the Philistine, Thou comest to me with a sword, and with a spear, and with a shield; but I come to thee in the name of the Lord of hosts, the God of the armies of Israel, whom thou hast defied. This day will the Lord deliver thee into mine hand; and I will smite thee, and take thine head from thee; and I will give the carcases of the host of the Philistines this day unto the fowls of the air, and to the wild beasts of the earth; that all the earth may know that there is a God in Israel. And all this assembly shall know that the Lord saveth not with sword and spear: for the battle is the Lord's, and he will give you into our hands.

And it came to pass, when the Philistine arose, and came and drew nigh to meet David, that David hasted, and ran toward the army to meet the Philistine. And David put his hand in his bag, and took thence a stone, and slang it, and smote the Philistine in his forehead, that the stone sunk into his forehead; and he fell upon his face to the earth. So David prevailed over the Philistine with a sling and with a stone, and smote the Philistine, and slew him; but there was no sword in the hand of David. Therefore David ran and stood upon the Philistine, and took his sword, and drew it out of the sheath thereof, and slew him, and cut off his head therewith. And when the Philistines saw their champion was dead, they fled. And the men of Israel and of Judah arose, and shouted, and pursued the Philistines, until thou come to the valley and to the gates of Ekron: and the wounded of the Philistines fell down by the way to Shaaraim, even unto Gath, and unto Ekron. And the children of Israel returned from chasing after the Philistines, and they spoiled their tents. And David took the head of the Philistine, and brought it to Jerusalem; but he put his armour in his tent.

XVII

A QUARREL WITH THE CAPTAIN

AFTER having, however, gloriously regaled myself with this food, I was washing it down with some good claret, with my wife and her friend in the cabin, when the captain's valet de chambre, head cook, house and ship steward, footman in livery and out on't, secretary and fore-mastman, all burst into the cabin at once, being indeed all but one person, and without saying, by your leave, began to pack half a hogshead of small beer in bottles, the necessary consequence of which must have been, either a total stop to conversation at that chearful season, when it is most agreeable, or the admitting that polyonymous officer aforesaid to the participation of it. I desired him, therefore, to delay his purpose a little longer, but he refused to grant my request; nor was he prevailed on to quit the room till he was threatened with having one bottle to pack more than his number, which then happened to stand empty within my reach.

With these menaces he retired at last, but not without muttering some menaces on his side, and which, to our great terror, he failed not to put into immediate execution.

Our captain was gone to dinner this day with his Swiss brother; and tho' he was a very sober man, was a little elevated with some champagne, which, as it cost the Swiss little or nothing, he dispensed at his table more liberally than our hospitable English noblemen put about those bottles, which the ingenious Peter Taylor teaches a led captain to avoid by distinguishing by the name of that generous liquor, which all humble companions are taught to postpone to the flavour of methuen or honest port.

While our two captains were thus regaling themselves, and celebrating their own heroic exploits, with all the inspiration which the liquor, at least, of wit could afford them, the polyonymous officer arrived, and being saluted by the name of honest Tom, was ordered to sit down and take his glass before he delivered his message; for every sailor is by turns his captain's mate over a can, except only that captain bashaw who presides in a man of war, and who upon earth has not other mate, unless it be another of the same bashaws.

Tom had no sooner swallowed his draught, than he hastily began his narrative, and faithfully related what had happened on board our ship; we say faithfully, tho' from what happened it may be suspected that Tom chose to add, perhaps, only five or six immaterial circumstances, as is always, I believe, the case, and may possibly have been done by me in relating this very story, tho' it happened not many hours ago.

No sooner was the captain informed of the interruption which had been given to his officer, and indeed to his orders, for he thought no time so convenient as than of his absence for causing any confusion in the cabin, than he leapt with such haste from his chair that he had like to have broke his sword, with which he always begirt himself when he walked out of his ship, and sometimes when he walked about in it, at the same time grasping eagerly that other implement called a cockade, which modern soldiers wear on their helmets, with the same view as the antients did their crests, to terrify the enemy; he muttered something, but so inarticulately, that the word *damn* was only intelligible; he then hastily took leave of the Swiss captain, who was too well bred to press his stay on such an occasion, and leapt first from the ship to his boat, and then from his boat to his own ship, with as much fierceness in his looks as he had ever express'd on boarding his defenceless prey, in the honourable calling of a privateer.

Having regained the middle-deck he paused a moment, while Tom and others loaded themselves with bottles, and then descending into the cabin exclaimed with a thundering voice, D——n me, why arn't the bottles stoed in, according to my orders?

I answered him very mildly, that I had prevented his man from doing it, as it was at an inconvenient time to me, and as in his absence, at least, I esteemed the cabin to be my own. 'Your cabin,' repeated he many times, 'no, d— me, 'tis my cabin. Your cabin! D— me! I have brought my hogs to a fair market. I suppose, indeed, you think it your cabin, and your ship, by your commanding in it; but I will command it, d—n me! I will shew the world I am the commander, and nobody but I! Did you think I sold you the command of my ship for that pitiful thirty pounds? I wish I had not seen you nor your thirty pounds aboard of her.' He then repeated the words thirty pounds often, with great disdain and with a contempt which, I own, the sum did not seem to deserve in my eye, either in itself, or on the present occasion; being, indeed, paid for the freight of —— weight of human flesh, which is above 50 per cent. dearer than the freight of any other luggage, whilst in reality it takes up less room, in fact no room at all.

In truth the sum was paid for nothing more than for a liberty to six persons (two of them servants) to stay on board a ship while she sails from one port to another, every shilling of which comes clear into the captain's pocket. Ignorant people may perhaps imagine, especially when they are told that the captain is obliged to sustain them, that their diet, at least, is worth something; which may probably be now and then so far the case, as to deduct a tenth part from the neat profits on this account; but it was otherwise at present: for when I had contracted with the captain at a price which I by no means thought moderate, I had some content in thinking I should have no more to pay for my voyage; but I was whispered that it was expected that passengers should find themselves in several things; such as tea, wine, and such-like; and particularly that gentlemen should stowe of the latter a much larger quantity than they could use, in order to leave the remainder as a present to the captain, at the end of the voyage; and it was expected, likewise, that gentlemen should put aboard some fresh stores, and the more of such things were put aboard, the welcomer they would be to the captain.

I was prevailed with by these hints, to follow the advice proposed, and accordingly, besides tea, and a large hamper of wine, with several hams and tongues, I caused a number of live chickens and sheep to be conveyed aboard; in truth, treble the quantity of provision which would have supported the persons I took with me, had the voyage continued three weeks, as it was supposed, with a bare possibility it might...

But, to return from so long a digression, to which the use of so improper an epithet gave occasion, and to which the novelty of the subject allured, I will make the reader amends by concisely telling him, that the captain poured forth such a torrent of abuse, that I very hastily, and very foolishly, resolved to quit the ship. I gave immediate orders to summons a hoy to carry me that evening to Dartmouth, without considering any consequence. Those orders I gave in no very low voice; so that those above stairs might possibly conceive there was more than one master in the cabin. In the same tone I likewise threatened the captain with that which, he afterward said, he feared more than any rock or quick sand. Nor can we wonder at this, when we are told he had been twice obliged, to bring to, and cast anchor there before, and had neither time escaped without the loss of almost his whole cargo.

The most distant sound of law thus frightened a man, who had often, I am convinced, heard numbers of cannon roar around him with intrepidity. Nor did he sooner see the hoy approaching the vessel, then he ran down again into the cabin, and, his rage being perfectly subsided, he tumbled on his knees, and a little too abjectly implored for mercy.

I did not suffer a brave man and an old man, to remain a moment in this posture; but I immediately forgave him.

And here, that I may not be thought the sly trumpeter of my own praises, I do utterly disclaim all praise on the occasion. Neither did the greatness of my mind dictate, nor the force of my Christianity exact this forgiveness. To speak truth, I forgave him from a motive which would make men much more forgiving, if they were much wiser than they are; because it was convenient for me so to do.

XVIII

BALLAD OF AGINCOURT

FAIR stood the wind for France,
  When we our sails advance,
  Nor now to prove our chance
    Longer will tarry;
But putting to the main,
At Caux, the mouth of Seine,
With all his martial train,
    Landed King Harry.

And taking many a fort,
Furnished in warlike sort,
Marcheth tow'rds Agincourt
    In happy hour;
Skirmishing day by day,
With those that stopp'd his way,
Where the French gen'ral lay
    With all his power.
Which in his height of pride,
King Henry to deride,
His ransom to provide
    To the king sending;
Which he neglects the while,
As from a nation vile,
Yet with an angry smile
    Their fall portending.
And turning to his men,
Quoth our brave Henry then,
'Though they to one be ten,
    Be not amazed.
Yet have we well begun,
Battles so bravely won,
Have ever to the sun
    By fame been raised.
And for myself (quoth he),
This my full rest shall be:
England ne'er mourn for me,
    Nor more esteem me:
Victor I will remain,
Or on this earth lie slain,
Never shall she sustain
    Loss to redeem me.
Poitiers and Cressy tell,
When most their pride did swell,
Under our swords they fell:
    No less our skill is
Than when our grandsire-great,
Claiming the regal seat,

By many a warlike feat
    Lopp'd the French lilies.'
The Duke of York so dread
The eager vaward led;
With the main, Henry sped,
    Amongst his hench-men.
Exeter had the rear,
A braver man not there,
O Lord, how hot they were,
    On the false Frenchmen!
They now to fight are gone,
Armour on armour shone,
Drum now to drum did groan,
    To hear was wonder;
That with the cries they make,
The very earth did shake,
Trumpet to trumpet spake,
    Thunder to thunder.
Well it thine age became,
O noble Erpingham,
Which didst the signal aim
    To our hid forces;
When from a meadow by,
Like a storm suddenly,
The English archery
    Stuck the French horses.
With Spanish yew so strong,
Arrows a cloth-yard long,
That like to serpents stung,
    Piercing the weather;
None from his fellow starts,
But playing manly parts,
And like true English hearts,
    Stuck close together.
When down their bows they threw,
And forth their bilbos drew,
And on the French they flew,
    Not one was tardy;

Arms were from shoulders sent,
Scalps to the teeth were rent,
Down the French peasants went,
    Our men were hardy.
This while our noble king,
His broad sword brandishing,
Down the French host did ding,
    As to o'erwhelm it,
And many a deep wound lent,
His arms with blood besprent,
And many a cruel dent
    Bruised his helmet.
Gloucester, that duke so good,
Next of the royal blood,
For famous England stood,
    With his brave brother;
Clarence, in steel so bright,
Though but a maiden knight,
Yet in that furious fight
    Scarce such another.
Warwick in blood did wade,
Oxford the foe invade,
And cruel slaughter made,
    Still as they ran up;
Suffolk his axe did ply,
Beaumont and Willoughby,
Bare them right doughtily,
    Ferrers and Fanhope.
Upon Saint Crispin's day
Fought was this noble fray,
Which fame did not delay
    To England to carry;
O when shall English men,
With such acts fill a pen,
Or England breed again
    Such a King Harry?

XIX

THE RIVER OF DEATH

AFTER this, I beheld until they were come unto the land of *Beulah*, where the Sun shineth night and day. Here, because they were weary, they betook themselves a while to rest. And because this country was common for Pilgrims, and because the orchards and vineyards that were here, belonged to the King of the Cœlestial Country, therefore they were licensed to make bold with any of his things. But a little while soon refreshed them here; for the bells did so ring, and the trumpets continually sound so melodiously, that they could not sleep, and yet they received as much refreshing, as if they had slept their sleep never so soundly. Here also all the noise of them that walked the streets, was, *More Pilgrims are come to town*. And another would answer, saying, And so many, went over the Water, and were let in at the Golden Gates to day. They would cry again, There is now a Legion of shining ones just come to town; by which, we know, that there are more Pilgrims upon the road; for here they come to wait for them, and to comfort them after all their sorrow. Then the Pilgrims got up, and walked to and fro: But how were their ears now filled with heavenly noises and their eyes delighted with Cœlestial Visions? In this land they *heard* nothing, *saw* nothing, *felt* nothing, *smelt* nothing, *tasted* nothing, that was offensive to their stomach or mind; only when they tasted of the water of the River, over which they were to go, they thought that tasted a little *bitterish* to the palate, but it proved sweeter when 'twas down.

In this place there was a Record kept of the names of them that had been Pilgrims of old, and a history of all the famous Acts that they had done. It was here also much discoursed, how the River to some had had its *flowings*, and what *ebbings* it has had while others have gone over. It has been in a manner *dry* for some, while it has overflowed its banks for others.

In this place, the Children of the town would go into the King's Gardens, and gather nosegays for the Pilgrims, and bring them to them with much affection. Here also grew *camphire*, with *spikenard*, and *saffron*, *calamus*, and *cinnamon*, with all its trees of *frankincense*, *myrrh*, and *aloes*, with all *chief* spices. With these the Pilgrims' chambers were perfumed while they staid here; and with these were their bodies anointed, to prepare them to go over the River, when the time appointed was come.

Now while they lay here, and waited for the good hour, there was a noise in the town, that there was a post come from the Cœlestial City, with matter of great importance to one *Christiana*, the wife of *Christian* the Pilgrim. So enquiry was made for her, and the house was found out where she was, so the post presented her with a letter: The contents whereof were, *Hail good woman! I bring thee tidings, that the Master calleth for thee, and expecteth that thou shouldest stand in his Presence, in clothes of Immortality, within this ten days.*

When he had read this letter to her, he gave her therewith a true token that he was a true messenger, and was come to bid her make haste to be gone, The token was, *an Arrow with a point sharpened with Love, let easily into her heart, which by degrees wrought so effectually with her, that at the time appointed she must be gone.*

When *Christiana* saw that her time was come, and that she was the first of this company that was to go over, she called for Mr. *Great-heart* her Guide, and told him how matters were. So he told her, he was heartily glad of the news, and could have been glad, had the post come for him. Then she bid that he should give advice how all things should be prepared for her Journey.

So he told her, saying, thus and thus it must be, and we that survive, will accompany you to the Riverside. Then she called for her children, and gave them *her Blessing*, and told them, that she yet read with comfort, the Mark that was set in their foreheads, and was glad to see them with her there, and that they had kept their garments so white.

Lastly, she bequeathed to the Poor that little she had, and commanded her sons and her daughters to be ready against the messenger should come for them.

When she had spoken these words to her Guide, and to her children, she called for Mr. *Valiant-for-Truth*, and said unto him, Sir, you have in all places shewed yourself truehearted, be *faithful unto Death*, and my King will give you a *Crown of Life*. I would also intreat you to have an eye to my children; and if at any time you see them faint, speak comfortably to them. For my daughters, my Sons' wives, they have been faithful, and a fulfilling of the Promise upon them will be their end. But she gave Mr. *Standfast* a ring.

Then she called for old Mr. *Honest*, and said of him, *Behold an Israelite indeed, in whom is no Guile*. Then said he, I wish you a fair day, when you set out for Mount *Sion*, and shall be glad to see that you go over the River dry-shod. But she answered, come *wet*, come *dry*, I long to be gone; for however the weather is in my Journey, I shall have time enough when I come there, to sit down and rest me, and dry me.

Then came in that good man Mr. *Ready-to-halt*, to see her. So she said to him, thy travel hither has been with difficulty; but that will make thy Rest the sweeter. But watch and be ready; for at an hour when you think not, the messenger may come.

After him came in Mr. *Despondency*, and his daughter *Much-afraid*; to whom she said, you ought, with Thankfulness, for ever, to remember your deliverance from the hand of Giant *Despair*, and out of *Doubting-Castle*. The effect of that mercy, is that you are brought with safety hither. Be ye watchful, and cast away Fear; be sober, and hope to the end.

Then she said to Mr. *Feeble-mind*, Thou wast delivered from the mouth of Giant *Slay-good*, that thou mightest live in the Light of the Living for ever, and see the King with comfort: Only I advise thee to repent thee of thy aptness to fear and doubt of his Goodness, before he sends for thee; lest thou shouldest, when he comes, be forced to stand before him for that fault, with blushing.

Now the day drew on, that *Christiana* must be gone. So the Road was full of people, to see her take her Journey. But behold all the banks beyond the River were full of horses and chariots, which were come down from above, to accompany her to the City Gate. So she came forth, and entred the *River*, with a *beckon* of farewell, to those that followed her to the River-side. The last word she was heard to say, here, was *I come, Lord, to be with thee, and bless thee.*

So her children and friends returned to their place, for that those that waited for *Christiana* had carried her out of their sight. So she went and called, and entred in at the Gate with all the ceremonies of Joy, that her husband *Christian* had done before her. At her departure her children wept, but Mr. *Great-heart* and Mr. *Valiant* play'd upon the well-tuned cymbal and harp for Joy. So all departed to their respective places.

In process of time, there came a post to the town again, and his business was with Mr. *Ready-to-halt*. So he enquired him out, and said to him, I am come to thee in the name of him whom thou hast Loved and followed, tho' upon *Crutches*: And my message is to tell thee, that he expects thee at his table to sup with him in his Kingdom, the next day after *Easter*; wherefore prepare thyself for thy Journey.

Then he also gave him a token that he was a true messenger, saying, *I have broken thy golden bowl, and loosed thy silver cord.*

After this, Mr. *Ready-to-halt* called for his fellow Pilgrims, and told them, saying, I am sent for, and God shall surely visit you also. So he desired Mr. *Valiant* to make his *Will*. And because he had nothing to bequeath to them that should survive him, but his *crutches*, and his *good wishes*, therefore thus he said: *These crutches I bequeath to my son, that shall tread in my steps, with an hundred warm wishes, that he may prove better than I have done.*

Then he thanked Mr. *Great-heart* for his conduct and kindness, and so addressed himself to his Journey. When he came at the brink of the River, he said, Now I shall have no more need of these *crutches*, since yonder are Chariots and Horses for me to ride on: The last words he was heard to say, was, *Welcome Life*. So he went his Way.

After this, Mr. *Feeble-mind* had tidings brought him, that the post sounded his horn at his chamber-door. Then he came in, and told him, saying, I am come to tell thee that thy Master has need of thee; and that in very little time thou must behold his Face in Brightness: And take this as a token of the truth of my message: *Those that look out at the windows, shall be darkned.*

Then Mr. *Feeble-mind* called for his friends, and told them what errand had been brought unto him, and what token he had received of the truth of the message. Then he said, Since I have nothing to bequeath to any, to what purpose should I make a will? As for my *feeble Mind*, that I will leave behind me, for that I have no need of that in the place whither I go; nor is it worth bestowing upon the poorest Pilgrims: Wherefore, when I am gone, I desire, that you, Mr. *Valiant*, would bury it in a dunghill. This done, and the day being come in which he was to depart, he entered the River as the rest: His last words were, *Hold out, Faith and Patience.* So he went over to the other side.

When days had many of them passed away, Mr. *Despondency* was sent for; for a post was come, and brought this message to him: *Trembling man, these are to summon thee to be ready with thy King by the next Lord's Day, to shout for Joy, for thy deliverance from all thy doubtings.*

And, said the messenger, that my message is true, take this for a proof. So he gave him the *grasshopper* to be a *burden* unto him. Now Mr. *Despondency's* daughter, whose name was *Much-afraid*, said, when she heard what was done, that she would go with her father. Then Mr. *Despondency* said to his friends; myself and my daughter, you know what we have been, and how troublesomely we have behaved ourselves in every company. My will, and my daughter's, is that our *Desponds* and slavish fears be by no man ever received, from the day of our departure, for ever: For I know, that after my death, they will offer themselves to others. For, to be plain with you, they are *ghosts*, the which we entertained when we first began to be Pilgrims, and could never shake them off after: And they will walk about, and seek entertainment of the Pilgrims; but for our sakes, shut ye the doors upon them.

When the time was come for them to depart, they went to the brink of the River. The last words of Mr. *Despondency*, were, *Farewel night, Welcome day*. His daughter went through the River singing, but none could understand what she said.

Then it came to pass a while after, that there was a post in the town, that enquired for Mr. *Honest*. So he came to his house, where he was, and delivered to his hands these lines: *Thou art commanded to be ready against this day sevennight, to present thyself before thy Lord, at his Father's house*. And for a token that my message is true, *All thy daughters of Musick shall be brought low*. Then Mr. *Honest* called for his friends, and said unto them, I die, but shall make no will. As for my Honesty, it shall go with me; let him that comes after, be told of this. When the day that he was to be gone was come, he addressed himself to go over the River. Now the River at that time over-flow'd the banks in some places; but Mr. *Honest* in his life-time had spoken to one *Good-Conscience* to meet him there, the which he also did, and lent him his hand, and so helped him over. The last words of Mr. *Honest* were, *Grace Reigns*: So he left the World.

After this, it was noised abroad, that Mr. *Valiant-for-Truth* was taken with a summons by the same post as the other; and had this for a token that the summons was true, *That his pitcher was broken at the fountain*. When he understood it, he called for his friends, and told them of it. Then, said he, I am going to my Father's, and tho' with great difficulty I am got hither, yet now I do not repent me of all the trouble I have been at to arrive where I am. *My Sword* I give to him that shall succeed me in my Pilgrimage, and my *Courage* and *Skill* to him that can get it. My *marks* and *scars* I carry with me, to be a witness for me, that I have fought His battles, who now will be my Rewarder. When the day that he must go hence was come, many accompany'd him to the River-side, into which as he went, he said, *Death, where is thy Sting?* And as he went down deeper, he said, *Grave, where is thy Victory?* So he passed over, and all the Trumpets sounded for him on the other side.

XX

AMYAS THROWS HIS SWORD INTO THE SEA

THE weary day wore on. The strip of blue sky was curtained over again, and all was dismal as before, though it grew sultrier every moment; and now and then a distant mutter shook the air to westward. Nothing could be done to lessen the distance between the ships, for the *Vengeance* had had all her boats carried away but one, and that was much too small to tow her: and while the men went down again to finish dinner, Amyas worked on at his sword, looking up every now and then suddenly at the Spaniard, as if to satisfy himself that it was not a vision which had vanished.

About two Yeo came up to him.

'He is ours safely now, sir. The tide has been running to the eastward for this two hours.'

'Safe as a fox in a trap. Satan himself cannot take him from us!'

'But God may,' said Brimblecombe, simply.

'Who spoke to you, sir? If I thought that He—There comes the thunder at last!'

And as he spoke an angry growl from the westward heavens seemed to answer his wild words, and rolled and loudened nearer and nearer, till right over their heads it crashed against some cloud-cliff far above, and all was still.

Each man looked in the other's face: but Amyas was unmoved.

'The storm is coming,' said he, 'and the wind in it. It will be Eastward-ho now, for once, my merry men all!'

'Eastward-ho never brought us luck,' said Jack in an undertone to Cary. But by this time all eyes were turned to the north-west, where a black line along the horizon began to define the boundary of sea and air, till now all dim in mist.

'There comes the breeze.'

'And there the storm, too.'

And with that strangely accelerating pace which some storms seem to possess, the thunder, which had been growling slow and seldom far away, now rang peal on peal along the cloudy floor above their heads.

'Here comes the breeze. Round with the yards, or we shall be taken aback.'

The yards creaked round; the sea grew crisp around them; the hot air swept their cheeks, tightened every rope, filled every sail, bent her over. A cheer burst from the men as the helm went up, and they staggered away before the wind right down upon the Spaniard, who lay still becalmed.

'There is more behind, Amyas,' said Cary. 'Shall we not shorten sail a little?'

'No. Hold on every stitch,' said Amyas. 'Give me the helm, man. Boatswain, pipe away to clear for fight.'

It was done, and in ten minutes the men were all at quarters, while the thunder rolled louder and louder overhead, and the breeze freshened fast.

'The dog has it now. There he goes!' said Cary.

'Right before the wind. He has no liking to face us.'

'He is running into the jaws of destruction,' said Yeo. 'An hour more will send him either right up the Channel, or smack on shore somewhere.'

'There! he has put his helm down. I wonder if he sees land?'

'He is like a March hare beat out of his country,' said Cary, 'and don't know whither to run next.'

Cary was right. In ten minutes more the Spaniard fell off again, and went away dead down wind, while the *Vengeance* gained on him fast. After two hours more, the four miles had diminished to one, while the lightning flashed nearer and nearer as the storm came up; and from the vast mouth of a black cloud-arch poured so fierce a breeze that Amyas yielded unwillingly to hints which were growing into open murmurs, and bade shorten sail.

On they rushed with scarcely lessened speed, the black arch following fast, curtained by one flat grey sheet of pouring rain, before which the water was boiling in a long white line; while every moment, behind the watery veil, a keen blue spark leapt down into the sea, or darted zigzag through the rain.

'We shall have it now, and with a vengeance; this will try your tackle, Master,' said Cary.

The functionary answered with a shrug, and turned up the collar of his rough frock, as the first drops flew stinging round his ears. Another minute, and the squall burst full upon them in rain which cut like hail,—hail which lashed the sea into froth, and wind which whirled off the heads of the surges, and swept the waters into one white seething waste. And above them, and behind them, and before them, the lightning leapt and ran, dazzling and blinding, while the deep roar of the thunder was changed to sharp ear-piercing cracks.

'Get the arms and ammunition under cover, and then below with you all,' shouted Amyas from the helm.

'And heat the pokers in the galley fire,' said Yeo, 'to be ready if the rain puts our linstocks out. I hope you'll let me stay on deck, sir, in case———'

'I must have some one, and who better than you? Can you see the chase?'

No; she was wrapped in the grey whirlwind. She might be within half a mile of them, for aught they could have seen of her.

And now Amyas and his old liegeman were alone. Neither spoke; each knew the other's thoughts, and knew that they were his own. The squall blew fiercer and fiercer, the rain poured heavier and heavier. Where was the Spaniard?

'If he has laid-to, we may overshoot him, sir!'

'If he has tried to lay-to, he will not have a sail left in the bolt-ropes, or perhaps a mast on deck. I know the stiff-neckedness of those Spanish tubs. Hurrah! there he is, right on our larboard bow!'

There she was indeed, two musket-shots off, staggering away with canvas split and flying.

'He has been trying to hull, sir, and caught a buffet,' said Yeo, rubbing his hands. 'What shall we do now?'

'Range alongside, if it blow live imps and witches, and try our luck once more. Pah! how this lightning dazzles!'

On they swept, gaining fast on the Spaniard.

'Call the men up, and to quarters; the rain will be over in ten minutes.'

Yeo ran forward to the gangway: and sprang back again, with a face white and wild—

'Land right ahead! Port your helm, sir! For the love of God, port your helm!'

Amyas, with the strength of a bull, jammed the helm down, while Yeo shouted to the men below.

She swung round. The masts bent like whips; crack went the fore-sail like a cannon. What matter? Within two hundred yards of them was the Spaniard; in front of her, and above her, a huge dark bank rose through the dense hail, and mingled with the clouds; and at its foot, plainer every moment, pillars and spouts of leaping foam.

'What is it, Morte? Hartland?'

It might be anything for thirty miles.

'Lundy!' said Yeo. 'The south end! I see the head of the Shutter in the breakers! Hard a-port yet, and get her close-hauled as you can, and the Lord may have mercy on us still! Look at the Spaniard!'

Yes, look at the Spaniard!

On their left, as they broached-to, the wall of granite sloped down from the clouds towards an isolated peak of rock, some two hundred feet in height. Then a hundred yards of roaring breaker upon a sunken shelf, across which the race of the tide poured like a cataract; then, amid a column of salt smoke, the Shutter, like a huge black fang, rose waiting for its prey; and between the Shutter and the land, the great galleon loomed dimly through the storm.

He, too, had seen his danger, and tried to broach-to. But his clumsy mass refused to obey the helm; he struggled a moment, half hid in foam; fell away again, and rushed upon his doom.

'Lost! lost! lost!' cried Amyas madly, and throwing up his hands, let go the tiller. Yeo caught it just in time.

'Sir, sir! What are you at? We shall clear the rock yet.'

'Yes!' shouted Amyas in his frenzy; 'but he will not!'

Another minute. The galleon gave a sudden jar, and stopped. Then one long heave and bound, as if to free herself. And then her bows lighted clean upon the Shutter.

An awful silence fell on every English soul. They heard not the roaring of wind and surge; they saw not the blinding flashes of the lightning; but they heard one long ear-piercing wail to every saint in heaven rise from five hundred human throats; they saw the mighty ship heel over from the wind, and sweep headlong down the cataract of the race, plunging her yards into the foam, and showing her whole black side even to her keel, till she rolled clean over, and vanished for ever and ever.

'Shame!' cried Amyas, hurling his sword far into the sea, 'to lose my right, my right! when it was in my very grasp! Unmerciful!'

A crack which rent the sky, and made the granite ring and quiver; a bright world of flame, and then a blank of utter darkness, against which stood out, glowing red-hot, every mast, and sail, and rock, and Salvation Yeo as he stood just in front of Amyas, the tiller in his hand. All red-hot, transfigured into fire; and behind, the black, black night.

XXI

THREE BALLADS

THE WIFE OF USHER'S WELL

THERE lived a wife at Usher's well,
    And a wealthy wife was she;
    She had three stout and stalwart sons,
And sent them o'er the sea.

They hadna been a week from her,
    A week but barely ane,
When word came to the carline wife
    That her three sons were gane.

They hadna been a week from her,
    A week but barely three,
When word came to the carline wife
    That her sons she'd never see.

'I wish the wind may never cease,
    Nor fashes in the flood,
Till my three sons come hame to me
    In earthly flesh and blood!'

It fell about the Martinmas,
    When nights are lang and mirk,
The carline wife's three sons came hame,
    And their hats were o' the birk.

It neither grew in syke nor ditch,
    Nor yet in ony sheugh;
But at the gates o' Paradise
    That birk grew fair eneugh.

'Blow up the fire, my maidens!
    Bring water from the well!
For a' my house shall feast this night,
    Since my three sons are well.'

And she has made to them a bed,
  She's made it large and wide;
And she's ta'en her mantle her about,
  Sat down at the bedside.

Up then crew the red, red cock,
  And up and crew the gray;
The eldest to the youngest said,
  ''Tis time we were away.'

The cock he hadna craw'd but once,
  And clapp'd his wings at a',
When the youngest to the eldest said,
  'Brother, we must awa'.

'The cock doth craw, the day doth daw,
  The channerin' worm doth chide;
Gin we be miss'd out o' our place,
  A sair pain we maun bide.'—

'Lie still, lie still but a little wee while,
  Lie still but if we may;
Gin my mother should miss us when she wakes,
  She'll go mad ere it be day.'—

'Fare ye well, my mother dear!
  Farewell to barn and byre!
And fare ye well, the bonny lass
  That kindles my mother's fire!'

SIR PATRICK SPENS

1. The Sailing

The king sits in Dunfermline town
  Drinking the blue-red wine;
'O where will I get a skeely skipper
  To sail this new ship o' mine?'

O up and spak an eldern knight,
  Sat at the king's right knee:
'Sir Patrick Spens is the best sailor
  That ever sail'd the sea.'

Our king has written a braid letter,
  And seal'd it with his hand,
And sent it to Sir Patrick Spens,
  Was walking on the strand.

'To Noroway, to Noroway,
  To Noroway o'er the faem;
The king's daughter of Noroway,
  'Tis thou must bring her hame.'

The first word that Sir Patrick read
  So loud, loud laugh'd he;
The neist word that Sir Patrick read
  The tear blinded his e'e.

'O wha is this has done this deed
  And tauld the king o' me,
To send us out, at this time o' year,
  To sail upon the sea?

'Be it wind, be it weet, be it hail, be it sleet,
  Our ship must sail the faem;
The king's daughter o' Noroway,
  'Tis we must fetch her hame.'

They hoysed their sails on Monenday morn
  Wi' a' the speed they may;
They hae landed in Noroway
  Upon a Wodensday.

II. THE RETURN

'Mak ready, mak ready, my merry men a'!
  Our gude ship sails the morn.'—
'Now ever alack, my master dear,
  I fear a deadly storm.

'I saw the new moon late yestreen
  Wi' the auld moon in her arm;
And if we gang to sea, master,
  I fear we'll come to harm.'

They hadna sail'd a league, a league,
  A league but barely three,
When the lift grew dark, and the wind blew loud,
  And gurly grew the sea.

The ankers brak, and the topmast lap,
  It was sic a deadly storm:
And the waves cam owre the broken ship
  Till a' her sides were torn.

'O where will I get a gude sailor
  To tak' my helm in hand,
Till I get up to the tall topmast
  To see if I can spy land?'—

'O here am I, a sailor gude,
  To tak' the helm in hand,
Till you go up to the tall topmast,
  But I fear you'll ne'er spy land.'

He hadna gane a step, a step,
  A step but barely ane,
When a bolt flew out of our goodly ship,
  And the saut sea it came in.

'Go fetch a web o' the silken claith,
  Another o' the twine,
And wap them into our ship's side,
  And let nae the sea come in.'

They fetch'd a web o' the silken claith,
  Another o' the twine,
And they wrapp'd them round that gude ship's side,
  But still the sea came in.

O laith, laith were our gude Scots lords
  To wet their cork-heel'd shoon;
But lang or a' the play was play'd
  They wat their hats aboon.

And mony was the feather bed
  That flatter'd on the faem;
And mony was the gude lord's son
  That never mair cam hame.

O lang, lang may the ladies sit,
  Wi' their fans into their hand,
Before they see Sir Patrick Spens
  Come sailing to the strand!

And lang, lang may the maidens sit
  Wi' their gowd kames in their hair,
A-waiting for their ain dear loves!
  For them they'll see nae mair.

Half-owre, half-owre to Aberdour,
  'Tis fifty fathoms deep;
And there lies gude Sir Patrick Spens,
  Wi' the Scots lords at his feet!

THE LOWLANDS O' HOLLAND

'My love has built a bonny ship, and set her on the sea,
With seven score good mariners to bear her company;
There's three score is sunk, and three score dead at sea,
And the Lowlands o' Holland has twin'd my love and me.

'My love he built another ship, and set her on the main,
And nane but twenty mariners for to bring her hame;
But the weary wind began to rise, and the sea began to rout,
My love then and his bonny ship turn'd wither-shins about.

'Then shall neither coif come on my head nor comb come
   in my hair;
Then shall neither coal nor candle-light shine in my bower
   mair;
Nor will I love another one until the day I die,
Sin' the Lowlands o' Holland has twin'd my love and me.'—

'O haud your tongue, my daughter dear, be still and be content;
There are mair lads in Galloway, ye neen nae sair lament.'—
'O there is none in Gallow, there's none at a' for me,
For I never loved a love but one, and he's drown'd in the
   sea.'

XXII

ABRAHAM LINCOLN

FELLOW-COUNTRYMEN: At this second appearing to take the oath of the presidential office, there is less occasion for an extended address than there was at the first. Then a statement, somewhat in detail, of a course to be pursued seemed fitting and proper. Now, at the expiration of four years, during which public declarations have been constantly called forth on every point and phase of the great contest which still absorbs the attention and engrosses the energies of the nation, little that is new could be presented. The progress of our arms, upon which all else chiefly depends, is as well known to the public as to myself; and it is, I trust, reasonably satisfactory and encouraging to all. With high hope for the future, no prediction in regard to it is ventured.

On the occasion corresponding to this four years ago, all thoughts were anxiously directed to an impending civil war. All dreaded it—all sought to avert it. While the inaugural address was being delivered from this place, devoted altogether to saving the Union without war, insurgent agents were in the city seeking to destroy it without war—seeking to dissolve the Union, and divide effects, by negotiation. Both parties deprecated war; but one of them would make war rather than let the nation survive; and the other would accept war rather than let it perish. And the war came.

One-eighth of the whole population were coloured slaves, not distributed generally over the Union, but localized in the Southern part of it. These slaves constituted a peculiar and powerful interest. All knew that this interest was, somehow, the cause of the war. To strengthen, perpetuate, and extend this interest was the object for which the insurgents would rend the Union, even by war; while the government claimed no right to do more than to restrict the territorial enlargement of it.

Neither party expected for the war the magnitude or the duration which it has already attained. Neither anticipated that the cause of the conflict might cease with, or even before, the conflict itself should cease. Each looked for an easier triumph, and a result less fundamental and astounding. Both read the same Bible, and pray to the same God; and each invokes his aid against the other. It may seem strange that any men should dare to ask a just God's assistance in wringing their bread from the sweat of other men's faces; but let us judge not, that we be not judged. The prayers of both could not be answered—that of neither has been answered fully.

The Almighty has his own purposes. 'Woe unto the world because of offences! for it must needs be that offences come; but woe to that man by whom the offence cometh.' If we shall suppose that American slavery is one of those offences which, in the providence of God, must needs come, but which, having continued through his appointed time, he now wills to remove, and that he gives to both North and South this terrible war, as the woe due to those by whom the offence came, shall we discern therein any departure from those divine attributes which the believers in a living God always ascribe to him? Fondly do we hope—fervently do we pray—that this mighty scourge of war may speedily pass away. Yet, if God wills that it continue until all the wealth piled by the bondman's two hundred and fifty years of unrequited toil shall be sunk, and until every drop of blood drawn with the lash shall be paid by another drawn with the sword, as was said three thousand years ago, so still it must be said, 'The judgments of the Lord are true and righteous altogether.'

With malice toward none; with charity for all; with firmness in the right, as God gives us to see the right, let us strive on to finish the work we are in; to bind up the nation's wounds; to care for him who shall have borne the battle, and for his widow, and his orphan—to do all which may achieve and cherish a just and lasting peace among ourselves, and with all nations.

XXIII

MR. TONY WELLER ON LITERATURE

'VELL, Sammy,' said the father.

'Vell, my Prooshan Blue,' responded the son, laying down his pen. 'What's the latest bulletin about mother-in-law?'

'Mrs. Veller passed a very good night, but is uncommon perwerse, and unpleasant this mornin'. Signed upon oath, S. Veller, Esquire, Senior. That's the last vun as was issued, Sammy,' replied Mr. Weller, untying his shawl.

'No better yet?' inquired Sam.

'All the symptoms aggerawated,' replied Mr. Weller, shaking his head. 'But wot's that, you're a doin' of? Pursuit of knowledge under difficulties, Sammy?'

'I've done now,' said Sam with slight embarrassment; 'I've been a writin'.'

'So I see,' replied Mr. Weller. 'Not to any young 'ooman, I hope, Sammy?'

'Why it's no use a sayin' it ain't,' replied Sam. 'It's a walentine.'

'A what!' exclaimed Mr. Weller, apparently horror-stricken by the word.

'A walentine,' replied Sam.

'Samivel, Samivel,' said Mr. Weller, in reproachful accents, 'I didn't think you'd ha' done it. Arter the warnin' you've had o' your father's wicious propensities; arter all I've said to you upon this here wery subject; arter actiwally seein' and bein' in the company o' your own mother-in-law, vich I should ha' thought wos a moral lesson as no man could never ha' forgotten to his dyin' day! I didn't think you'd ha' done it, Sammy, I didn't think you'd ha' done it!' These reflections were too much for the good old man. He raised Sam's tumbler to his lips and drank off its contents.

'Wot's the matter now?' said Sam.

'Nev'r mind, Sammy,' replied Mr. Weller, 'it'll be a wery agonizin' trial to me at my time of life, but I'm pretty tough, that's vun consolation, as the wery old turkey remarked wen the farmer said he wos afeerd he should be obliged to kill him for the London market.'

'Wot'll be a trial?' inquired Sam.

'To see you married, Sammy—to see you a dilluded wictim, and thinkin' in your innocence that it's all wery capital,' replied Mr. Weller. 'It's a dreadful trial to a father's feelin's, that 'ere, Sammy.'

'Nonsense,' said Sam. 'I ain't a goin' to get married, don't you fret yourself about that; I know you're a judge of these things. Order in your pipe, and I'll read you the letter. There!'

We cannot distinctly say whether it was the prospect of the pipe, or the consolatory reflection that a fatal disposition to get married ran in the family and couldn't be helped, which calmed Mr. Weller's feelings, and caused his grief to subside. We should be rather disposed to say that the result was attained by combining the two sources of consolation, for he repeated the second in a low tone, very frequently; ringing the bell meanwhile, to order in the first. He then divested himself of his upper coat; and lighting the pipe and placing himself in front of the fire with his back towards it, so that he could feel its full heat, and recline against the mantelpiece at the same time, turned towards Sam, and, with a countenance greatly mollified by the softening influence of tobacco, requested him to 'fire away.'

Sam dipped his pen into the ink to be ready for any corrections, and began with a very theatrical air:

' "Lovely——" '

'Stop,' said Mr. Weller, ringing the bell. 'A double glass o' the inwariable, my dear.'

'Very well, sir,' replied the girl; who with great quickness appeared, vanished, returned, and disappeared.

'They seem to know your ways here,' observed Sam.

'Yes,' replied his father, 'I've been here before, in my time. Go on, Sammy.'

' "Lovely creetur," ' repeated Sam.

' 'Tain't in poetry, is it?' interposed his father.

'No, no,' replied Sam.

'Werry glad to hear it,' said Mr. Weller. 'Poetry's unnat'ral; no man ever talked poetry 'cept a beadle on boxin' day, or Warren's blackin', or Rowland's oil, or some o' them low fellows; never you let yourself down to talk poetry, my boy. Begin agin, Sammy.'

Mr. Weller resumed his pipe with critical solemnity, and Sam once more commenced, and read as follows:

' "Lovely creetur i feel myself a dammed" '—.

'That ain't proper,' said Mr. Weller, taking his pipe from his mouth.

'No; it ain't "dammed," ' observed Sam, holding the letter up to the light, 'it's "shamed," there's a blot there—"I feel myself ashamed." '

'Werry good,' said Mr. Weller. 'Go on.'

' "Feel myself ashamed, and completely cir—" I forget what this here word is,' said Sam, scratching his head with the pen, in vain attempts to remember.

'Why don't you look at it, then?' inquired Mr. Weller.

'So I *am* a lookin' at it,' replied Sam, 'but there's another blot. Here's a "c," and a "i," and a "d." '

'Circumwented, p'haps,' suggested Mr. Weller.

'No, it ain't that,' said Sam, 'circumscribed; that's it.'

'That ain't as good a word as circumwented, Sammy,' said Mr. Weller, gravely.

'Think not?' said Sam.

'Nothin' like it,' replied his father.

'But don't you think it means more?' inquired Sam.

'Vell p'raps it is a more tenderer word,' said Mr. Weller, after a few moments' reflection. 'Go on, Sammy.'

' "Feel myself ashamed and completely circumscribed in a dressin' of you, for you *are* a nice gal and nothin' but it." '

'That's a werry pretty sentiment,' said the elder Mr. Weller, removing his pipe to make way for the remark.

'Yes, I think it is rayther good,' observed Sam, highly flattered.

'Wot I like in that 'ere style of writin',' said the elder Mr. Weller, 'is, that there ain't no callin' names in it,—no Wenuses, nor nothin' o' that kind. Wot's the good o' callin' a young 'ooman a Wenus or a angel, Sammy?'

'Ah! what, indeed?' replied Sam.

'You might jist as well call her a griffin, or a unicorn, or a king's arms at once, which is werry well known to be a col-lection o' fabulous animals,' added Mr. Weller.

'Just as well,' replied Sam.

'Drive on, Sammy,' said Mr. Weller.

Sam complied with the request, and proceeded as follows; his father continuing to smoke, with a mixed expression of wisdom and complacency, which was particularly edifying.

' "Afore I see you, I thought all women was alike." '

'So they are,' observed the elder Mr. Weller parenthetically.

' "But now," ' continued Sam, ' "now I find what a reg'lar soft-headed, inkred'lous turnip I must ha' been; for there ain't nobody like you, though *I* like you better than nothin' at all." I thought it best to make that rayther strong,' said Sam, looking up.

Mr. Weller nodded approvingly, and Sam resumed.

' "So I take the privilidge of the day, Mary, my dear—as

the gen'l'm'n in difficulties did, ven he valked out of a Sunday, —to tell you that the first and only time I see you, your likeness was took on my hart in much quicker time and brighter colours than ever a likeness was took by the profeel macheen (wich p'raps you may have heerd on Mary my dear) altho it *does* finish a portrait and put the frame and glass on complete, with a hook at the end to hang it up by, and all in two minutes and a quarter."'

'I am afeerd that werges on the poetical, Sammy,' said Mr. Weller, dubiously.

'No it don't,' replied Sam, reading on very quickly, to avoid contesting the point:

'"Except of me Mary my dear as your walentine and think over what I've said.—My dear Mary I will now conclude." That's all,' said Sam.

'That's rather a sudden pull up, ain't it, Sammy?' inquired Mr. Weller.

'Not a bit on it,' said Sam; 'she'll vish there wos more, and that's the great art o' letter writin'.'

'Well,' said Mr. Weller, 'there's somethin' in that; and I wish your mother-in-law 'ud only conduct her conwersation on the same gen-teel principle. Ain't you agoin' to sign it?'

'That's the difficulty,' said Sam; 'I don't know what *to* sign it.'

'Sign it, Veller,' said the oldest surviving proprietor of that name.

'Won't do,' said Sam. 'Never sign a walentine with your own name.'

'Sign it "Pickvick," then,' said Mr. Weller; 'it's a werry good name, and a easy one to spell.'

'The wery thing,' said Sam. 'I *could* end with a werse; what do you think?'

'I don't like it, Sam,' rejoined Mr. Weller. 'I never know'd a respectable coachman as wrote poetry, 'cept one, as made an affectin' copy o' werses the night afore he wos hung for a highway robbery; and *he* wos only a Cambervell man, so even that's no rule.'

But Sam was not to be dissuaded from the poetical idea that had occurred to him, so he signed the letter,
'Your love-sick
Pickwick.'

XXIV

A NIGHT ATTACK

WE all weighed that night; the *Tinker* bearing up for Jamaica, while we kept by the wind steering for Gonaives in St. Domingo. The third day we were off Cape St. Nicholas, and getting a slant of wind from the westward, we ran up the Bight of Leogane all that night, but towards morning it fell calm; we were close in under the high-land, about two miles from the shore, and the night was the darkest I ever was out in anywhere. There were neither moon nor stars to be seen, and the dark clouds settled down, until they appeared to rest upon our mastheads, compressing, as it were, the hot steamy air upon us until it became too dense for breathing. In the early part of the night it had rained in heavy showers now and then, and there were one or two faint flashes of lightning, and some heavy peals of thunder, which rolled amongst the distant hills in loud shaking reverberations, which gradually became fainter and fainter, until they grumbled away in the distance in hoarse murmurs, like the low notes of an organ in one of our old cathedrals; but now there was neither rain nor wind—all nature seemed fearfully hushed; for where we lay, in the smooth bight, there was no swell, not even a ripple on the glasslike sea; the sound of the shifting of a handspike, or the tread of the men, as they ran to haul on a rope, or the creaking of the rudder, sounded loud and distinct. The sea in our neighbourhood was strongly phosphorescent, so that the smallest chip thrown overboard struck fire from the water, as if it had been a piece of iron cast on flint; and when you looked over the quarter, as I delight to do, and tried to penetrate into the dark clear profound beneath, you every now and then saw a burst of pale light, like a halo, far down in the depths of the green sea, caused by the motion of some fish, or of what Jack, no great natural philosopher, usually calls *blubbers*; and when the dolphin or skipjack leapt into the air, they sparkled out from the still bosom of the deep dark water like rockets, until they fell again into their element in a flash of fire. This evening the corvette had showed no lights, and although I conjectured she was not far from us, still I could not with any certainty indicate her whereabouts. It might now have been about three o'clock, and I was standing on the aftermost gun on the starboard side, peering into the impervious darkness over the tafferel, with my dear old dog Sneezer by my side, nuzzling and fondling after his affectionate fashion, while the pilot, Peter Mangrove, stood within handspike length of me. The dog had been growling, but all in fun, and snapping at me, when in a moment he hauled off, planted his paws on the rail, looked forth into the night and gave a short anxious bark, like the solitary pop of the sentry's musket to alarm the mainguard in outpost work.

Peter Mangrove advanced, and put his arm round the dog's neck. 'What you see, my shild?' said the black pilot.

Sneezer uplifted his voice, and gave a long continuous growl.

'Ah!' said Mangrove, sharply, 'Massa Captain, something near we—never doubt dat—de dog yeerie someting we can't yeerie, and see something we can't see.'

I had lived long enough never to despise any caution, from whatever quarter it proceeded. So I listened, still as a stone. Presently I thought I heard the distant splash of oars. I placed my hand behind my ear, and waited with breathless attention. Immediately I saw the sparkling dip of them in the calm black water, as if a boat, and a large one, was pulling very fast towards us. 'Look out, hail that boat,' said I.

'Boat ahoy!' sung out the man, to whom I had spoken. No answer. 'Coming here?' reiterated the seaman. No better success. The boat or canoe, or whatever it might be, was by this time close aboard of us, within pistol-shot at the farthest—no time to be lost, so I hailed myself, and this time the challenge did produce an answer.

'*Sore boat—fruit and wegitab.*'

'Shore boat, with fruit and vegetables, at this time of night —I don't like it,' said I. 'Boatswain's mate,—all hands— pipe away the boarders. Cutlasses, men—quick, a piratical row-boat is close to.' And verily we had little time to lose, when a large canoe or row-boat, pulling twelve oars at the fewest and carrying twenty-five men, or thereabouts, swept up on our larboard quarter, hooked on, and the next moment upwards of twenty unlooked-for visitors scrambled up our shallow side, and jumped on board. All this took place so suddenly that there were not ten of my people ready to receive them, but those ten were the prime men of the ship.

'Surrender, you scoundrels—surrender. You have boarded a man-of-war. Down with your arms, or we shall kill you to a man.'

But they either did not understand me, or did not believe me, for the answer was a blow from a cutlass, which, if I had not parried with my night-glass, which it broke in pieces, might have effectually stopped my promotion.

'Cut them down, boarders, down with them—they are pirates,' shouted I; 'heave cold shot into their boat alongside —all hands, Mr. Rousemout,' to the boatswain, 'call all hands.'

We closed. The assailants had no firearms, but they were armed with swords and long knives, and as they fought with desperation, several of our people were cruelly haggled; and after the first charge, the combatants on both sides became so blended, that it was impossible to strike a blow, without running the risk of cutting down a friend. By this time all hands were on deck; the boat alongside had been swamped by the cold shot that had been hove crashing through her bottom, when down came a shower from the surcharged clouds, or waterspout—call it which you will—that absolutely deluged the decks, the scuppers being utterly unable to carry off the water. So long as the pirates fought in a body, I had no fear, as, dark as it was, our men, who held together, knew where to strike and thrust; but when the torrent of rain descended in bucketfuls, the former broke away, and were pursued singly into various corners about the deck, all escape being cut off from the swamping of their boat. Still they were not vanquished, and I ran aft to the binnacle, where a blue light was stowed away,—one of several that we had got on deck to burn that night, in order to point out our whereabouts to the *Firebrand*. I fired it, and rushing forward cutlass-in-hand, we set on the gang of black desperadoes with such fury, that after killing two of them outright, and wounding and taking prisoners seven, we drove the rest overboard into the sea, where the small-armed men, who by this time had tackled to their muskets, made short work of them, guided as they were by the sparkling of the dark water, as they struck out and swam for their lives. The blue light was immediately answered by another from the corvette, which lay about a mile off; but before her boats, two of which were immediately armed and manned, could reach us, we had defeated our antagonists, and the rain had increased to such a degree, that the heavy drops, as they fell with a strong rushing noise into the sea, flashed it up into one entire sheet of fire.

We secured our prisoners, all blacks and mulattoes, the most villainous-looking scoundrels I had ever seen, and shortly after it came on to thunder and lighten, as if heaven and earth had been falling together. A most vivid flash— it almost blinded me. Presently the *Firebrand* burnt another blue light, whereby we saw that her maintopmast was gone close by the cap, with the topsail, and upper spars, and yards, and gear, all hanging down in a lumbering mass of confused wreck; she had been struck by the levin brand, which had killed four men, and stunned several more.

By this time the cold grey streaks of morning appeared in the eastern horizon, and soon after the day broke; and by two o'clock in the afternoon, both corvette and schooner were at anchor at Gonaives.

XXV

THE QUEENSFERRY DILIGENCE

> 'Go call a coach, and let a coach be call'd,
> And let the man who calleth be the caller:
> And in his calling let him nothing call,
> But Coach! Coach! Coach! O for a coach, ye gods!'

IT was early on a fine summer's day, near the end of the eighteenth century, when a young man, of genteel appearance, journeying towards the north-east of Scotland, provided himself with a ticket in one of those public carriages which travel between Edinburgh and the Queensferry, at which place, as the name implies, and as is well-known to all my northern readers, there is a passage-boat for crossing the Frith of Forth. The coach was calculated to carry six regular passengers, besides such interlopers as the coachman could pick up by the way, and intrude upon those who were legally in possession. The tickets, which conferred right to a seat in this vehicle of little ease, were dispensed by a sharp-looking old dame, with a pair of spectacles on a very thin nose, who inhabited a 'laigh shop,' *anglicè*, a cellar opening to the High-street by a strait and steep stair, at the bottom of which she sold tape, thread, needles, skeans of worsted, coarse linen cloth, and such feminine gear, to those who had the courage and skill to descend to the profundity of her dwelling, without falling headlong themselves, or throwing down any of the numerous articles which, piled on each side of the descent, indicated the profession of the trader below.

The written hand-bill, which, pasted on a projecting board, announced that the Queensferry Diligence, or Hawes Fly, departed precisely at twelve o'clock on Tuesday, the fifteenth July, 17—, in order to secure for travellers the opportunity of passing the Frith with the flood-tide, lied on the present occasion like a bulletin; for although that hour was pealed from Saint Giles's steeple, and repeated by the Tron, no coach appeared upon the appointed stand. . . .

The young gentleman, who began to grow somewhat impatient, was now joined by a companion in this petty misery of human life—the person who had taken out the other place. ... He was a good-looking man of the age of sixty, perhaps older, but his hale complexion and firm step announced that years had not impaired his strength or health. ...

He arrived with a hurried pace, and, casting an alarmed glance towards the dial-plate of the church, then looking at the place where the coach should have been, exclaimed, 'Deil's in it—I am too late after all!' The young man relieved his anxiety, by telling him the coach had not yet appeared. The old gentleman, apparently conscious of his own want of punctuality, did not at first feel courageous enough to censure that of the coachman. ...

At length, after one or two impatient glances at the progress of the minute-hand of the clock, having compared it with his own watch, a huge and antique gold repeater, and having twitched about his features to give due emphasis to one or two peevish pshaws, he hailed the old lady of the cavern.

'Good woman,—what the d—l is her name?—Mrs. Macleuchar!'

Mrs. Macleuchar, aware that she had a defensive part to sustain in the encounter which was to follow, was in no hurry to hasten the discussion by returning a ready answer.

'Mrs. Macleuchar—Good woman,' (with an elevated voice)—then apart, 'Old doited hag, she's as deaf as a post—I say, Mrs. Macleuchar!'

'I am just serving a customer.—Indeed, hinny, it will no be a bodle cheaper than I tell ye.'

'Woman,' reiterated the traveller, 'do you think we can stand here all day till you have cheated that poor servant wench out of her half-year's fee and bountith?'

'Cheated!' retorted Mrs. Macleuchar, eager to take up the quarrel upon a defensible ground; 'I scorn your words, sir; you are an uncivil person, and I desire you will not stand there to slander me at my ain stairhead.'

'The woman,' said the senior, looking with an arch glance

at his destined travelling companion, 'does not understand the words of action.—Woman,' again turning to the vault, 'I arraign not thy character, but I desire to know what is become of thy coach?'

'What's your wull?' answered Mrs. Macleuchar, relapsing into deafness.

'We have taken places, ma'am,' said the younger stranger, 'in your diligence for Queensferry.'—'Which should have been half-way on the road before now,' continued the elder and more impatient traveller, rising in wrath as he spoke; 'and now in all likelihood we shall miss the tide, and I have business of importance on the other side—and your cursed coach———'

'The coach?—gude guide us, gentlemen, is it no on the stand yet?' answered the old lady, her shrill tone of expostulation sinking into a kind of apologetic whine. 'Is it the coach ye hae been waiting for?'

'What else could have kept us broiling in the sun by the side of the gutter here, you—you faithless woman? Eh?'

Mrs. Macleuchar now ascended her trap stair (for such it might be called, though constructed of stone), until her nose came upon a level with the pavement; then, after wiping her spectacles to look for that which she well knew was not to be found, she exclaimed, with well-feigned astonishment, 'Gude guide us—saw ever ony body the like o' that!'

'Yes, you abominable woman,' vociferated the traveller, 'many have seen the like of it, and all will see the like of it, that have any thing to do with your trolloping sex'; then, pacing with great indignation before the door of the shop, still as he passed and repassed, like a vessel who gives her broadside as she comes abreast of a hostile fortress, he shot down complaints, threats, and reproaches, on the embarrassed Mrs. Macleuchar. He would take a post-chaise—he would call a hackney-coach—he would take four horses—he must —he would be on the north side to-day—and all the expense of his journey, besides damages, direct and consequential, arising from delay, should be accumulated on the devoted head of Mrs. Macleuchar.

There was something so comic in his pettish resentment, that the younger traveller, who was in no such pressing hurry to depart, could not help being amused with it, especially as it was obvious, that every now and then the old gentleman, though very angry, could not help laughing at his own vehemence. But when Mrs. Macleuchar began also to join in the laughter, he quickly put a stop to her ill-timed merriment.

'Woman,' said he, 'is that advertisement thine?' showing a bit of crumpled printed paper: 'Does it not set forth, that, God willing, as you hypocritically express it, the Hawes Fly, or Queensferry Diligence, would set forth to-day at twelve o'clock; and is it not, thou falsest of creatures, now a quarter past twelve, and no such fly or diligence to be seen?—Dost thou know the consequence of seducing the lieges by false reports?—Dost thou know it might be brought under the statute of leasing-making? Answer; and for once in thy long, useless, and evil life, let it be in the words of truth and sincerity—hast thou such a coach?—Is it *in rerum natura?*—or is this base annunciation a mere swindle on the incautious, to beguile them of their time, their patience, and three shillings of sterling money of this realm?—Hast thou, I say, such a coach? ay or no?'

'O dear, yes, sir; the neighbours ken the diligence weel, green picked out wi' red—three yellow wheels and a black ane.'

'Woman, thy special description will not serve—it may be only a lie with a circumstance.'

'O, man, man!' said the overwhelmed Mrs. Macleuchar, totally exhausted by having been so long the butt of his rhetoric, 'take back your three shillings, and mak me quit o' ye.'

'Not so fast, not so fast, woman—will three shillings transport me to Queensferry, agreeably to thy treacherous program?—or will it requite the damage I may sustain by leaving my business undone, or repay the expenses which I must disburse if I am obliged to tarry a day at the South Ferry for lack of tide?—Will it hire, I say, a pinnace, for which alone the regular price is five shillings?'

Here his argument was cut short by a lumbering noise, which proved to be the advance of the expected vehicle, pressing forward with all the dispatch to which the broken-winded jades that drew it could possibly be urged. With ineffable pleasure, Mrs. Macleuchar saw her tormentor deposited in the leathern convenience; but still, as it was driving off, his head thrust out of the window reminded her, in words drowned amid the rumbling of the wheels, that, if the diligence did not attain the Ferry in time to save the flood-tide, she, Mrs. Macleuchar, should be held responsible for all the consequences that might ensue. . . .

So much time was consumed by [the] interruptions of their journey, that when they descended the hill above the Hawes (for so the inn on the southern side of the Queensferry is denominated,) the experienced eye of the Antiquary at once discerned, from the extent of wet sand, and the number of black stones and rocks, covered with sea-weed, which were visible along the skirts of the shore, that the hour of tide was past. The young traveller expected a burst of indignation; but whether, as Croaker says in 'The Good-natured Man,' our hero had exhausted himself in fretting away his misfortunes beforehand, so that he did not feel them when they actually arrived, or whether he found the company in which he was placed too congenial to lead him to repine at anything which delayed his journey, it is certain that he submitted to his lot with much resignation.

'The d—l's in the diligence and the old hag it belongs to! —Diligence, quoth I? Thou shouldst have called it the Sloth—Fly!—quoth she? why, it moves like a fly through a glue-pot, as the Irishman says. But, however, time and tide tarry for no man; and so, my young friend, we'll have a snack here at the Hawes, which is a very decent sort of a place, and I'll be very happy to finish the account I was giving you of the difference between the mode of entrenching *castra stativa* and *castra æstiva*, things confounded by too many of our historians. Lack-a-day, if they had ta'en the pains to satisfy their own eyes, instead of following each other's blind guidance!—Well! we shall be pretty comfortable at the Hawes; and besides, after all, we must have dined somewhere, and it will be pleasanter sailing with the tide of ebb and the evening breeze.'

In this Christian temper of making the best of all occurrences, our travellers alighted at the Hawes.

XXVI

L'ALLEGRO

HENCE, loathéd Melancholy,
    Of Cerberus and blackest Midnight born
    In Stygian cave forlorn
'Mongst horrid shapes, and shrieks, and sights unholy!
Find out some uncouth cell
    Where brooding Darkness spreads his jealous wings
And the night-raven sings;
    There under ebon shades, and low-brow'd rocks
As ragged as thy locks,
    In dark Cimmerian desert ever dwell.

But come, thou Goddess fair and free,
In heaven yclep'd Euphrosyne,
And by men, heart-easing Mirth,
Whom lovely Venus at a birth
With two sister Graces more
To ivy-crownéd Bacchus bore:
Or whether (as some sager sing)
The frolic wind that breathes the spring
Zephyr, with Aurora playing,
As he met her once a-Maying—
There on beds of violets blue
And fresh-blown roses wash'd in dew
Fill'd her with thee, a daughter fair,
So buxom, blithe, and debonair.
    Haste thee, Nymph, and bring with thee
Jest, and youthful jollity,

Quips, and cranks, and wanton wiles,
Nods, and becks, and wreathéd smiles
Such as hang on Hebe's cheek,
And love to live in dimple sleek;
Sport that wrinkled Care derides,
And Laughter holding both his sides:—
Come, and trip it as you go
On the light fantastic toe;
And in thy right hand lead with thee
The mountain nymph, sweet Liberty;
And if I give thee honour due,
Mirth, admit me of thy crew,
To live with her, and live with thee
In unreprovéd pleasures free;
To hear the lark begin his flight
And singing startle the dull night
From his watch-tower in the skies,
Till the dappled dawn doth rise;
Then to come, in spite of sorrow,
And at my window bid good-morrow
Through the sweetbriar, or the vine,
Or the twisted eglantine:
While the cock with lively din
Scatters the rear of darkness thin,
And to the stack, or the barn-door,
Stoutly struts his dames before:
Oft listening how the hounds and horn
Cheerly rouse the slumbering morn,
From the side of some hoar hill,
Through the high wood echoing shrill:
Sometime walking, not unseen,
By hedge-row elms, on hillocks green,
Right against the eastern gate
Where the great Sun begins his state
Robed in flames and amber light,
The clouds in thousand liveries dight,
While the ploughman, near at hand,
Whistles o'er the furrow'd land,

And the milkmaid singeth blithe,
And the mower whets his scythe,
And every shepherd tells his tale
Under the hawthorn in the dale.
    Straight mine eye hath caught new pleasures
Whilst the landscape round it measures;
Russet lawns, and fallows grey,
Where the nibbling flocks do stray;
Mountains, on whose barren breast
The labouring clouds do often rest;
Meadows trim with daisies pied,
Shallow brooks and rivers wide;
Towers and battlements it sees
Bosom'd high in tufted trees,
Where perhaps some Beauty lies,
The Cynosure of neighbouring eyes.
    Hard by, a cottage chimney smokes
From betwixt two aged oaks,
Where Corydon and Thyrsis, met,
Are at their savoury dinner set
Of herbs, and other country messes
Which the neat-handed Phillis dresses;
And then in haste her bower she leaves
With Thestylis to bind the sheaves;
Or, if the earlier season lead,
To the tann'd haycock in the mead.
    Sometimes with secure delight
The upland hamlets will invite,
When the merry bells ring round,
And the jocund rebecks sound
To many a youth and many a maid,
Dancing in the chequer'd shade;
And young and old come forth to play
On a sun-shine holy-day,
Till the live-long day-light fail:
Then to the spicy nut-brown ale,
With stories told of many a feat,
How Faery Mab the junkets eat;

She was pinch'd, and pull'd, she said;
And he, by Friar's lantern led,
Tells how the drudging Goblin sweat
To earn his cream-bowl duly set,
When in one night, ere glimpse of morn,
His shadowy flail hath thresh'd the corn
That ten day-labourers could not end;
Then lies him down the lubber fiend,
And, stretch'd out all the chimney's length,
Basks at the fire his hairy strength;
And crop-full out of doors he flings
Ere the first cock his matin rings.
  Thus done the tales, to bed they creep,
By whispering winds soon lull'd asleep.
  Tower'd cities please us then
And the busy hum of men,
Where throngs of knights and barons bold
In weeds of peace high triumphs hold,
With store of ladies, whose bright eyes
Rain influence, and judge the prize
Of wit or arms, while both contend
To win her grace whom all commend.
There let Hymen oft appear
In saffron robe, with taper clear,
And pomp, and feast, and revelry,
With mask, and antique pageantry;
Such sights as youthful poets dream
On summer eves by haunted stream.
Then to the well-trod stage anon,
If Jonson's learned sock be on,
Or sweetest Shakespeare, Fancy's child,
Warble his native wood-notes wild.
  And ever against eating cares
Lap me in soft Lydian airs
Married to immortal verse,
Such as the meeting soul may pierce
In notes, with many a winding bout
Of linkéd sweetness long drawn out,

With wanton heed and giddy cunning,
The melting voice through mazes running,
Untwisting all the chains that tie
The hidden soul of harmony;
That Orpheus' self may heave his head
From golden slumber, on a bed
Of heap'd Elysian flowers, and hear
Such strains as would have won the ear
Of Pluto, to have quite set free
His half-regain'd Eurydice.

    These delights if thou canst give,
Mirth, with thee I mean to live.

XXVII

[Copy.]

ADMIRALTY INSTRUCTIONS

RELATIVE TO HORSES AND DOGS

The Commander-in-Chief,
H.M. Ships and Vessels,
Portsmouth.

Captain,
Ship *Excellent*.
Portsmouth.
Submitted.

WITH reference to your signal, there is nothing laid down in the Admiralty instructions as regards naval officers in charge of a battalion of seamen riding.

Their Lordships have hitherto left it to the discretion of the officers themselves whether they ride or walk, and it was hoped that naval officers would not ride unless they were capable of withstanding the cup and ball motion which is so closely connected with equestrian exercise.

This hope, however, has not always been realized, and

the disappearance into the big drum of the Grenadiers made by a commanding officer of the Naval Brigade on the occasion of a review at Windsor, together with a record made by a midshipman from Whitehall to Hyde Park Corner at the Jubilee Review, has not encouraged their Lordships to issue an order that naval officers should be mounted.

On such occasions as I have seen naval officers mounted, the uniform has been breeches and boots, but there is no mention of these articles in the uniform regulations.

I enclose a photograph of saddlery supplied or otherwise obtained by this establishment for the use of naval officers at functions. The extreme height of the pommel and the crupper of the saddle is to give extra stability to the officer while in the perilous position of being balanced astride the horse.

The only instructions issued here with regard to equestrian drill are that rolling and pitching should be avoided as much as possible, the animal's way should be checked when rounding corners, and extreme deflection never applied except at slow speeds; in mounting and dismounting the port side only is used, and spurs are not to be used to hold on by.

If not under control four red lights need not be hoisted; placing the hand behind the back is sufficient warning to the next astern not to close.

The animal is steered in the same way as a boat with a yoke, except that whereas in a boat the yoke is at the stern, with a horse it is in the bows. The yoke lines are called reins.

The initial velocity of the animal depends upon the mark and upon the food given. If it is a good mark and much food has been given, great care must be exercised by the naval officer in getting into the saddle.

CAPTAIN

I am directed by my Lords Commissioners of the Admiralty to inform you that they have had under consideration your submission of February 13 last with reference to that portion of their Lordships' directions contained in Admiralty letter N.S. 2168/349 of January 2, '05, whereby caretakers employed upon ineffective vessels are required to provide a dog for that purpose that would meet with their Lordships' approval.

I am to inform you that their Lordships—having in view the purpose for which these dogs are to be employed—are of opinion that the samples cited by you—that is to say, a half-bred dachshund and a toy pug—are not suitable; and my Lords, while desirous of not limiting the choice of animals unduly, are of opinion that the dogs employed should be of active habits and able to bark effectively, that is with reference to the size of ship on which they are employed.

My Lords are of opinion that one of the sample dogs quoted in your correspondence—a Pekin spaniel of 3 lbs. weight—would not be effective on a battleship, but might be suitable for a gun vessel. You are, therefore, to make such arrangements in this respect as will, in your opinion, carry out the intentions of their Lordships most effectively.

COMMODORE TRUNNION'S HUNT

The Commodore and his crew had, by dint of turning, almost weathered the parson's house that stood to windward of the church, when the notes of a pack of hounds unluckily reached the ears of the two hunters which Trunnion and the Lieutenant bestrode. These fleet animals no sooner heard the enlivening sound, than, eager for the chace, they sprung away all of a sudden, and strained every nerve to partake of the sport, flew across the fields with incredible speed, overleaped hedges and ditches, and every thing in their way, without the least regard to their unfortunate riders.

The Lieutenant, whose steed had got the heels of the others, finding it would be great folly and presumption in him to pretend to keep the saddle with his wooden leg, very wisely took the opportunity of throwing himself off in his passage through a field of rich clover, among which he lay at his ease; and seeing his captain advancing at full gallop, hailed him with the salutation of 'What cheer? ho!' The Commodore, who was in infinite distress, eyeing him askance, as he passed, replied with a faultering voice, 'O damn ye! you are safe at an anchor; I wish to God I were as fast moored.' Nevertheless, conscious of his disabled heel, he would not venture to try the experiment which had succeeded so well with Hatchway, but resolved to stick as close as possible to his horse's back, until providence should interpose in his behalf. With this view he dropped his whip, and with his right hand laid fast hold on the pummel, contracting every muscle in his body to secure himself in the seat, and grinning most formidably, in consequence of this exertion. In this attitude he was hurried on a considerable way, when all of a sudden his view was comforted by a five-bar gate that appeared before him, as he never doubted that there the career of his hunter must necessarily end. But, alas! he reckoned without his host: Far from halting at this obstruction, the horse sprung over it with amazing agility, to the utter confusion and disorder of his owner, who lost his hat and periwig in the leap, and now began to think in good earnest, that he was actually mounted on the back of the devil. He recommended himself to God, his reflection forsook him, his eye-sight and all his other senses failed, he quitted the reins, and, fastening by instinct on the mane, was in this condition conveyed into the midst of the sportsmen, who were astonished at the sight of such an apparition. Neither was their surprise to be wondered at, if we reflect on the figure that presented itself to their view. The Commodore's person was at all times an object of admiration; much more so on this occasion, when every singularity was aggravated by the circumstances of his dress and disaster.

He had put on in honour of his nuptials his best coat of blue broad cloth, cut by a tailor of Ramsgate, and trimmed with five dozen of brass buttons, large and small; his breeches were of the same piece, fastened at the knees with large bunches of tape; his waistcoat was of red plush lapelled with green velvet, and garnished with vellum holes; his boots bore an infinite resemblance, both in colour and shape, to a pair of leather buckets; his shoulder was graced with a broad buff belt, from whence depended a huge hanger with a hilt like that of a backsword; and on each side of his pummel appeared a rusty pistol rammed in a case covered with a bearskin. The loss of his tie-periwig and laced hat, which were curiosities of the kind, did not at all contribute to the improvement of the picture, but, on the contrary, by exhibiting his bald pate, and the natural extension of his lantern jaws, added to the peculiarity and extravagance of the whole. Such a spectacle could not have failed of diverting the whole company from the chace, had his horse thought proper to pursue a different route, but the beast was too keen a sporter to choose any other way than that which the stag followed; and, therefore, without stopping to gratify the curiosity of the spectators, he in a few minutes outstripped every hunter in the field. There being a deep hollow way betwixt him and the hounds, rather than ride round about the length of a furlong to a path that crossed the lane, he transported himself at one jump, to the unspeakable astonishment and terror of a waggoner who chanced to be underneath, and saw this phenomenon fly over his carriage. This was not the only adventure he achieved. The stag having taken a deep river that lay in his way, every man directed his course to a bridge in the neighbourhood; but our bridegroom's courser, despising all such conveniences, plunged into the stream without hesitation, and swam in a twinkling to the opposite shore. This sudden immersion into an element of which Trunnion was properly a native, in all probability helped to recruit the exhausted spirits of his rider, who, at his landing on the other side, gave some tokens of sensation, by hollowing aloud for assistance, which he could not possibly receive, because his horse still maintained the advantage he had gained, and would not allow himself to be overtaken.

In short, after a long chace that lasted several hours, and extended to a dozen miles at least, he was the first in at the death of the deer, being seconded by the Lieutenant's gelding, which, actuated by the same spirit, had, without a rider, followed his companion's example.

XXVIII

THE UPPER THAMES

PRESENTLY at a place where the river flowed round a headland of the meadows, we stopped a while for rest and victuals, and settled ourselves on a beautiful bank which almost reached the dignity of a hill-side: the wide meadows spread before us, and already the scythe was busy amidst the hay. One change I noticed amidst the quiet beauty of the fields—to wit, that they were planted with trees here and there, often fruit-trees, and that there was none of the niggardly begrudging of space to a handsome tree which I remembered too well; and though the willows were often polled (or shrowded, as they call it in that country-side), this was done with some regard to beauty: I mean that there was no polling of rows on rows so as to destroy the pleasantness of half a mile of country, but a thoughtful sequence in the cutting, that prevented a sudden bareness anywhere. To be short, the fields were everywhere treated as a garden made for the pleasure as well as the livelihood of all, as old Hammond told me was the case.

On this bank or bent of the hill, then, we had our midday meal; somewhat early for dinner, if that mattered, but we had been stirring early: the slender stream of the Thames winding below us between the garden of a country I have been telling of; a furlong from us was a beautiful little islet begrown with graceful trees; on the slopes westward of us was a wood of varied growth overhanging the narrow meadow on the south side of the river; while to the north was a wide stretch of mead rising very gradually from the river's edge. A delicate spire of an ancient building rose up from out of the trees in the middle distance, with a few grey houses clustered about it; while nearer to us, in fact not half a furlong from the water, was a quite modern stone house—a wide quadrangle of one story, the buildings that made it being quite low. There was no garden between it and the river, nothing but a row of pear-trees still quite young and slender;

and though there did not seem to be much ornament about it, it had a sort of natural elegance, like that of the trees themselves.

*   *   *   *   *

Presently we saw before us a bank of elm-trees, which told us of a house amidst them, though I looked in vain for the grey walls that I expected to see there. As we went, the folk on the bank talked indeed, mingling their kind voices with the cuckoo's song, the sweet strong whistle of the blackbirds, and the ceaseless note of the corn-crake as he crept through the long grass of the mowing-field; whence came waves of fragrance from the flowering clover amidst of the ripe grass.

In a few minutes we had passed through a deep eddying pool into the sharp stream that ran from the ford, and beached our craft on a tiny strand of limestone-gravel, and stepped ashore into the arms of our up-river friends, our journey done.

I disentangled myself from the merry throng, and mounting on the cart-road that ran along the river some feet above the water, I looked round about me. The river came down through a wide meadow on my left, which was grey now with the ripened seeding grasses; the gleaming water was lost presently by a turn of the bank, but over the meadow I could see the mingled gables of a building where I knew the lock must be, and which now seemed to combine a mill with it. A low wooded ridge bounded the river-plain to the south and south-east, whence we had come, and a few low houses lay about its feet and up its slope. I turned a little to my right, and through the hawthorn sprays and long shoots of the wild roses could see the flat country spreading out far away under the sun of the calm evening, till something that might be called hills with a look of sheep-pastures about them bounded it with a soft blue line. Before me, the elm-boughs still hid most of what houses there might be in this river-side dwelling of men; but to the right of the cart-road a few grey buildings of the simplest kind showed here and there.

There I stood in a dreamy mood, and rubbed my eyes as if I were not wholly awake, and half expected to see the gay-clad company of beautiful men and women change to two or three spindle-legged back-bowed men and haggard, hollow-eyed, ill-favoured women, who once wore down the soil of this land with their heavy hopeless feet, from day to day, and season to season, and year to year. But no change came as yet, and my heart swelled with joy as I thought of all the beautiful grey villages, from the river to the plain and the plain to the uplands, which I could picture to myself so well all peopled now with this happy and lovely folk, who had cast away riches and attained to wealth.

* * * * *

Almost without my will my feet moved on along the road they knew. The raised way led us into a little field bounded by a backwater of the river on one side; on the right hand we could see a cluster of small houses and barns, new and old, and before us a grey stone barn and a wall partly overgrown with ivy, over which a few grey gables showed. The village road ended in the shallow of the aforesaid backwater. We crossed the road, and again almost without my will my hand raised the latch of a door in the wall, and we stood presently on a stone path which led up to the old house to which fate in the shape of Dick had so strangely brought me in this new world of men. My companion gave a sigh of pleased surprise and enjoyment; nor did I wonder, for the garden between the wall and the house was redolent of the June flowers, and the roses were rolling over one another with that delicious super-abundance of small well-tended gardens which at first sight takes away all thought from the beholder save that of beauty. The blackbirds were singing their loudest, the doves were cooing on the roof-ridge, the rooks in the high elm-trees beyond were garrulous among the young leaves, and the swifts wheeled whining about the gables. And the house itself was a fit guardian for all the beauty of this heart of summer.

Once again Ellen echoed my thoughts as she said: 'Yes, friend, this is what I came out for to see; this many-gabled old house built by the simple country-folk of the long-past times, regardless of all the turmoil that was going on in cities and courts, is lovely still amidst all the beauty which these latter days have created; and I do not wonder at our friends tending it carefully and making much of it. It seems to me as if it had waited for these happy days, and held in it the gathered crumbs of happiness of the confused and turbulent past.'

She led me up close to the house, and laid her shapely sun-browned hand and arm on the lichened wall as if to embrace it, and cried out, 'O me! O me! How I love the earth, and the seasons, and weather, and all things that deal with it, and all that grows out of it,—as this has done!'

O June, O June, that we desired so,
Wilt thou not make us happy on this day?
Across the river thy soft breezes blow
Sweet with the scent of beanfields far away,
Above our heads rustle the aspens grey,
Calm is the sky with harmless clouds beset,
No thought of storm the morning vexes yet.

  See, we have left our hopes and fears behind
To give our very hearts up unto thee;
What better place than this then could we find
By this sweet stream that knows not of the sea,
That guesses not the city's misery,
This little stream whose hamlets scarce have names,
This far-off, lonely mother of the Thames?

XXIX

MR. PECKSNIFF AT THE BOARDING-HOUSE

MR. PECKSNIFF had followed his younger friends up stairs, and taken a chair at the side of Mrs. Todgers. He had also spilt a cup of coffee over his legs without appearing to be aware of the circumstance; nor did he seem to know that there was muffin on his knee.

'And how have they used you down stairs, sir?' asked the hostess.

'Their conduct has been such, my dear madam,' said Mr. Pecksniff, 'as I can never think of without emotion, or remember without a tear. Oh, Mrs. Todgers!'

'My goodness!' exclaimed that lady. 'How low you are in your spirits, sir!'

'I am a man, my dear madam,' said Mr. Pecksniff, shedding tears, and speaking with an imperfect articulation, 'but I am also a father. I am also a widower. My feelings, Mrs. Todgers, will not consent to be entirely smothered, like the young children in the Tower. They are grown up, and the more I press the bolster on them, the more they look round the corner of it.'

He suddenly became conscious of the bit of muffin, and stared at it intently: shaking his head the while, in a forlorn and imbecile manner, as if he regarded it as his evil genius, and mildly reproached it.

'She was beautiful, Mrs. Todgers,' he said, turning his glazed eye again upon her, without the least preliminary notice. 'She had a small property.'

'So I have heard,' cried Mrs. Todgers with great sympathy.'

'Those are her daughters,' said Mr. Pecksniff, pointing out the young ladies, with increased emotion.

Mrs. Todgers had no doubt of it.

'Mercy and Charity,' said Mr. Pecksniff, 'Charity and Mercy. Not unholy names, I hope?'

'Mr. Pecksniff!' cried Mrs. Todgers. 'What a ghastly smile! Are you ill, sir?'

He pressed his hand upon her arm, and answered in a solemn manner, and a faint voice, 'Chronic.'

'Cholic?' cried the frightened Mrs. Todgers.

'Chron-ic,' he repeated with some difficulty. 'Chron-ic. A chronic disorder. I have been its victim from childhood. It is carrying me to my grave.'

'Heaven forbid!' cried Mrs. Todgers.

'Yes it is,' said Mr. Pecksniff, reckless with despair. 'I am rather glad of it, upon the whole. You are like her, Mrs. Todgers.'

'Don't squeeze me so tight, pray, Mr. Pecksniff. If any of the gentlemen should notice us.'

'For her sake,' said Mr. Pecksniff. 'Permit me. In honour of her memory. For the sake of a voice from the tomb. You are *very* like her, Mrs. Todgers! What a world this is!'

'Ah! Indeed you may say that!' cried Mrs. Todgers.

'I'm afraid it is a vain and thoughtless world,' said Mr. Pecksniff, overflowing with despondency. 'These young people about us. Oh! what sense have they of their responsibilities? None. Give me your other hand, Mrs. Todgers.'

That lady hesitated, and said 'she didn't like.'

'Has a voice from the grave no influence?' said Mr. Pecksniff, with dismal tenderness. 'This is irreligious! My dear creature.'

'Hush!' urged Mrs. Todgers. 'Really you mustn't.'

'It's not me,' said Mr. Pecksniff. 'Don't suppose it's me: it's the voice; it's her voice.'

Mrs. Pecksniff, deceased, must have had an unusually thick and husky voice for a lady, and rather a stuttering voice, and to say the truth somewhat of a drunken voice, if it had ever borne much resemblance to that in which Mr. Pecksniff spoke just then. But perhaps this was delusion on his part.

'It has been a day of enjoyment, Mrs. Todgers, but still it has been a day of torture. It has reminded me of my loneliness. What am I in the world?'

'An excellent gentleman, Mr. Pecksniff,' said Mrs. Todgers.

'There is consolation in that too,' cried Mr. Pecksniff. 'Am I?'

'There is no better man living,' said Mrs. Todgers, 'I am sure.'

Mr. Pecksniff smiled through his tears, and slightly shook his head. 'You are very good,' he said, 'thank you. It is a great happiness to me, Mrs. Todgers, to make young people happy. The happiness of my pupils is my chief object. I dote upon 'em. They dote upon me too. Sometimes.'

'Always,' said Mrs. Todgers.

'When they say they haven't improved, ma'am,' whispered Mr. Pecksniff, looking at her with profound mystery, and motioning to her to advance her ear a little closer to his mouth. 'When they say they haven't improved, ma'am, and the premium was too high, they lie! I shouldn't wish it to be mentioned; you will understand me; but I say to you as to an old friend, they lie.'

'Base wretches they must be!' said Mrs. Todgers.

'Madam,' said Mr. Pecksniff, 'you are right. I respect you for that observation. A word in your ear. To Parents and Guardians. This is in confidence, Mrs. Todgers?'

'The strictest, of course!' cried that lady.

'To Parents and Guardians,' repeated Mr. Pecksniff. 'An eligible opportunity now offers, which unites the advantages of the best practical architectural education with the comforts of a home, and the constant association with some, who, however humble their sphere and limited their capacity—observe! —are not unmindful of their moral responsibilities.'

Mrs. Todgers looked a little puzzled to know what this might mean, as well she might; for it was, as the reader may perchance remember, Mr. Pecksniff's usual form of advertisement when he wanted a pupil; and seemed to have no particular reference, at present, to anything. But Mr. Pecksniff held up his finger as a caution to her not to interrupt him.

'Do you know any parent or guardian, Mrs. Todgers,' said Mr. Pecksniff, 'who desires to avail himself of such an opportunity for a young gentleman? An orphan would be preferred. Do you know of any orphan with three or four hundred pound?'

Mrs. Todgers reflected, and shook her head.

'When you hear of an orphan with three or four hundred pound,' said Mr. Pecksniff, 'let that dear orphan's friends apply, by letter post-paid, to S. P., Post-office, Salisbury. I don't know who he is, exactly. Don't be alarmed, Mrs. Todgers,' said Mr. Pecksniff, falling heavily against her: 'Chronic—chronic! Let's have a little drop of something to drink.'

'Bless my life, Miss Pecksniffs!' cried Mrs. Todgers, aloud, 'your dear pa's took very poorly!'

Mr. Pecksniff straightened himself by a surprising effort, as every one turned hastily towards him; and standing on his feet, regarded the assembly with a look of ineffable wisdom. Gradually it gave place to a smile; a feeble, helpless, melancholy smile; bland, almost to sickliness. 'Do not repine, my friends,' said Mr. Pecksniff, tenderly. 'Do not weep for me. It is chronic.' And with these words, after making a futile attempt to pull off his shoes, he fell into the fire-place.

The youngest gentleman in company had him out in a second. Yes, before a hair upon his head was singed, he had him on the hearthrug.—Her father!

She was almost beside herself. So was her sister. Jinkins consoled them both. They all consoled them. Everybody had something to say, except the youngest gentleman in company, who with a noble self-devotion did the heavy work, and held up Mr. Pecksniff's head without being taken notice of by anybody. At last they gathered round, and agreed to carry him up stairs to bed. The youngest gentleman in company was rebuked by Jinkins for tearing Mr. Pecksniff's coat! Ha, ha! But no matter.

They carried him up stairs, and crushed the youngest gentleman at every step. His bedroom was at the top of the house, and it was a long way; but they got him there in course of time. He asked them frequently on the road for a little drop of something to drink. It seemed an idiosyncrasy. The youngest gentleman in company proposed a draught of water. Mr. Pecksniff called him opprobrious names for the suggestion.

Jinkins and Gander took the rest upon themselves, and made him as comfortable as they could, on the outside of his bed; and when he seemed disposed to sleep, they left him. But before they had all gained the bottom of the staircase, a vision of Mr. Pecksniff, strangely attired, was seen to flutter on the top landing. He desired to collect their sentiments, it seemed, upon the nature of human life.

'My friends,' cried Mr. Pecksniff, looking over the banisters, 'let us improve our minds by mutual inquiry and discussion. Let us be moral. Let us contemplate existence. Where is Jinkins?'

'Here,' cried that gentleman. 'Go to bed again!'

'To bed!' said Mr. Pecksniff. 'Bed! 'Tis the voice of the sluggard, I hear him complain, you have woke me too soon, I must slumber again. If any young orphan will repeat the remainder of that simple piece from Doctor Watts's collection an eligible opportunity now offers.'

Nobody volunteered.

'This is very soothing,' said Mr. Pecksniff, after a pause. 'Extremely so. Cool and refreshing, particularly to the legs! The legs of the human subject, my friends, are a beautiful production. Compare them with wooden legs, and observe the difference between the anatomy of nature and the anatomy of art. Do you know,' said Mr. Pecksniff, leaning over the banisters, with an odd recollection of his familiar manner among new pupils at home, 'that I should very much like to see Mrs. Todgers's notion of a wooden leg, if perfectly agreeable to herself!'

As it appeared impossible to entertain any reasonable hopes of him after this speech, Mr. Jinkins and Mr. Gander went up stairs again, and once more got him into bed.

XXX

JOHN GILPIN

JOHN GILPIN was a Citizen
    Of credit and renown;
  A Train-Band Captain eke was he
    Of famous London Town.
John Gilpin's Spouse said to her Dear,
    'Though wedded we have been
These twice ten tedious years; yet we
    No holiday have seen!

To-morrow is our Wedding Day,
    And we will then repair
Unto the *Bell* at Edmonton,
    All in a chaise and pair.
My sister and my sister's child,
    Myself and children three,
Will fill the chaise; so you must ride
    On horseback after we!'
He soon replied, 'I do admire
    Of womankind but one;
And you are She, my dearest Dear!
    Therefore it shall be done!
I am a Linendraper bold,
    As all the World does know;
And my good friend, the Calender,
    Will lend his horse to go.'
Quoth Mrs. Gilpin, 'That's well said;
    And for that wine is dear,
We will be furnished with our own,
    Which is so bright and clear.'
John Gilpin kissed his loving Wife;
    O'erjoyed was he to find,
That, though on pleasure she was bent,
    She had a frugal mind.
The morning came. The chaise was brought;
    But yet was not allowed
To drive up to the door, lest all
    Should say that she was proud!
So, three doors off the chaise was stayed,
    Where they did all get in;
Six precious Souls, and all agog
    To dash through thick and thin.
Smack went the whip, round went the wheels;
    Were never folks so glad!
The stones did rattle underneath,
    As if Cheapside were mad!
John Gilpin, at his horse's side,
    Seized fast the flowing mane;

And up he got in haste to ride,
    But soon came down again:
For saddletree scarce reached had he,
    His journey to begin,
When, turning round his face, he saw
    Three customers come in.
So down he came; for loss of time,
    Although it grieved him sore;
Yet loss of pence, full well he knew,
    Would grieve him still much more!
'Twas long before the customers
    Were suited to their mind;
When Betty screamed into his ears,
    'The wine is left behind!'
'Good lack!' quoth he, 'yet bring it me!
    My leathern belt likewise;
In which I bear my trusty sword,
    When I do exercise.'
Now, Mistress Gilpin, careful Soul!
    Had two stone bottles found,
To hold the liquor which she loved,
    And keep it safe and sound.
Each bottle had two curling ears,
    Through which the belt he drew;
He hung one bottle on each side,
    To make his balance true.
Then, over all, that he might be
    Equipped from top to toe,
His long red cloak, well brushed and neat,
    He manfully did throw.
Now, see him, mounted once again
    Upon his nimble steed,
Full slowly pacing o'er the stones,
    With caution and good heed.
But, finding soon a smoother road
    Beneath his well-shod feet,
The snorting beast began to trot;
    Which galled him in his seat.

So, 'Fair and softly!' John did cry;
  But John, he cried in vain!
That trot became a gallop soon,
  In spite of curb or rein.
So stooping down, as he needs must,
  Who cannot sit upright,
He grasped the mane with both his hands,
  And eke with all his might!
Away went Gilpin, neck or nought!
  Away went hat and wig!
He little dreamt, when he set out,
  Of running such a rig!
The horse, who never had before
  Been handled in this kind,
Affrighted, fled! and, as he flew,
  Left all the World behind.
The wind did blow, the cloak did fly
  Like streamer long and gay,
Till, loop and button failing both,
  At last, it flew away!
Then might all people well discern
  The bottles he had slung,
A bottle swinging at each side,
  As has been said, or sung.
The dogs did bark, the children screamed,
  Up flew the windows all;
And ev'ry Soul cried out, 'Well done!'
  As loud as he could bawl.
Away went Gilpin, who but he!
  His fame soon spread around.
'He carries weight! He rides a race!
  'Tis for a Thousand Pound!'
And still, as fast as he drew near,
  'Twas wonderful to view
How, in a trice, the Turnpike-men
  Their Gates wide open threw!
And now, as he went, bowing down
  His reeking head full low,

The bottles twain, behind his back,
    Were shattered at a blow.
Down ran the wine into the road,
    Most piteous to be seen;
And made his horse's flanks to smoke,
    As he had basted been.
But still he seemed to carry weight,
    With leathern girdle braced,
For still the bottle-necks were left
    Both dangling at his waist.
Thus, all through merry Islington,
    These gambols he did play,
And till he came unto the Wash
    Of Edmonton so gay.
And there he threw the Wash about
    On both sides of the way;
Just like unto a trundling mop,
    Or a wild goose at play.
At Edmonton, his loving Wife,
    From the balcony espied
Her tender Husband; wond'ring much
    To see how he did ride.
'Stop! Stop! John Gilpin! Here's the house!'
    They all at once did cry,
'The dinner waits; and we are tired!'
    Said Gilpin, 'So am I!'
But, ah! his horse was not a whit
    Inclined to tarry there,
For why? His owner had a house
    Full ten miles off, at Ware.
So like an arrow swift he flew,
    Shot by an Archer strong;
So did he fly! which brings me to
    The middle of my Song.
Away went Gilpin, out of breath,
    And sore against his will,
Till at his friend's, the Calender's,
    His horse at last stood still.

The Calender, surprised to see
    His friend in such a trim,
Laid down his pipe, flew to the gate.
    And thus accosted him.
'What news? What news? The tidings tell!
    Make haste, and tell me all!
Say, Why, bare-headed, you are come?
    Or why you come at all?'
Now Gilpin had a pleasant wit,
    And loved a timely joke,
And thus unto the Calender,
    In merry strains he spoke.
'I came, because your horse would come;
    And, if I well forebode,
My hat and wig will soon be here!
    They are upon the road!'
The Calender, right glad to find
    His friend in merry pin,
Returned him not a single word;
    But to the house went in.
Whence straight he came, with hat and wig:
    A wig that drooped behind,
A hat not much the worse for wear;
    Each comely in its kind.
He held them up; and, in his turn,
    Thus shewed his ready wit.
'My head is twice as big as yours;
    They therefore needs must fit!
But let me scrape the dirt away
    That hangs about your face!
And stop and eat! for well you may
    Be in a hungry case.'
Said John, 'It is my Wedding Day;
    And folks would gape and stare,
If Wife should dine at Edmonton,
    And I should dine at Ware!'
Then speaking to his horse, he said,
    'I am in haste to dine!

'Twas for your pleasure you came here!
 You shall go back for mine!'
Ah! luckless word and bootless boast;
 For which he paid full dear!
For, while he spoke, a braying ass
 Did sing most loud and clear:
Whereat his horse did snort, as if
 He heard a lion roar;
And galloped off with all his might,
 As he had done before.
Away went Gilpin! and away,
 Went Gilpin's hat and wig!
He lost them sooner than at first!
 For why? They were too big!
Now Gilpin's Wife, when she had seen
 Her Husband posting down
Into the country far away,
 She pulled out Half a Crown.
And thus unto the Youth she said,
 That drove them to the *Bell,*
'This shall be yours, when you bring back
 My Husband safe and well!'
The Youth did ride, and soon they met;
 He tried to stop John's horse,
By seizing fast the flowing rein,
 But only made things worse:
For, not performing what he meant
 And gladly would have done,
He thereby frighted Gilpin's horse,
 And made him faster run.
Away went Gilpin; and away
 Went Post-boy at his heels!
The Post-boy's horse right glad to miss
 The lumber of the wheels.
Six Gentlemen, upon the road,
 Thus seeing Gilpin fly,
With Post-boy scamp'ring in the rear,
 They raised the Hue and Cry!

'Stop thief! Stop thief! A highwayman!'
  Not one of them was mute!
So they, and all that passed that way,
  Soon joined in the pursuit.
But all the Turnpike Gates again
  Flew open, in short space;
The men still thinking, as before,
  That Gilpin rode a race.
And so he did; and won it too!
  For he got first to Town;
Nor stopped till, where he first got up,
  He did again get down.
Now let us sing, 'Long live the King!
  And Gilpin, long live he!'
And when he next does ride abroad,
  May I be there to see!

XXXI

KING WILLIAM ENTERS EXETER

EXETER, in the meantime, was greatly agitated. Lamplugh, the bishop, as soon as he heard that the Dutch were at Torbay, set off in terror for London. The Dean fled from the deanery. The magistrates were for the King, the body of the inhabitants for the Prince. Everything was in confusion when, on the morning of Thursday, the eighth of November, a body of troops, under the command of Mordaunt, appeared before the city. With Mordaunt came Burnet, to whom William had entrusted the duty of protecting the clergy of the Cathedral from injury and insult. The Mayor and Aldermen had ordered the gates to be closed, but yielded on the first summons. The deanery was prepared for the reception of the Prince. On the following day, Friday the ninth, he arrived. The magistrates had been pressed to receive him in state at the entrance of the city, but had steadfastly refused. The pomp of that day, however, could well spare them. Such a sight had never been seen in Devonshire. Many of the citizens went forth half a day's journey to meet the champion of their religion. All the neighbouring villages poured forth their inhabitants.

A great crowd, consisting chiefly of young peasants, brandishing their cudgels, had assembled on the top of Haldon Hill, whence the army, marching from Chudleigh, first descried the rich valley of the Exe, and the two massive towers rising from the cloud of smoke which overhung the capital of the West. The road, all down the long descent, and through the plain to the banks of the river, was lined, mile after mile, with spectators. From the West Gate to the Cathedral Close, the pressing and shouting on each side was such as reminded Londoners of the crowds on the Lord Mayor's day. The houses were gaily decorated. Doors, windows, balconies, and roofs were thronged with gazers. An eye accustomed to the pomp of war would have found much to criticize in the spectacle. For several toilsome marches in the rain, through roads where one who travelled on foot sank at every step up to the ankles in clay, had not improved the appearance either of the men or of their accoutrements. But the people of Devonshire, altogether unused to the splendour of well ordered camps, were overwhelmed with delight and awe. Descriptions of the martial pageant were circulated all over the kingdom. They contained much that was well fitted to gratify the vulgar appetite for the marvellous. For the Dutch army, composed of men who had been born in various climates, and had served under various standards, presented an aspect at once grotesque, gorgeous, and terrible to islanders who had, in general, a very indistinct notion of foreign countries. First rode Macclesfield at the head of two hundred gentlemen, mostly of English blood, glittering in helmets and cuirasses, and mounted on Flemish war horses. Each was attended by a negro, brought from the sugar plantations on the coast of Guiana. The citizens of Exeter, who had never seen so many specimens of the African race, gazed with wonder on those black faces set off by embroidered turbans and white feathers. Then, with drawn broadswords, came a squadron of Swedish horsemen in black armour and fur cloaks. They were regarded with a strange interest; for it was rumoured that they were natives of a land where the ocean was frozen and where the night lasted through half the year, and that they had themselves slain the huge bears whose skins they wore. Next, surrounded by a goodly company of gentlemen and pages, was borne aloft the Prince's banner. On its broad folds the crowd which covered the roofs and filled the windows read with delight that memorable inscription, 'The Protestant religion and the liberties of England.'

But the acclamations redoubled when, attended by forty running footmen, the Prince himself appeared, armed on back and breast, wearing a white plume and mounted on a white charger. With how martial an air he curbed his horse, how thoughtful and commanding was the expression of his ample forehead and falcon eye, may still be seen on the canvas of Kneller. Once those grave features relaxed into a smile. It was when an ancient woman, perhaps one of the zealous Puritans who, through twenty-eight years of persecution, had waited with firm faith for the consolation of Israel, perhaps the mother of some rebel who had perished in the carnage of Sedgemoor, or in the more fearful carnage of the Bloody Circuit, broke from the crowd, rushed through the drawn swords and curveting horses, touched the hand of the deliverer, and cried out that now she was happy. Near to the Prince was one who divided with him the gaze of the multitude. That, men said, was the great Count Schomberg, the first soldier in Europe, since Turenne and Condé were gone, the man whose genius and valour had saved the Portuguese monarchy on the field of Montes Claros, the man who had earned a still higher glory by resigning the truncheon of a Marshal of France for the sake of the true religion. It was not forgotten that the two heroes, who, indissolubly united by their common Protestantism, were entering Exeter together, had twelve years before been opposed to each other under the walls of Maestricht, and that the energy of the young Prince had not then been found a match for the cool science of the veteran who now rode in friendship by his side. Then came a long column of the whiskered infantry of Switzerland, distinguished in all the Continental wars of two centuries by pre-eminent valour and discipline, but never till that week seen on English ground. And then marched a succession of bands, designated, as was the fashion of that age, after their leaders, Bentinck, Solmes, and Ginkell, Talmash and Mackay. With peculiar pleasure Englishmen might look on one gallant regiment which still bore the name of the honoured and lamented Ossory.

The effect of the spectacle was heightened by the recollection of more than one renowned event in which the warriors now pouring through the West Gate had borne a share. For they had seen service very different from that of the Devonshire militia, or of the camp at Hounslow. Some of them had repelled the fiery onset of the French on the field of Seneff; and others had crossed swords with the infidels in the cause of Christendom on that great day when the siege of Vienna was raised. The very senses of the multitude were fooled by imagination. Newsletters conveyed to every part of the kingdom fabulous accounts of the size and strength of the invaders. It was affirmed that they were, with scarcely an exception, above six feet high, and that they wielded such huge pikes, swords, and muskets, as had never before been seen in England. Nor did the wonder of the population diminish when the artillery arrived, twenty-one heavy pieces of brass cannon, which were with difficulty tugged along by sixteen cart horses to each. Much curiosity was excited by a strange structure mounted on wheels. It proved to be a movable smithy, furnished with all tools and materials necessary for repairing arms and carriages. But nothing caused so much astonishment as the bridge of boats, which was laid with great speed on the Exe for the conveyance of waggons, and afterwards as speedily taken to pieces and carried away. It was made, if report said true, after a pattern contrived by the Christians who were warring against the Great Turk on the Danube. The foreigners inspired as much good will as admiration. Their politic leader took care to distribute the quarters in such a manner as to cause the smallest possible inconvenience to the inhabitants of Exeter and of the neighbouring villages. The most rigid discipline was maintained. Not only were pillage and outrage effectually prevented, but the troops were required to demean themselves with civility towards all classes. Those who had formed their notions of an army from the conduct of Kirke and his Lambs were amazed to see soldiers who never swore at a landlady or took an egg without paying for it. In return for this moderation the people furnished the troops with provisions in great abundance and at reasonable prices.

XXXII

THE GREEN SPECTACLES

AS we were now to hold up our heads a little higher in the world, it would be proper to sell the colt, which was grown old, at a neighbouring fair, and buy us a horse that would carry single or double upon an occasion, and make a pretty appearance at church or upon a visit. This at first I opposed stoutly; but it was as stoutly defended. However, as I weakened, my antagonist gained strength, till at last it was resolved to part with him.1

As the fair happened on the following day, I had intentions of going myself; but my wife persuaded me that I had got a cold, and nothing could prevail upon her to permit me from home. 'No, my dear,' said she, 'our son Moses is a discreet boy, and can buy and sell to a very good advantage: you know all our great bargains are of his purchasing. He always stands out and higgles, and actually tires them till he gets a bargain.'

As I had some opinion of my son's prudence, I was willing enough to entrust him with this commission: and the next morning I perceived his sisters mighty busy in fitting out Moses for the fair; trimming his hair, brushing his buckles, and cocking his hat with pins. The business of the toilet being over, we had at last the satisfaction of seeing him mounted upon the colt, with a deal box before him to bring home groceries in. He had on a coat made of that cloth they call thunder-and-lightning, which though grown too short, was much too good to be thrown away. His waistcoat was of gosling green, and his sisters had tied his hair with a broad black riband. We all followed him several paces from the door, bawling after him, 'Good luck! good luck!' till we could see him no longer.

He was scarce gone, when Mr. Thornhill's butler came to congratulate us upon our good fortune, saying that he overheard his young master mention our names with great commendation.

Good fortune seemed resolved not to come alone. Another footman from the same family followed, with a card for my daughters, importing that the two ladies had received such pleasing accounts from Mr. Thornhill of us all, that after a few previous inquiries they hoped to be perfectly satisfied. 'Ay,' cried my wife, 'I now see it is no easy matter to get into the families of the great; but when one once gets in, then, as Moses says, one may go to sleep.' To this piece of humour, for she intended it for wit, my daughters assented with a loud laugh of pleasure. In short, such was her satisfaction at this message, that she actually put her hand in her pocket, and gave the messenger sevenpence halfpenny.

This was to be our visiting day. The next that came was Mr. Burchell, who had been at the fair. He brought œy little ones a pennyworth of gingerbread each, which my wife undertook to keep for them, and give them by letters at a time. He brought my daughters also a couple of boxes, in which they might keep wafers, snuff, patches, or even money, when they got it. My wife was unusually fond of a weasel-skin purse, as being the most lucky; but this by the by. We had still a regard for Mr. Burchell, though his late rude behaviour was in some measure displeasing; nor could we now avoid communicating our happiness to him, and asking his advice: although we seldom followed advice, we were all ready enough to ask it. When he read the note from the two ladies, he shook his head, and observed, that an affair of this sort demanded the utmost circumspection. This air of diffidence highly displeased my wife. 'I never doubted, sir,' cried she, 'your readiness to be against my daughters and me. You have more circumspection than is wanted. However, I fancy when we come to ask advice, we will apply to persons who seem to have made use of it themselves.' —'Whatever my own conduct may have been, madam,' replied he, 'is not the present question: though, as I have made no use of advice myself, I should in conscience give it to those that will.' As I was apprehensive this answer might draw on a repartee, making up by abuse what it wanted in wit, I changed the subject, by seeming to wonder what could keep our son so long at the fair, as it was now almost nightfall. 'Never mind our son,' cried my wife; 'depend upon it he knows what he is about. I'll warrant we'll never see him sell his hen of a rainy day. I have seen him buy such bargains as would amaze one. I'll tell you a good story about that, that will make you split your sides with laughing. —But, as I live, yonder comes Moses, without a horse, and the box at his back.'

As she spoke, Moses came slowly on foot, and sweating under the deal box, which he had strapped round his shoulders like a pedlar. 'Welcome, welcome, Moses! well, my boy, what have you brought us from the fair?'—'I have brought you myself,' cried Moses, with a sly look, and resting the box on the dresser. 'Ay, Moses,' cried my wife, 'that we know; but where is the horse?'—'I have sold him,' cried Moses, 'for three pounds, five shillings and twopence.'— 'Well done, my good boy,' returned she; 'I knew you would touch them off. Between ourselves, three pounds five shillings and twopence is no bad day's work. Come, let us have it then.'—'I have brought back no money,' cried Moses again. 'I have laid it all out in a bargain, and here it is,' pulling out a bundle from his breast: 'here they are; a gross of green spectacles, with silver rims and shagreen cases.'— 'A gross of green spectacles!' repeated my wife in a faint

THE SOLITARY REAPER

Behold her, single in the field,
Yon solitary Highland Lass!
Reaping and singing by herself;
Stop here, or gently pass!
Alone she cuts and binds the grain,
And sings a melancholy strain;
O listen! for the Vale profound
Is overflowing with the sound.

No Nightingale did ever chaunt
More welcome notes to weary bands
Of travellers in some shady haunt,
Among Arabian sands:
A voice so thrilling ne'er was heard
In spring-time from the Cuckoo-bird,
Breaking the silence of the seas
Among the farthest Hebrides.

Will no one tell me what she sings?—
Perhaps the plaintive numbers flow
For old, unhappy, far-off things,
And battles long ago:
Or is it some more humble lay,
Familiar matter of to-day?
Some natural sorrow, loss, or pain,
That has been, and may be again?

Whate'er the theme, the Maiden sang
As if her song could have no ending;
I saw her singing at her work,
And o'er the sickle bending;—
I listened, motionless and still;
And, as I mounted up the hill,
The music in my heart I bore,
Long after it was heard no more.

THE DAFFODILS

I wandered lonely as a cloud
That floats on high o'er vales and hills,
When all at once I saw a crowd,
A host, of golden daffodils;
Beside the lake, beneath the trees,
Fluttering and dancing in the breeze.

Continuous as the stars that shine
And twinkle on the milky way,
They stretched in never-ending line
Along the margin of a bay:
Ten thousand saw I at a glance,
Tossing their heads in sprightly dance.

The waves beside them danced; but they
Out-did the sparkling waves in glee:
A poet could not but be gay,
In such a jocund company:
I gazed—and gazed—but little thought
What wealth the show to me had brought:

For oft, when on my couch I lie
In vacant or in pensive mood,
They flash upon that inward eye
Which is the bliss of solitude;
And then my heart with pleasure fills,
And dances with the daffodils.

Most sweet it is with unuplifted eyes
To pace the ground, if path be there or none,
While a fair region round the traveller lies
Which he forbears again to look upon;
Pleased rather with some soft ideal scene,
The work of Fancy, or some happy tone
Of meditation, slipping in between
The beauty coming and the beauty gone.

If Thought and Love desert us, from that day
Let us break off all commerce with the Muse:
With Thought and Love companions of our way,
Whate'er the senses take or may refuse,
The Mind's internal heaven shall shed her dews
Of inspiration on the humblest lay.

XXXIV

SIR ROGER AT CHURCH

I AM always very well pleased with a country Sunday, and think, if keeping holy the seventh day were only a human institution, it would be the best method that could have been thought of for the polishing and civilizing of mankind. It is certain the country people would soon degenerate into a kind of savages and barbarians, were there not such frequent returns of a stated time in which the whole village meet together with their best faces, and in their cleanliest habits, to converse with one another upon indifferent subjects, hear their duties explained to them, and join together in adoration of the Supreme Being. Sunday clears away the rust of the whole week, not only as it refreshes in their minds the notions of religion, but as it puts both the sexes upon appearing in their most agreeable forms, and exerting all such qualities as are apt to give them a figure in the eye of the village. A country fellow distinguishes himself as much in the churchyard, as a citizen does upon the Change, the whole parish politics being generally discussed in that place either after sermon or before the bell rings.

My friend Sir Roger, being a good churchman, has beautified the inside of his church with several texts of his own choosing; he has likewise given a handsome pulpit-cloth, and railed in the communion table at his own expense. He has often told me, that at his coming to his estate, he found his parishioners very irregular; and that in order to make them kneel and join in the responses, he gave every one of them a hassock and a common prayer-book: and at the same time employed an itinerant singing master, who goes about the country for that purpose, to instruct them rightly in the tunes of the psalms; upon which they now very much value themselves, and indeed outdo most of the country churches that I have ever heard.

As Sir Roger is landlord to the whole congregation, he keeps them in very good order, and will suffer nobody to sleep in it besides himself; for if by chance he has been surprised into a short nap at sermon, upon recovering out of it he stands up and looks about him, and if he sees anybody else nodding, either wakes them himself, or sends his servants to them. Several other of the old knight's particularities break out upon these occasions: sometimes he will be lengthening out a verse in the singing-psalms, half a minute after the rest of the congregation have done with it; sometimes, when he is pleased with the matter of his devotion, he pronounces *Amen* three or four times to the same prayer; and sometimes stands up when everybody else is upon their knees, to count the congregation, or see if any of his tenants are missing.

I was yesterday very much surprised to hear my old friend, in the midst of the service, calling out to one John Matthews to mind what he was about, and not disturb the congregation. This John Matthews it seems is remarkable for being an idle fellow, and at that time was kicking his heels for his diversion. This authority of the knight, though exerted in that odd manner which accompanies him in all circumstances of life, has a very good effect upon the parish, who are not polite enough to see anything ridiculous in his behaviour; besides that the general good sense and worthiness of his character makes his friends observe these little singularities as foils that rather set off than blemish his good qualities.

As soon as the sermon is finished, nobody presumes to stir till Sir Roger is gone out of the church. The knight walks down from his seat in the chancel between a double row of his tenants, that stand bowing to him on each side; and every now and then inquires how such an one's wife, or mother, or son, or father do, whom he does not see at church; which is understood as a secret reprimand to the person that is absent.

The chaplain has often told me, that upon a catechizing

day, when Sir Roger has been pleased with a boy that answers well, he has ordered a bible to be given him next day for his encouragement; and sometimes accompanies it with a flitch of bacon to his mother. Sir Roger has likewise added five pounds a year to the clerk's place; and that he may encourage the young fellows to make themselves perfect in the church service, has promised, upon the death of the present incumbent, who is very old, to bestow it according to merit.

The fair understanding between Sir Roger and his chaplain, and their mutual concurrence in doing good, is the more remarkable, because the very next village is famous for the differences and contentions that rise between the parson and the 'squire, who live in a perpetual state of war. The parson is always preaching at the 'squire, and the 'squire to be revenged on the parson never comes to church. The 'squire has made all his tenants atheists, and tithe-stealers; while the parson instructs them every Sunday in the dignity of his order, and insinuates to them in almost every sermon that he is a better man than his patron. In short, matters are come to such an extremity, that the 'squire has not said his prayers either in public or private this half year; and that the parson threatens him, if he does not mend his manners, to pray for him in the face of the whole congregation.

Feuds of this nature, though too frequent in the country, are very fatal to the ordinary people; who are so used to be dazzled with riches, that they pay as much deference to the understanding of a man of an estate, as of a man of learning: and are very hardly brought to regard any truth, how important soever it may be, that is preached to them, when they know there are several men of five hundred a year who do not believe it.

THE VICAR

Some years ago, ere time and taste
   Had turned our parish topsy-turvy,
When Darnel Park was Darnel Waste,
   And roads as little known as scurvy,

The man who lost his way, between
  St. Mary's Hill and Sandy Thicket,
Was always shown across the green,
  And guided to the Parson's wicket.

Back flew the bolt of lissom lath;
  Fair Margaret, in her tidy kirtle,
Led the lorn traveller up the path,
  Through clean clipt rows of box and myrtle;
And Don and Sancho, Tramp and Tray,
  Upon the parlour steps collected,
Wagged all their tails, and seemed to say—
  'Our master knows you—you're expected.'

Uprose the Reverend Dr. Brown,
  Uprose the Doctor's winsome marrow;
The lady laid her knitting down,
  Her husband clasped his ponderous Barrow!
Whate'er the stranger's caste or creed,
  Pundit or Papist, saint or sinner,
He found a stable for his steed,
  And welcome for himself, and dinner.

If, when he reached his journey's end,
  And warmed himself in Court or College,
He had not gained an honest friend
  And twenty curious scraps of knowledge,—
If he departed as he came,
  With no new light on love or liquor,—
Good sooth, the traveller was to blame,
  And not the Vicarage, nor the Vicar.

His talk was like a stream, which runs
  With rapid change from rocks to roses:
It slipped from politics to puns,
  It passed from Mahomet to Moses;
Beginning with the laws which keep
  The planets in their radiant courses,
And ending with some precept deep
  For dressing eels, or shoeing horses.

He was a shrewd and sound Divine,
   Of loud Dissent the mortal terror;
And when, by dint of page and line,
   He 'stablished Truth, or startled Error,
The Baptist found him far too deep;
   The Deist sighed with saving sorrow;
And the lean Levite went to sleep,
   And dreamed of tasting pork to-morrow.

His sermon never said or showed
   That Earth is foul, that Heaven is gracious,
Without refreshment on the road
   From Jerome, or from Athanasius:
And sure a righteous zeal inspired
   The hand and head that penned and planned them,
For all who understood admired,
   And some who did not understand them.

He wrote, too, in a quiet way,
   Small treatises, and smaller verses,
And sage remarks on chalk and clay,
   And hints to noble Lords—and nurses;
True histories of last year's ghost,
   Lines to a ringlet, or a turban,
And trifles for the Morning Post,
   And nothings for Sylvanus Urban.

He did not think all mischief fair,
   Although he had a knack of joking;
He did not make himself a bear,
   Although he had a taste for smoking;
And when religious sects ran mad,
   He held, in spite of all his learning,
That if a man's belief is bad,
   It will not be improved by burning.

THE VICAR

And he was kind, and loved to sit
   In the low hut or garnished cottage,
And praise the farmer's homely wit,
   And share the widow's homelier pottage:
At his approach complaint grew mild;
   And when his hand unbarred the shutter,
The clammy lips of fever smiled
   The welcome which they could not utter.

He always had a tale for me
   Of Julius Cæsar, or of Venus;
From him I learnt the rule of three,
   Cat's cradle, leap frog, and *Quae genus*:
I used to singe his powdered wig,
   To steal the staff he put such trust in,
And make the puppy dance a jig,
   When he began to quote Augustine.

Alack the change! in vain I look
   For haunts in which my boyhood trifled,—
The level lawn, the trickling brook,
   The trees I climbed, the beds I rifled:
The church is larger than before;
   You reach it by a carriage entry;
It holds three hundred people more,
   And pews are fitted up for gentry.

Sit in the Vicar's seat: you'll hear
   The doctrine of a gentle Johnian,
Whose hand is white, whose tone is clear,
   Whose phrase is very Ciceronian.
Where is the old man laid?—look down
   And construe on the slab before you,
'*Hic jacet* GVLIELMVS BROWN,
   Vir nullâ non donandus lauru.'

XXXV

FROM BURNS

MY BONNIE MARY

GO fetch to me a pint o' wine,
    And fill it in a silver tassie;
    That I may drink before I go,
A service to my bonnie lassie.
The boat rocks at the pier o' Leith,
    Fu' loud the wind blows frae the Ferry;
The ship rides by the Berwick-law,
    And I maun leave my bonnie Mary.

The trumpets sound, the banners fly,
    The glittering spears are rankèd ready;
The shouts o' war are heard afar,
    The battle closes thick and bloody;
But it's not the roar o' sea or shore
    Wad make me langer wish to tarry;
Nor shouts o' war that's heard afar—
    It's leaving thee, my bonnie Mary.

A RED, RED ROSE

O my luve's like a red, red rose,
    That's newly sprung in June:
O my luve's like the melodie,
    That's sweetly played in tune.
As fair art thou, my bonnie lass,
    So deep in luve am I:
And I will luve thee still, my dear,
    Till a' the seas gang dry.

Till a' the seas gang dry, my dear,
    And the rocks melt wi' the sun;
I will luve thee still, my dear,
    While the sands o' life shall run.

And fare thee weel, my only luve!
 And fare thee weel awhile!
And I will come again, my luve,
 Though it were ten thousand mile.

MARY MORRISON

Oh, Mary, at thy window be,
 It is the wished, the trysted hour!
Those smiles and glances let me see,
 That make the miser's treasure poor:
How blithely wad I bide the stoure,
 A weary slave frae sun to sun,
Could I the rich reward secure,
 The lovely Mary Morrison.

Yestreen when to the trembling string,
 The dance gaed through the lighted ha',
To thee my fancy took its wing,
 I sat, but neither heard nor saw.
Though this was fair, and that was braw,
 And yon the toast of a' the town,
I sighed, and said amang them a',
 'Ye are na Mary Morrison.'

Oh, Mary, canst thou wreck his peace,
 Wha for thy sake wad gladly die?
Or canst thou break that heart of his,
 Whase only faut is loving thee?
If love for love thou wilt na gie,
 At least be pity to me shown;
A thought ungentle canna be
 The thought o' Mary Morrison.

JOHN ANDERSON

John Anderson my jo, John,
 When we were first acquent,
Your locks were like the raven,
 Your bonnie brow was brent;

> But now your brow is beld, John,
>   Your locks are like the snaw;
> But blessings on your frosty pow,
>   John Anderson my jo.
>
> John Anderson my jo, John,
>   We clamb the hill thegither,
> And mony a canty day, John,
>   We've had wi' ane anither:
> Now we maun totter down, John,
>   But hand in hand we'll go,
> And sleep thegither at the foot,
>   John Anderson my jo.

XXXVI

A NIGHT AMONG THE PINES

> 'The bed was made, the room was fit,
>   By punctual eve the stars were lit;
> The air was still, the water ran;
>   No need there was for maid or man,
> When we put up, my ass and I,
>   At God's green caravanserai.'

FROM *Bleymard* after dinner, although it was already late, I set out to scale a portion of the *Lozère*. An ill-marked stony drove road guided me forward; and I met nearly half a dozen bullock-carts descending from the woods, each laden with a whole pine-tree for the winter's firing. At the top of the woods, which do not climb very high upon this cold ridge, I struck leftward by a path among the pines, until I hit on a dell of green turf, where a streamlet made a little spout over some stones to serve me for a water-tap. 'In a more sacred or sequestered bower . . . nor nymph, nor faunus, haunted.' The trees were not old, but they grew thickly round the glade: there was no outlook, except north-eastward upon distant hill-tops, or straight upward to the sky; and the encampment felt secure and private like a room. By the time I had made my arrangements and fed *Modestine*, the day was already beginning to decline. I buckled myself to the knees into my sack and made a hearty meal; and as soon as the sun went down, I pulled my cap over my eyes and fell asleep.

Night is a dead monotonous period under a roof; but in the open world it passes lightly, with its stars and dews and perfumes, and the hours are marked by changes in the face of Nature. What seems a kind of temporal death to people choked between walls and curtains, is only a light and living slumber to the man who sleeps a-field. All night long he can hear Nature breathing deeply and freely; even as she takes her rest, she turns and smiles; and there is one stirring hour unknown to those who dwell in houses, when a wakeful influence goes abroad over the sleeping hemisphere, and all the outdoor world are on their feet. It is then that the cock first crows, not this time to announce the dawn, but like a cheerful watchman speeding the course of night. Cattle awake on the meadows; sheep break their fast on dewy hillsides, and change to a new lair among the ferns; and houseless men, who have lain down with the fowls, open their dim eyes and behold the beauty of the night.

At what inaudible summons, at what gentle touch of Nature, are all these sleepers thus recalled in the same hour to life? Do the stars rain down an influence, or do we share some thrill of mother earth below our resting bodies? Even shepherds and old country-folk, who are the deepest read in these arcana, have not a guess as to the means or purpose of this nightly resurrection. Towards two in the morning they declare the thing takes place; and neither know nor inquire further. And at least it is a pleasant incident. We are disturbed in our slumber only, like the luxurious *Montaigne*, 'that we may the better and more sensibly relish it.' We have a moment to look upon the stars. And there is a special pleasure for some minds in the reflection that we share the impulse with all outdoor creatures in our neighbourhood, that we have escaped out of the *Bastille* of civilization, and are become, for the time being, a mere kindly animal and a sheep of Nature's flock.

When that hour came to me among the pines, I wakened thirsty. My tin was standing by me half full of water. I emptied it at a draught; and feeling broad awake after this internal cold aspersion, sat upright to make a cigarette. The stars were clear, coloured, and jewel-like, but not frosty. A faint silvery vapour stood for the *Milky Way*. All around me the black fir-points stood upright and stock-still. By the whiteness of the pack-saddle I could see *Modestine* walking round and round at the length of her tether; I could hear her steadily munching at the sward; but there was not another sound, save the indescribable quiet talk of the runnel over the stones. I lay lazily smoking and studying the colour of the sky, as we call the void of space, from where it showed a reddish grey behind the pines to where it showed a glossy blue-black between the stars. As if to be more like a pedlar, I wear a silver ring. This I could see faintly shining as I raised or lowered the cigarette; and at each whiff the inside of my hand was illuminated, and became for a second the highest light in the landscape.

A faint wind, more like a moving coolness than a stream of air, passed down the glade from time to time; so that even in my great chamber the air was being renewed all night long. I thought with horror of the inn at *Chasseradès* and the congregated nightcaps; with horror of the nocturnal prowesses of clerks and students, of hot theatres and pass-keys and close rooms. I have not often enjoyed a more serene possession of myself, nor felt more independent of material aids. The outer world, from which we cower into our houses, seemed after all a gentle habitable place; and night after night a man's bed, it seemed, was laid and waiting for him in the fields, where God keeps an open house. I thought I had rediscovered one of those truths which are revealed to savages and hid from political economists: at the least, I had discovered a new pleasure for myself. And yet even while I was exulting in my solitude I became aware of a strange lack. I wished a companion to lie near me in the starlight, silent and not moving, but ever within touch. For there is a fellowship more quiet even than solitude, and which, rightly understood, is solitude made perfect. And to live out of doors with the woman a man loves is of all lives the most complete and free.

As I thus lay, between content and longing, a faint noise stole towards me through the pines. I thought, at first, it was the crowing of cocks or the barking of dogs at some very distant farm; but steadily and gradually it took articulate shape in my ears, until I became aware that a passenger was going by upon the high-road in the valley, and singing loudly as he went. There was more of good-will than grace in his performance; but he trolled with ample lungs; and the sound of his voice took hold upon the hill-side and set the air shaking in the leafy glens. I have heard people passing by night in sleeping cities; some of them sang; one, I remember, played loudly on the bagpipes. I have heard the rattle of a cart or carriage spring up suddenly after hours of stillness, and pass, for some minutes, within the range of my hearing as I lay abed. There is a romance about all who are abroad in the black hours, and with something of a thrill we try to guess their business. But here the romance was double: first, this glad passenger, lit internally with wine, who sent up his voice in music through the night; and then I, on the other hand, buckled into my sack, and smoking alone in the pine-woods between four and five thousand feet towards the stars.

When I awoke again (*Sunday, 29th September*), many of the stars had disappeared; only the stronger companions of the night still burned visibly overhead; and away towards the east I saw a faint haze of light upon the horizon, such as had been the *Milky Way* when I was last awake. Day was at hand. I lit my lantern, and by its glowworm light put on my boots and gaiters; then I broke up some bread for *Modestine*, filled my can at the water-tap, and lit my spirit-lamp to boil myself some chocolate. The blue darkness lay long in the glade where I had so sweetly slumbered; but soon there was a broad streak of orange melting into gold along the mountain-tops of *Vivarais*. A solemn glee possessed my mind at this gradual and lovely coming in of day. I heard the runnel with delight; I looked round me for something beautiful and unexpected; but the still black pine-trees, the hollow glade, the munching ass, remained unchanged in figure. Nothing had altered but the light, and that, indeed, shed over all a spirit of life and of breathing peace, and moved me to a strange exhilaration.

I drank my water chocolate, which was hot if it was not rich, and strolled here and there, and up and down about the glade. While I was thus delaying, a gush of steady wind, as long as a heavy sigh, poured direct out of the quarter of the morning. It was cold, and set me sneezing. The trees near at hand tossed their black plumes in its passage; and I could see the thin distant spires of pine along the edge of the hill rock slightly to and fro against the golden east. Ten minutes after, the sunlight spread at a gallop along the hill-side, scattering shadows and sparkles, and the day had come completely.

I hastened to prepare my pack, and tackle the steep ascent that lay before me; but I had something on my mind. It was only a fancy; yet a fancy will sometimes be importunate. I had been most hospitably received and punctually served in my green caravanserai. The room was airy, the water excellent, and the dawn had called me to a moment. I say nothing of the tapestries or the inimitable ceiling, nor yet of the view which I commanded from the windows; but I felt I was in some one's debt for all this liberal entertainment. And so it pleased me, in a half-laughing way, to leave pieces of money on the turf as I went along, until I had left enough for my night's lodging. I trust they did not fall to some rich and churlish drover.

XXXVII

MR. COLLINS PROPOSES

MRS. BENNET and Kitty walked off, and as soon as they were gone Mr. Collins began.

'Believe me, my dear Miss Elizabeth, that your modesty, so far from doing you any disservice, rather adds to your other perfections. You would have been less amiable in my eyes had there *not* been this little unwillingness; but allow me to assure you that I have your respected mother's permission for this address. You can hardly doubt the purport of my discourse, however your natural delicacy may lead you to dissemble; my attentions have been too marked to be mistaken. Almost as soon as I entered the house, I singled you out as the companion of my future life. But before I am run away with by my feelings on this subject, perhaps it would be advisable for me to state my reasons for marrying—and, moreover, for coming into Hertfordshire with the design of selecting a wife, as I certainly did.'

The idea of Mr. Collins, with all his solemn composure, being run away with by his feelings, made Elizabeth so near laughing, that she could not use the short pause he allowed in any attempt to stop him farther, and he continued:—

'My reasons for marrying are, first, that I think it a right thing for every clergyman in easy circumstances (like myself) to set the example of matrimony in his parish; secondly, that I am convinced it will add very greatly to my happiness; and thirdly—which, perhaps, I ought to have mentioned earlier—that it is the particular advice and recommendation of the very noble lady whom I have the honour of calling patroness. Twice has she condescended to give me her opinion (unasked, too!) on this subject; and it was but the very Saturday night before I left Hunsford—between our pools at quadrille, while Mrs. Jenkinson was arranging Miss de Bourgh's footstool, that she said, "Mr. Collins, you must marry. A clergyman like you must marry. Choose properly, choose a gentlewoman for *my* sake; and for your *own*, let her be an active, useful sort of person, not brought up high, but able to make a small income go a good way. This is my advice. Find such a woman as soon as you can, bring her to Hunsford, and I will visit her." Allow me, by the way, to observe, my fair cousin, that I do not reckon the notice and kindness of Lady Catherine de Bourgh as among the least of the advantages in my power to offer. You will find her manners beyond anything I can describe; and your wit and vivacity, I think, must be acceptable to her, especially when tempered with the silence and respect which her rank will inevitably excite. Thus much for my general intention in favour of matrimony; it remains to be told why my views were directed to Longbourn instead of my own neighbourhood, where I assure you there are many amiable young women. But the fact is, that being, as I am, to inherit this estate after the death of your honoured father (who, however, may live many years longer), I could not satisfy myself without resolving to choose a wife from among his daughters, that the loss to them might be as little as possible, when the melancholy event takes place—which, however, as I have already said, may not be for several years. This has been my motive, my fair cousin, and I flatter myself it will not sink me in your esteem. And now nothing remains for me but to assure you in the most animated language of the violence of my affection. To fortune I am perfectly indifferent, and shall make no demand of that nature on your father, since I am well aware that it could not be complied with; and that one thousand pounds in the 4 per cents., which will not be yours till after your mother's decease, is all that you may ever be entitled to. On that head, therefore, I shall be uniformly silent; and you may assure yourself that no ungenerous reproach shall ever pass my lips when we are married.'

It was absolutely necessary to interrupt him now.

'You are too hasty, sir,' she cried. 'You forget that I have made no answer. Let me do it without further loss of time. Accept my thanks for the compliment you are paying me. I am very sensible of the honour of your proposals, but it is impossible for me to do otherwise than decline them.'

'I am not now to learn,' replied Mr. Collins, with a formal wave of the hand, 'that it is usual with young ladies to reject the addresses of the man whom they secretly mean to accept, when he first applies for their favour; and that sometimes the refusal is repeated a second or even a third time. I am therefore by no means discouraged by what you have just said, and shall hope to lead you to the altar ere long.'

'Upon my word, sir,' cried Elizabeth, 'your hope is rather an extraordinary one after my declaration. I do assure you that I am not one of those young ladies (if such young ladies there are) who are so daring as to risk their happiness on the chance of being asked a second time. I am perfectly serious in my refusal. You could not make *me* happy, and I am convinced that I am the last woman in the world who would make *you* so. Nay, were your friend Lady Catherine to know me, I am persuaded she would find me in every respect ill qualified for the situation.'

'Were it certain that Lady Catherine would think so,' said Mr. Collins, very gravely—'but I cannot imagine that her ladyship would at all disapprove of you. And you may be certain that when I have the honour of seeing her again, I shall speak in the highest terms of your modesty, economy, and other amiable qualifications.'

'Indeed, Mr. Collins, all praise of me will be unnecessary. You must give me leave to judge for myself, and pay me the compliment of believing what I say. I wish you very happy and very rich, and by refusing your hand, do all in my power to prevent your being otherwise. In making me the offer, you must have satisfied the delicacy of your feelings with regard to my family, and may take possession of Longbourn estate whenever it falls, without any self-reproach. This matter may be considered, therefore, as finally settled.' And rising as she thus spoke, she would have quitted the room, had not Mr. Collins thus addressed her:—

'When I do myself the honour of speaking to you next on the subject, I shall hope to receive a more favourable answer than you have now given me; though I am far from accusing you of cruelty at present, because I know it to be the established custom of your sex to reject a man on the first application, and perhaps you have even now said as much to encourage my suit as would be consistent with the true delicacy of the female character.'

'Really, Mr. Collins,' cried Elizabeth with some warmth, 'you puzzle me exceedingly. If what I have hitherto said can appear to you in the form of encouragement, I know not how to express my refusal in such a way as may convince you of its being one.'

'You must give me leave to flatter myself, my dear cousin, that your refusals of my addresses are merely words of course. My reasons for believing it are briefly these:—It does not appear to me that my hand is unworthy your acceptance, or that the establishment I can offer would be any other than highly desirable. My situation in life, my connections with the family of De Bourgh, and my relationship to your own, are circumstances highly in my favour; and you should take it into further consideration, that in spite of your manifold attractions, it is by no means certain that another offer of marriage may ever be made to you. Your portion is unhappily so small, that it will in all likelihood undo the effects of your loveliness and amiable qualifications. As I must therefore conclude that you are not serious in your rejection of me, I shall choose to attribute it to your wish of increasing my love by suspense, according to the usual practice of elegant females.'

'I do assure you, sir, that I have no pretensions whatever to that kind of elegance which consists in tormenting a respectable man. I would rather be paid the compliment of being believed sincere. I thank you again and again for the honour you have done me in your proposals, but to accept them is absolutely impossible. My feelings in every respect forbid it. Can I speak plainer? Do not consider me now as an elegant female, intending to plague you, but as a rational creature, speaking the truth from her heart.'

'You are uniformly charming!' cried he, with an air of awkward gallantry; 'and I am persuaded that when sanctioned by the express authority of both your excellent parents, my proposals will not fail of being acceptable.'

To such perseverance in wilful self-deception Elizabeth would make no reply, and immediately and in silence withdrew.

XXXVIII

MR. JORROCKS ON 'UNTING

PRECISELY at eight o'clock Mr. Jorrocks ascended the platform, attended by Captain Doleful, Roger Swizzle, Romeo Simpkins, and Abel Snorem, and was received with the most enthusiastic cheering. He wore the full-dress uniform of the hunt: sky-blue coat lined with pink silk, canary coloured shorts, and white silk stockings. His neckcloth and waistcoat were white, and a finely plaited shirt-frill protruded through the stand-up collar of the latter. Bunches of white ribbon dangled at his knees. In his hand he held a roll of notes, while some books of reference and a tumbler of brandy and water were placed by Benjamin on a table at the back of the platform. Benjamin had on his new red frock with blue collar, cord breeches, and white stockings.

After bowing most familiarly to the company, Mr. Jorrocks cleared his voice with a substantial *hem*, and then addressed the meeting.

'Beloved 'earers! beloved I may call you, for though I have not the pleasure of knowin' many of you, I hope werry soon to make your intimate acquaintance. Beloved 'earers, I say I have come 'ere this evenin' for the double purpose of seeing you, and instructin' of you on those matters that have brought me to this your beautiful and salubrisome town. (Cheers.) Beautiful I may call it, for its architectural proportions are grand, and salubrisome it must be when it boasts so many cheerful, wigorous countenances as I now see gathered around me. (Loud applause.) And if by my comin' I shall spread the great light of sportin' knowledge, and enable you to preserve those glowin' mugs when far removed from these waters, then shall I be a better doctor than either Swizzle or Sebastian, and the day that drew John Jorrocks from the sugars of retirement in Great Coram Street will henceforth remain red-lettered in the mental calendar of his existence. (Loud cheers.) Red-lettered did I say? Ah! wot a joyous colour to denote a great and glorious ewent! Believe me there is no colour like red—no sport like 'unting.

'Blue coats and canaries,' observed Mr. Jorrocks, looking down at his legs, 'are well enough for dancin' in, but the man wot does much dancin' will not do much 'unting. But to business—Lectorin' is all the go—and why should sportin' be excluded? Is it because sportin' is its own champion? Away with the idea! Are there no pints on which grey experience can show the beacon lights to 'ot youth and indiscretion? Assuredly there are! Full then of hardour—full of keenness, one pure concentrated essence of 'unting, John Jorrocks comes to enlighten all men capable of instruction on pints that all wish to be considered conversant with.

'Well did that great man, I think it was Walter Scott, but if it war'nt, 'twas little Bartley, the bootmaker, say, that there was no young man wot would not rather have a himputation on his morality than on his 'ossmanship, and yet, how few there are wot really know anything about the matter! Oh, but if hignorance be bliss 'ow 'appy must they be! (Loud cheers and laughter.)

''Unting is the sport of kings, the image of war without its guilt, and only five-and-twenty per cent. of its danger! In that word, "'unting," what a ramification of knowledge is compressed! The choice of an 'oss—the treatment of him when got—the groomin' at home, the ridin' abroad—the boots, the breeches, the saddle, the bridle, the 'ound, the 'untsman, the feeder, the Fox! Oh, how that beautiful word, Fox, gladdens my 'eart, and warms the declinin' embers of my age. (Cheers.) The 'oss and the 'ound were made for each other, and natur threw in the Fox as a connectin' link between the two. (Loud cheers.) He's perfect symmetry, and my affection for him is a perfect paradox. In the summer I loves him with all hardour of affection; not an 'air of his beautiful 'ead would I hurt; the sight of him is more glorious nor the Lord Mayor's show! but when the hautumn comes—when the brownin' copse and cracklin' stubble proclaim the farmer's fears are past, then, dash my vig, 'ow I glories in pursuing of him to destruction, and holdin' him above the bayin' pack! (Loud cheers.)

'And yet,' added Mr. Jorrocks thoughtfully, 'it ar'nt that I loves the fox less, but that I loves the 'ound more, as the chap says in the play, when he sticks his friend in the gizzard. (Roars of laughter and applause.)

'The 'oss loves the 'ound, and I loves both; and it is that love wot brings me to these parts, to follow the all-glorious callin' of the chase, and to enlighten all men capable of illumination. To-night I shall instruct you with a lecture on dealin'.

'There is a wast of fancy about dealin'—far more than relates to the mere colour; indeed some say that colour is immaterial, and there is an old saw about a good 'oss never being of a bad colour, but the first question a green 'orn asks is the colour of the prad. Old Steropes says, if you have no predilection that way, choose a mouse-coloured dun, for it has the peculiar adwantage of lookin' equally well all the year round. A black list down the back makes it still more desirable, as the bystanders will suppose you are ridin' with a crupper, a practice no finished 'ossmen ought to neglect. This latter point, however, is confuted by Gambado, who says, "be werry shy of a crupper if your 'oss naturally throws his saddle forward. It will certainlie make his tail sore, set him a kickin', and werry likely bring you into trouble."

'How perplexin' must all this be to a beginner,' exclaimed Mr. Jorrocks, throwing up his hands.

'The height of an 'oss, Gambado says, is perfectly immaterial, prowided he is higher behind than before. Nothin' is more pleasin' to a traveller than the sensation of continually gettin' forward; whereas the ridin' of an 'oss of a contrary make is like swarmin' the banisters of a staircase, when, though perhaps you really advance, you feel as if you were goin' backwards.

'Gambado says nothin' about the size of an 'oss's head, but he says he should carry it low, that he may have an eye to the ground and see the better where he steps. Some say the 'ead should be as large as possible, inasmuch as the weight tends to prewent the 'oss from rearin', which is a wice dangerous in the highest degree; my idea is, that the size of the 'ead is immaterial, for the 'oss doesn't go on it, at least he didn't ought to do I know.

'The ears cannot well be too long, Gambado says, for a judicious rider steers his course by fixin' his eyes between them. This, however, is a disputed point, and old Dickey Lawrence recommends that they should be large and loppin' in a horizontal direction, by which position no rain can possibly enter, and the 'oss will have no occasion to shake his 'ead, a habit which he says not only disturbs the brain, but frequently brings on the mad staggers.

'Here again the doctors differ!

'It seem agreed on all hand that the less a 'oss lifts his forelegs, the easier he will move for his rider, and he will likewise brush all the stones out of his way, which might otherwise throw him down. Gambado thinks if he turns his toes well out, he will disperse them right and left, and not have the trouble of kickin' the same stone a second time, but I don't see much adwantage in this, and think he might as well be kickin' the same stone as a fresh one.

'There can be no doubt that a Roman nose like Arterxerxes's adds greatly to the gravity of an 'oss's countenance. It has a fine substantial yeoman-like appearance, and well becomes the father of a family, a Church dignitary, or a man in easy circumstances.—Roman nose and a shovel hat are quite unique.—Some think a small eye a recommendation, as they are less exposed to injuries than large ones, but that is matter of fancy. The nostrils, Lawrence says, should be small, and the lips thick and leathery, which latter property aids the sensibility of the mouth werry considerably.—Some prefer an arched neck to a ewe, but the latter has a fine consequential hair, and ought not to be slighted.

'It may be prejudice, but I confess I likes an 'oss's back wot inclines to a hog bend.—Your slack backs are all very well for carryin' millers' sacks, but rely upon it there's nothin' like the outward bow for makin' them date their leaps properly. Many men in the Surrey remember my famous 'oss Star-gazer. He was made in that form, and in his leaps threw an arch like the dome of St. Paul's. A long back is a grand thing for a family 'oss.—I've seen my cousin Joe clap six of his brats and his light porter on the back of the old Crockerdile, and the old nag would have carried another if his tail had been tied up.—In the 'unting field, however, one seldom sees more than one man on an 'oss, at a time. Two don't look sportin', and the world's governed by appearances.

'Some people object to high blowers, that is, 'osses wot make a noise like steam-engines as they go. I don't see no great objection to them myself, and think the use they are of in clearin' the way in crowded thoroughfares, and the protection they afford in dark nights by preventin' people ridin' against you, more than counterbalance any disconwenience. —Gambado says, a bald face, wall eyes, and white legs, answer the same purpose, but if you can get all four, it will be so much the better.

'Broken knees is nothin'.—Where, let me ax, is the man with the 'oss that he will swear will never tumble down?

'At an American 'oss sale, I read of t'other day, a buyer exclaims—

' "Vy, he's broken knee'd!"

' "Not at all, you mister," cried the hauctioneer pertly. "The gen'leman wot sells this 'oss always marks his stud on the knee, that he may know 'em again"—haw! haw! haw' chuckled Mr. Jorrocks; ' "Lofty hactioned 'oss!—struck his knee again his tooth!" I once heard a dealer declare on behalf of a broken-kneed 'un in the City.

'But let us narrow the field of 'oss speckilation, and view our buyer on the road to a dealer's in search of an 'unter. No man should go there in black silk stockin's; dress trousers are also out of character. . . .

'When three men enter a yard, a dealer seldom opens out. Two are plenty for business—if the buyer is pea-green, he had better get some riper friend to play first fiddle, and he must be spectator. If he has a button at his 'at and 'olds his tongue, he may pass for a quiet fox-'unter, and so command respect. There's "Masonry" in fox-'unting, and a loop in at the linin' or a button behind, will do more than all the swagger and bluster in the world.

'Thus, my beloved 'earers,' concluded Mr. Jorrocks, 'have I conducted you through the all-perilous journey of your first deal, showin' how warious and conflictin' are the opinions relative to 'osses, and how, as in many cases, wot is one man's meat is anither man's puzzon. Far be it from me to say that you will be much wizer from anything you have heard, for the old stager will find nothin' but what he knew before, while all that can be taught the beginner is not to be too sanguinary in his expectations.'

XXXIX

MRS. WILFER'S WEDDING-DAY

'WELL, Ma,' returned Lavvy, 'since you will force it out of me, I must respectfully take leave to say that your family are no doubt under the greatest obligations to you for having an annual toothache on your wedding-day, and that it's very disinterested in you, and an immense blessing to them. Still, on the whole, it is possible to be too boastful even of that boon.'

'You incarnation of sauciness,' said Mrs. Wilfer, 'do you speak like that to me? On this day of all days in the year? Pray do you know what would have become of you, if I had not bestowed my hand upon R. W., your father, on this day?'

'No, Ma,' replied Lavvy, 'I really do not; and, with the greatest respect for your abilities and information, I very much doubt if you do either.'

Whether or no the sharp vigour of this sally on a weak point of Mrs. Wilfer's entrenchments might have routed that heroine for the time is rendered uncertain by the arrival of a flag of truce in the person of Mr. George Sampson: bidden to the feast as a friend of the family, whose affections were now understood to be in course of transference from Bella to Lavinia, and whom Lavinia kept—possibly in remembrance of his bad taste in having overlooked her in the first instance—under a course of stinging discipline.

'I congratulate you, Mrs. Wilfer,' said Mr. George Sampson, who had meditated this neat address while coming along, 'on the day.' Mrs. Wilfer thanked him with a magnanimous sigh, and again became an unresisting prey to that inscrutable toothache.

'I am surprised,' said Mr. Sampson feebly, 'that Miss Bella condescends to cook.'

Here Miss Lavinia descended on the ill-starred young gentleman with a crushing supposition that at all events it was no business of his. This disposed of Mr. Sampson in a melancholy retirement of spirit, until the cherub arrived, whose amazement at the lovely woman's occupation was great.

However, she persisted in dishing the dinner as well as cooking it, and then sat down, bibless and apronless, to partake of it as an illustrious guest: Mrs. Wilfer first responding to her husband's cheerful 'For what we are about to receive—' with a sepulchral Amen, calculated to cast a damp upon the stoutest appetite.

'But what,' said Bella, as she watched the carving of the fowls, 'makes them pink inside, I wonder, Pa! Is it the breed?'

'No, I don't think it's the breed, my dear,' returned Pa. 'I rather think it is because they are not done.'

'They ought to be,' said Bella.

'Yes, I'm aware they ought to be, my dear,' rejoined her father, 'but they—ain't.'

So, the gridiron was put in requisition, and the good-tempered cherub, who was often as un-cherubically employed in his own family as if he had been in the employment of some of the Old Masters, undertook to grill the fowls. Indeed, except in respect of staring about him (a branch of the public service to which the pictorial cherub is much addicted), this domestic cherub discharged as many odd functions as his prototype; with the difference, say, that he performed with a blacking-brush on the family's boots, instead of performing on enormous wind instruments and double-basses, and that he conducted himself with cheerful alacrity to much useful purpose, instead of foreshortening himself in the air with the vaguest intentions.

Bella helped him with his supplemental cookery, and made him very happy, but put him in mortal terror too by asking him when they sat down at table again, how he supposed they cooked fowls at the Greenwich dinners, and whether he believed they really were such pleasant dinners as people said? His secret winks and nods of remonstrance, in reply, made the mischievous Bella laugh until she choked, and then Lavinia was obliged to slap her on the back, and then she laughed the more.

But her mother was a fine corrective at the other end of the table; to whom her father, in the innocence of his good fellowship, at intervals appealed with: 'My dear, I am afraid you are not enjoying yourself?'

'Why so, R. W.?' she would sonorously reply.

'Because, my dear, you seem a little out of sorts.'

'Not at all,' would be the rejoinder, in exactly the same tone.

'Would you take a merry-thought, my dear?'

'Thank you. I will take whatever you please, R. W.'

'Well, but, my dear, do you like it?'

'I like it as well as I like anything, R. W.' The stately woman would then, with a meritorious appearance of devoting herself to the general good, pursue her dinner as if she were feeding somebody else on high public grounds.

Bella had brought dessert and two bottles of wine, thus shedding unprecedented splendour on the occasion. Mrs. Wilfer did the honours of the first glass by proclaiming: 'R. W., I drink to you.'

'Thank you, my dear. And I to you.'

'Pa and Ma!' said Bella.

'Permit me,' Mrs. Wilfer interposed, with outstretched glove. 'No. I think not. I drank to your Pa. If, however, you insist on including me, I can in gratitude offer no objection.'

'Why, Lor, Ma,' interposed Lavvy the bold, 'isn't it the day that made you and Pa one and the same? I have no patience.'

'By whatever other circumstances the day may be marked, it is not the day, Lavinia, on which I will allow a child of mine to pounce upon me. I beg—nay, command!—that you will not pounce. R. W., it is appropriate to recall that it is for you to command and for me to obey. It is your house, and you are master at your own table. Both our healths!' drinking the toast with tremendous stiffness.

'I really am a little afraid, my dear,' hinted the cherub meekly, 'that you are not enjoying yourself?'

'On the contrary,' returned Mrs. Wilfer, 'quite so. Why should I not?'

'I thought, my dear, that perhaps your face might——'

'My face might be a martyrdom, but what would that import, or who should know it if I smiled?'

And she did smile; manifestly freezing the blood of Mr. George Sampson by so doing. For that young gentleman, catching her smiling eye, was so very much appalled by its expression as to cast about in his thoughts concerning what he had done to bring it down upon himself.

'The mind naturally falls,' said Mrs. Wilfer, 'shall I say into a reverie, or shall I say into a retrospect? on a day like this.'

Lavvy, sitting with defiantly folded arms, replied (but not audibly), 'For goodness' sake say whichever of the two you like best, Ma, and get it over.'

'The mind,' pursued Mrs. Wilfer in an oratorical manner, 'naturally reverts to Papa and Mamma—I here allude to my parents—at a period before the earliest dawn of this day. I was considered tall; perhaps I was. Papa and Mamma were unquestionably tall. I have rarely seen a finer woman than my mother; never than my father.'

The irrepressible Lavvy remarked aloud, 'Whatever grandpapa was, he wasn't a female.'

'Your grandpapa,' retorted Mrs. Wilfer, with an awful look, and in an awful tone, 'was what I describe him to have been, and would have struck any of his grandchildren to the earth who presumed to question it. It was one of mamma's cherished hopes that I should become united to a tall member of society. It may have been a weakness, but if so, it was equally the weakness, I believe, of King Frederick of Prussia.' These remarks being offered to Mr. George Sampson, who had not the courage to come out for single combat but lurked with his chest under the table and his eyes cast down, Mrs. Wilfer proceeded, in a voice of increasing sternness and impressiveness, until she should force that skulker to give himself up. 'Mamma would appear to have had an indefinable foreboding of what afterwards happened, for she would frequently urge upon me, "Not a little man. Promise me, my child, not a little man. Never, never, never marry a little man!" Papa also would remark to me (he possessed extraordinary humour), "that a family of whales must not ally themselves with sprats." His company was eagerly sought, as may be supposed, by the wits of the day, and our house was their continual resort. I have known as many as three copper-plate engravers exchanging the most exquisite sallies and retorts there, at one time.' (Here Mr. Sampson delivered himself captive, and said, with an uneasy movement on his chair, that three was a large number, and it must have been highly entertaining.) 'Among the most prominent members of that distinguished circle, was a gentleman measuring six feet four in height. *He* was *not* an engraver.' (Here Mr. Sampson said, with no reason whatever, Of course not.) 'This gentleman was so obliging as to honour me with attentions which I could not fail to understand.' (Here Mr. Sampson murmured that when it came to that, you could always tell.) 'I immediately announced to both my parents that those attentions were misplaced, and that I could not favour his suit. They inquired was he too tall? I replied it was not the stature, but the intellect was too lofty. At our house, I said, the tone was too brilliant, the pressure was too high, to be maintained by me, a mere woman, in every-day domestic life. I well remember mamma's clasping her hands, and exclaiming, "This will end in a little man!"'

(Here Mr. Sampson glanced at his host and shook his head with despondency.) 'She afterwards went so far as to predict that it would end in a little man whose mind would be below the average, but that was in what I may denominate a paroxysm of maternal disappointment. Within a month,' said Mrs. Wilfer, deepening her voice, as if she were relating a terrible ghost story, 'within a month, I first saw R. W., my husband. Within a year I married him. It is natural for the mind to recall these dark coincidences on the present day.'

XL

THE FAMOUS BALLAD OF THE JUBILEE CUP

YOU may lift me up in your arms, lad, and turn my face to the sun
    For a last look back at the dear old track where the Jubilee Cup was won;
And draw your chair to my side, lad—no, thank ye, I feel no pain—
For I'm going out with the tide, lad, but I'll tell you the tale again.

I'm seventy-nine, or nearly, and my head it has long turned grey,
But it all comes back as clearly as though it was yesterday—
The dust, and the bookies shouting around the clerk of the scales,
And the clerk of the course, and the nobs in force, and 'Is 'Ighness, the Pr*nce of W*les.

'Twas a nine-hole thresh to wind'ard, but none of us cared for that,
With a straight run home to the service tee, and a finish along the flat.

'Stiff?' Ah, well you may say it! Spot-barred, and at five-stone-ten!
But at two and a bisque I'd ha' run the risk; for I was a greenhorn then.

So we stripped to the B. Race signal, the old red swallow-tail—
There was young Ben Bolt, and the Portland colt, and Aston Villa, and Yale;
And W. G., and Steinitz, Leander, and The Saint,
And the German Emperor's Meteor, a-looking as fresh as paint;

John Roberts (scratch), and Safety Match, The Lascar, and Lorna Doone,
Oom Paul (a bye), and Romany Rye, and me upon Wooden Spoon;
And some of us cut for partners, and some of us strung to baulk,
And some of us tossed for stations—But there, what use to talk?

Three-quarter-back on the Kingsclere crack was station enough for me,
With a fresh jackyarder blowing and the Vicarage goal a-lee!
And I leaned and patted her centre-bit, and eased the quid in her cheek,
With a 'Soh, my lass!' and a 'Woa, you brute!'—for she could do all but speak.

She was geared a thought too high, perhaps; she was trained a trifle fine;
But she had the grand reach forward! *I* never saw such a line!
Smooth-bored, clean-run, from her fiddle head with its dainty ear half-cock,
Hard-bit, *pur sang*, from her overhang to the heel of her off hind sock.

THE JUBILEE CUP

Sir Robert he walked beside me as I worked her down to the mark;
'There's money on this, my lad,' said he, 'and most of 'em's running dark;
But ease the sheet if you're bunkered, and pack the scrimmages tight,
And use your slide at the distance, and we'll drink to your health to-night!'

But I bent and tightened my stretcher. Said I to myself, said I,—
'John Jones, this here is the Jubilee Cup, and you have to do or die.'
And the words weren't hardly spoken when the umpire shouted 'Play!'
And we all kicked off from the Gasworks end with a 'Yoicks!' and a 'Gone away!'

And at first I thought of nothing, as the clay flew by in lumps,
But stuck to the old Ruy Lopez, and wondered who'd call for trumps,
And luffed her close to the cushion, and watched each one as it broke,
And in triple file up the Rowley mile we went like a trail of smoke.

The Lascar made the running: but he didn't amount to much,
For old Oom Paul was quick on the ball, and headed it back to touch;
And the whole first flight led off with the right, as The Saint took up the pace,
And drove it clean to the putting green and trumped it there with an ace.

John Roberts had given a miss in baulk, but Villa cleared with a punt;
And keeping her service hard and low, The Meteor forged to the front,
With Romany Rye to windward at dormy and two to play,
And Yale close up—but a Jubilee Cup isn't run for every day.

We laid our course for the Warner—I tell you the pace was hot!
And again off Tattenham Corner, a blanket covered the lot.
Check side! Check side! Now steer her wide! and barely an inch of room,
With The Lascar's tail over our lee rail, and brushing Leander's boom!

We were running as strong as ever—eight knots—but it couldn't last;
For the spray and the bails were flying, the whole field tailing fast;
And the Portland colt had shot his bolt, and Yale was bumped at the Doves,
And The Lascar resigned to Steinitz, stale-mated in fifteen moves.

It was bellows to mend with Roberts—starred three for a penalty kick:
But he chalked his cue and gave 'em the butt, and Oom Paul scored the trick—
'Off-side—no ball—and at fourteen all! Mark cock! and two for his nob!'—
When W. G. ran clean through his lee, and yorked him twice with a lob.

He yorked him twice on a crumbling pitch, and wiped his eye with a brace,
But his guy-rope split with the strain of it, and he dropped back out of the race;

THE JUBILEE CUP

And I drew a bead on The Meteor's lead, and challenging none too soon,
Bent over and patted her garboard strake, and called upon Wooden Spoon.

She was all of a shiver forward, the spoondrift thick on her flanks,
But I'd brought her an easy gambit, and nursed her over the banks;
She answered her helm—the darling!—and woke up now with a rush,
While The Meteor's jock he sat like a rock—he knew we rode for his brush!

There was no one else left in it. The Saint was using his whip,
And Safety Match, with a lofting catch, was pocketed deep at slip;
And young Ben Bolt with his niblick took miss at Leander's lunge,
But topped the net with the ricochet, and Steinitz threw up the sponge.

But none of the lot could stop the rot—nay, don't ask *me* to stop!—
The Villa had called for lemons, Oom Paul had taken his drop,
And both were kicking the referee. Poor fellow! he done his best;
But, being in doubt, he'd ruled them out—which he always did when pressed.

So, inch by inch, I tightened the winch, and chucked the sandbags out—
I heard the nursery cannons pop, I heard the bookies shout:
'The Meteor wins!' 'No, Wooden Spoon!' 'Check!' 'Vantage!' 'Leg before!'
'Last lap!' 'Pass Nap!' At his saddle-flap I put up the helm and wore.

You may overlap at the saddle-flap, and yet be loo'd on the
   tape:
And it all depends upon changing ends, how a seven-year-
   old will shape;
It was tack and tack to the Lepe and back—a fair ding-dong
   to the Ridge,
And he led by his forward canvas yet as we shot 'neath Ham-
   mersmith Bridge.

He led by his forward canvas—he led from his strongest
   suit—
But along we went on a roaring scent, and at Fawley I gained
   a foot.
He fisted off with his jigger, and gave me his wash—too
   late!
Deuce—vantage—check! By neck and neck, we rounded
   into the straight.

I could hear the 'Conquering 'Ero' a-crashing on Godfrey's
   band,
And my hopes fell sudden to zero, just there with the race
   in hand—
In sight of the Turf's Blue Ribbon, in sight of the umpire's
   tape,
As I felt the tack of her spinnaker crack, as I heard the steam
   escape!

Had I lost at that awful juncture my presence of mind? . . .
   but no!
I leaned and felt for the puncture, and plugged it there with
   my toe . . .
Hand over hand by the Members' Stand I lifted and eased
   her up,
Shot—clean and fair—to the crossbar there, and landed the
   Jubilee Cup!

'The odd by a head, and leg before,' so the Judge he gave the
   word:
And the Umpire shouted 'Over!' but I neither spoke nor
   stirred.

They crowded round: for there on the ground I lay in a
   dead-cold swoon,
Pitched neck and crop on the turf atop of my beautiful
   Wooden Spoon.

Her dewlap tire was punctured, her bearings all red-hot;
She'd a lolling tongue, and her bowsprit sprung, and her
   running gear in a knot;
And amid the sobs of her backers, Sir Robert loosened her
   girth
And led her away to the knacker's. She had raced her last
   on earth!

But I mind me well of the tear that fell from the eye of our
   noble Pr*nce,
And the things he said as he tucked me in bed—and I've lain
   there ever since;
Tho' it all gets mixed up queerly that happened before my
   spill,—
But I draw my thousand yearly: it'll pay for the doctor's bill.

I'm going out with the tide, lad.—You'll dig me a humble
   grave,
And whiles you will bring your bride, lad, and your sons (if
   sons you have),
And there, when the dews are weeping, and the echoes
   murmur 'Peace!'
And the salt, salt tide comes creeping and covers the popping-
   crease,

In the hour when the ducks deposit their eggs with a boasted
   force,
They'll look and whisper 'How was it?' and you'll take them
   over the course.
And your voice will break as you try to speak of the glorious
   first of June,
When the Jubilee Cup, with John Jones up, was won upon
   Wooden Spoon.

XLI

SAINT GEORGE OF ENGLAND

SAINT GEORGE was a knight and born in Cappadocia. On a time he came in to the province of Libya, to a city which is said Silene. And by this city was a stagne or a pond like a sea, wherein was a dragon which envenomed all the country. And on a time the people were assembled for to slay him, and when they saw him they fled. And when he came nigh the city he venomed the people with his breath, and therefore the people of the city gave to him every day two sheep for to feed him, because he should do no harm to the people, and when the sheep failed there was taken a man and a sheep. Then was an ordinance made in the town that there should be taken the children and young people of them of the town by lot, and every each one as it fell, were he gentle or poor, should be delivered when the lot fell on him or her. So it happed that many of them of the town were then delivered, insomuch that the lot fell upon the king's daughter, whereof the king was sorry, and said unto the people: For the love of the gods take gold and silver and all that I have, and let me have my daughter. They said: How sir! ye have made and ordained the law, and our children be now dead, and ye would do the contrary. Your daughter shall be given, or else we shall burn you and your house.

When the king saw he might no more do, he began to weep, and said to his daughter: Now shall I never see thine espousals. Then returned he to the people and demanded eight days' respite, and they granted it to him. And when the eight days were passed they came to him and said: Thou seest that the city perisheth: Then did the king do array his daughter like as she should be wedded, and embraced her, kissed her and gave her his benediction, and after, led her to the place where the dragon was.

When she was there S. George passed by, and when he saw the lady he demanded the lady what she made there and

SAINT GEORGE OF ENGLAND

she said: Go ye your way, fair young man, that ye perish not also. Then said he: Tell to me what have ye and why weep ye, and doubt ye of nothing. When she saw that he would know, she said to him how she was delivered to the dragon. Then said S. George: Fair daughter, doubt ye no thing hereof for I shall help thee in the name of Jesu Christ. She said: For God's sake, good knight, go your way, and abide not with me, for ye may not deliver me. Thus as they spake together the dragon appeared and came running to them, and S. George was upon his horse, and drew out his sword and garnished him with the sign of the cross, and rode hardily against the dragon which came towards him, and smote him with his spear and hurt him sore and threw him to the ground. And after said to the maid: Deliver to me your girdle, and bind it about the neck of the dragon and be not afeard. When she had done so the dragon followed her as it had been a meek beast and debonair. Then she led him into the city, and the people fled by mountains and valleys, and said: Alas! alas! we shall be all dead. Then S. George said to them: Ne doubt ye no thing, without more, believe ye in God, Jesu Christ, and do ye to be baptized and I shall slay the dragon. Then the king was baptized and all his people, and S. George slew the dragon and smote off his head, and commanded that he should be thrown in the fields, and they took four carts with oxen that drew him out of the city.

Then were there well fifteen thousand men baptized, without women and children, and the king did do make a church there of our Lady and of S. George, in the which yet sourdeth a fountain of living water, which healeth sick people that drink thereof. After this the king offered to S. George as much money as there might be numbered, but he refused all and commanded that it should be given to poor people for God's sake; and enjoined the king four things, that is, that he should have charge of the churches and that he should honour the priests and hear their service diligently, and that he should have pity on the poor people, and after, kissed the king and departed.

Now it happed that in the time of Diocletian and Maximian, which were emperors, was so great persecution of christian men that within a month were martyred well twenty-two thousand, and therefore they had so great dread that some renied and forsook God and did sacrifice to the idols. When S. George saw this, he left the habit of a knight and sold all that he had, and gave it to the poor, and took the habit of a christian man, and went into the middle of the paynims and began to cry: All the gods of the paynims and gentiles be devils, my God made the heavens and is very God. Then said the provost to him: Of what presumption cometh this to thee, that thou sayest that our gods be devils? And say to us what thou art and what is thy name. He answered anon and said: I am named George, I am a gentleman, a knight of Cappadocia, and have left all for to serve the God of heaven. Then the provost enforced himself to draw him unto his faith by fair words, and when he might not bring him thereto he did do raise him on a gibbet; and so much beat him with great staves and broches of iron, that his body was all tobroken in pieces. And after he did do take brands of iron and join them to his sides, and his bowels which then appeared he did do frot with salt, and so sent him into prison, but our Lord appeared to him the same night with great light and comforted him much sweetly. And by this great consolation he took to him so good heart that he doubted no torment that they might make him suffer. Then, when Dacian the provost saw that he might not surmount him, he called his enchanter and said to him: I see that these christian people doubt not our torments. The enchanter bound himself, upon his head to be smitten off, if he overcame not his crafts. Then he did take strong venom and meddled it with wine, and made invocation of the names of his false gods, and gave it to S. George to drink. S. George took it and made the sign of the cross on it, and anon drank it without grieving him any thing. Then the enchanter made it more stronger than it was tofore of venom, and gave it him to drink, and it grieved him nothing. When the enchanter saw that, he kneeled down at the feet of S. George and prayed him that he would make him christian. And when Dacian knew that he was become christian he made to smite off his head. And after, on the morn, he made S. George to be set between two wheels, which were full of swords, sharp and cutting on both sides, but anon the wheels were broken and S. George escaped without hurt. And then commanded Dacian that they should put him in a caldron full of molten lead, and when S. George entered therein, by the virtue of our Lord it seemed that he was in a bath well at ease. Then Dacian seeing this began to assuage his ire, and to flatter him by fair words, and said to him: George, the patience of our gods is over great unto thee which hast blasphemed them, and done to them great despite, then fair, and right sweet son, I pray thee that thou return to our law and make sacrifice to the idols, and leave thy folly, and I shall enhance thee to great honour and worship. Then began S. George to smile, and said to him: Wherefore saidst thou not to me thus at the beginning? I am ready to do as thou sayest. Then was Dacian glad and made to cry over all the town that all the people should assemble for to see George make sacrifice which so much had striven there against. Then was the city arrayed and feast kept throughout all the town, and all came to the temple for to see him.

When S. George was on his knees, and they supposed that he would have worshipped the idols, he prayed our Lord God of heaven that he would destroy the temple and the idol in the honour of his name, for to make the people to be converted. And anon the fire descended from heaven and burnt the temple, and the idols, and their priests, and sith the earth opened and swallowed all the cinders and ashes that were left. Then Dacian made him to be brought tofore him, and said to him: What be the evil deeds that thou hast done, and also great untruth? Then said to him S. George: Ah, sir, believe it not, but come with me and see how I shall sacrifice. Then said Dacian to him: I see well thy fraud and thy barat, thou wilt make the earth to swallow me, like as thou hast the temple and my gods. Then said S. George: O caitiff, tell me how may thy gods help thee when they may not help themselves! Then was Dacian so angry that he said to his wife: I shall die for anger if I may not surmount and overcome this man. Then said she to him: Evil and cruel tyrant! ne seest thou not the great virtue of the christian people? I said to thee well that thou shouldst not do to them any harm, for their God fighteth for them, and know thou well that I will become christian. Then was Dacian much abashed and said to her: Wilt thou be christian? Then he took her by the hair, and did do beat her cruelly. Then demanded she of S. George: What may I become because I am not christened? Then answered the blessed George: Doubt thee nothing, fair daughter, for thou shalt be baptized in thy blood. Then began she to worship our Lord Jesu Christ, and so she died and went to heaven. On the morn Dacian gave his sentence that S. George should be drawn through all the city, and after, his head should be smitten off. Then made he his prayer to our Lord that all they that desired any boon might get it of our Lord God in his name, and a voice came from heaven which said that it which he had desired was granted; and after he had made his orison his head was smitten off, about the year of our Lord two hundred and eighty-seven. When Dacian went homeward from the place where he was beheaded towards his palace, fire fell down from heaven upon him and burnt him and all his servants. . . .

This blessed and holy martyr S. George is patron of this realm of England and the cry of men of war. In the worship of whom is founded the noble order of the garter, and also a noble college in the castle of Windsor by kings of England, in which college is the heart of S. George, which Sigismund, the emperor of Almayne, brought and gave for a great and a precious relique to King Harry the fifth. And also the said Sigismund was a brother of the said garter, and also there is a piece of his head, which college is nobly endowed to the honour and worship of Almighty God and his blessed martyr S. George. Then let us pray unto him that he be special protector and defender of this realm.

XLII

RIDING TO SELL

NOTHING could be further from Mr. Sawyer's wishes than to find himself, on the present occasion, in a conspicuous position with the Quorn hounds. Had he wanted to be singled out in front of all that talent and beauty, Marathon was certainly the last animal he would have chosen on which to make an appearance in such choice company; nevertheless, the force of circumstances is beyond the control even of men like Mr. Sawyer, and however averse he might be to 'achieve greatness,' he found, most unwillingly, 'greatness thrust upon him.' For awhile he had lost sight of everybody, and was in the act of pulling out his cigar-case to enjoy one of his Laranagas in solitude and repose, proposing to hang on the line, keeping a little down wind, and as soon as he should spy the second-horses, mount the grey, and send Marathon straight home. Crasher, he thought, would buy the horse without asking any more questions.

Scarcely, however, had he got his weed fairly *under weigh*, than the music of a pack of hounds broke suddenly on his ear from behind a high impervious bullfinch that sheltered one side of the grass-lane along which he was proceeding so leisurely. 'Confound the brutes!' said Sawyer to himself, 'here they are again!' As he opened the gate through which the track led into a sixty-acre pasture, the whole pack swept under his horse's nose, running with sufficient energy to denote what sportsmen call a holding scent; they carried a capital head, and were forcing their fox at a pace which kept him going, but was not good enough to come up with him. It was just the sort of gallop that enables people who ride to hounds to look about them, and enjoy not only the sport, but the accompanying humours of the scene. . . .

Had he been riding a donkey, it was not in Mr. Sawyer's nature to abstain from turning the animal's head towards the hounds under such temptation; moreover, he distinguished amongst the first flight his Harborough companions, including the pale face of the Honourable Crasher, who by 'bucketing' Boadicea most unmercifully, had got there somehow, and appeared quite satisfied with his situation. What could our friend do, but cut in, and go to work at once?

Marathon, excited by the turmoil, was fain to set his back up once more. He found, however, that the kicking was now all the other way. Taking him in a grasp that would have lifted a ton, Mr. Sawyer drove his spurs into the half-bred brute, and set him going close to the hounds at the best pace he could command. For a short distance, and when held well together, Marathon could stride away in a very imposing form. The sensation of having a lead is, in itself, provocative of emulation; behind our friend were four or five intimate companions, who were not likely to let him hear the last of any instance of 'shirking' that should come under their notice. Close on their track were the flower of Leicestershire; and these again were succeeded, so to speak, by a whole army of camp-followers, 'maddening in the rear.' Had the Styx been in front of him, he must have charged it 'in or over.'

Instead of the waters of Acheron, however, there was nothing more formidable in his line than a straggling, overgrown bullfinch at the far end of the field; just such a fence, indeed, as Marathon was in the habit of declining, but yet which he hoped the turmoil behind, the general excitement, and the persuasive powers of his own spurs, would enable him to induce his horse to face. He had plenty of time to scan it as he approached. Half a mile or so of ridge and furrow, even at a hunter's best pace, gives leisure for consideration. Ere the hounds had strung through it in single file, he was aware of a wide ditch *to* him; on the further side was obviously a grass-field, *and* an uncertainty!

Marking with his eye the weakest place, through which, nevertheless, he could not see daylight, Mr. Sawyer crammed his hat on his head, and set his horse resolutely at the fence; Marathon, according to custom, when he expected anything out of the common, *shutting up* every stride he went. Had it not been rather downhill, even his master's consummate horsemanship would have failed to bring him close to it. The fall of the ground, however, and the pace he was going, forbade the bay to stop. *Crash!* he plunged into the very middle of the fence—broke through it from sheer velocity, to jerk both knees against a strong oak rail beyond—blundered on to his nose over that—slid half a dozen yards on his head—nearly recovered himself—stumbled once more, and finally got up again, with his curb-rein turned over his ears; the rider's feet out of both stirrups, hat off, a contusion on his left eyebrow, and the horse's nostrils full of mud, but *no fall!* 'By the powers, that's a *rum one*,' said Mr. Sawyer, as he cantered slowly up the opposite slope, repairing damages the while, and turned round to see the first flight charge the obstacle, which had so nearly disposed of his own chance.

Lusty as eagles, ravenous as wolves, jealous as girls, down came the four *gluttons* at the fence, each man having chosen his own place, and scorning to deviate one hair's breadth from his line. None, however, had made so judicious a selection as Mr. Sawyer. The rail, which had so nearly discomfited the latter, would neither bend nor break, but he had the luck of getting it where it was lowest and nearest to the fence; everywhere else it was not only high, but stood out a horse's length into the field, just the place which must catch the cleverest hunter in the world, if ridden to do it all in its stride.

The scene that met Mr. Sawyer's eyes was amusing, though alarming. Four *imperial crowners* at one and the same instant—four loose horses galloping wildly away—four red coats rising simultaneously from Mother Earth—eight top-booted legs shuffling in ludicrous haste after the departing steeds. Had our friend been Briareus himself, he could not have caught *all* their horses. He was a man, however, who seldom lost an opportunity, and was not likely to miss such a chance as the present. Selecting Boadicea, he galloped after her, and succeeded in pinning her against a pound: notwithstanding that the mare lashed out at him more than once, he brought her back in triumph to her panting owner.

Meanwhile, the four dismounted sportsmen condoled breathlessly with each other, as they laboured up the grassy slope. . . .

'My chestnut mare would have jumped it!' exclaimed Major Brush, inwardly registering a vow to abstain from 'oxers' for the future; whilst the Honourable, though he held his tongue, was thinking what a capital horse that was of Sawyer's, and dismally reflecting that if Boadicea hadn't kicked at him when he was down, he never would have been such a tailor as to let her go.

'Catch hold!' said Mr. Sawyer, throwing the mare's reins to her owner, whose gratitude he thereby earned for the rest of his life. 'There's no hurry,' he added, as the Honourable dived wildly at his stirrup; 'they've over-run it a mile back, and checked in the next field.'

The latter part of the sentence was true enough. His quick eye had shown him the pack at fault, as he secured Boadicea in the corner where the pound stood; the former was a bit of what theatrical people call 'gag.' It was as much as to say, 'Whilst you fellows are hustling and spurting, and tumbling about, I am so well mounted that I can observe matters as coolly as if I was hunting in a balloon.'

It was not without its effect on his listener. As they rode through the hand-gate together into the enclosure where the hounds were at fault, the Honourable Crasher no longer scanned Marathon with the eye of a purchaser. He looked on the horse now as his own property. He was determined to have him.

By some mysterious law of nature, whenever one individual succeeds either in what is termed *pounding* a field, or in getting such a start of them that nobody shall have a chance of catching him whilst the pace holds—and this, be it observed, is no everyday occurrence in countries where the best riders in England congregate for the express purpose of riding as well as they can—it invariably happens that the immediate failure of scent, or some such untoward contingency, robs the lucky one of his anticipated triumph. On the present occasion, much to Mr. Sawyer's delight, they never hit off their fox again. By degrees, the tail of the field straggled up, having found their way by every available gate and gap; then came the second-horses, carefully ridden, cool, and comparatively clean, not having turned a hair; lastly, arrived a man in a gig, by a convenient bridle-road, hotter than any one present, wiping his face on a coloured handkerchief, which he afterwards put in the crown of his hat.

Whilst sandwiches were being munched, and silver horns drained of their contents, ginger-cordial, orange-brandy, V.O.P., and other enticing fluids, Mr. Sawyer was giving The Boy stringent orders about taking Marathon home. He could not feel thoroughly comfortable till that impostor was fairly out of sight, and he should find himself established on the unassuming little grey.

When he had made up his mind, the Honourable Crasher was a man of few words. Refreshed by a mouthful of sherry, not unacceptable after a rattling fall, and comfortably perched on the back of Confidence, a delightful animal that a child could ride, and perhaps the best and safest hunter in his stable, he ranged alongside of our friend, and plunged at once *in medias res.*

'So you want to sell the bay horse you have just sent home?' said he, with none of the hesitation and beating about the bush to which Mr. Sawyer had hitherto been accustomed in his horse-dealing operations. 'If you do, and will name the price you ask for him, I should like to buy him.'

The owner could not resist the impulse of enhancing the value of his horse, by affecting unwillingness to sell him, and, in so doing, nearly lost the chance of disposing of him, altogether.

'I don't think I ought to part with him,' said he reflectively; 'it strikes me he's about the best in my stable.'

Crasher fell back apparently satisfied. It was evident he did not attach so much importance to the act of 'exchange or barter' as did our friend. Mr. Sawyer picked himself up without loss of time. 'I shouldn't like to sell him to *everybody*,' said he affectionately, 'but if you fancy him very much,

I wouldn't mind letting you have him,' he added, after a pause, and in the tone of a man who makes a painful sacrifice in the cause of friendship.

'I'll give you two hundred and fifty for him,' drawled out the Honourable, with apparently about as much interest as he would have felt in paying three-and-sixpence for a pair of gloves.

'Guineas!' stipulated Mr. Sawyer; 'Guineas,' was the answer; and in this simple manner the deal was concluded.

XLIII

MY FIRST PLAY

AT the north end of Cross-court there yet stands a portal, of some architectural pretensions, though reduced to humble use, serving at present for an entrance to a printing-office. This old door-way, if you are young, reader, you may not know was the identical pit entrance to Old Drury—Garrick's Drury—all of it that is left. I never pass it without shaking some forty years from off my shoulders, recurring to the evening when I passed through it to see *my first play*. The afternoon had been wet, and the condition of our going (the elder folks and myself) was, that the rain should cease. With what a beating heart did I watch from the window the puddles, from the stillness of which I was taught to prognosticate the desired cessation! I seem to remember the last spurt, and the glee with which I ran to announce it.

We went with orders, which my godfather F. had sent us. He kept the oil shop (now Davies's) at the corner of Featherstone-building, in Holborn. F. was a tall grave person, lofty in speech, and had pretensions above his rank. He associated in those days with John Palmer, the comedian, whose gait and bearing he seemed to copy; if John (which is quite as likely) did not rather borrow somewhat of his manner from my godfather. He was also known to, and visited by,

Sheridan. It was to his house in Holborn that young Brinsley brought his first wife on her elopement with him from a boarding-school at Bath—the beautiful Maria Linley. My parents were present (over a quadrille table) when he arrived in the evening with his harmonious charge.—From either of these connexions it may be inferred that my godfather could command an order for the then Drury-lane theatre at pleasure—and, indeed, a pretty liberal issue of those cheap billets, in Brinsley's easy autograph, I have heard him say was the sole remuneration which he had received for many years' nightly illumination of the orchestra and various avenues of that theatre—and he was content it should be so. The honour of Sheridan's familiarity—or supposed familiarity— was better to my godfather than money.

F. was the most gentlemanly of oilmen; grandiloquent, yet courteous. His delivery of the commonest matters of fact was Ciceronian. He had two Latin words almost constantly in his mouth (how odd sounds Latin from an oilman's lips!), which my better knowledge since has enabled me to correct. In strict pronunciation they should have been sounded *vice versa*—but in those young years they impressed me with more awe than they would now do, read aright from Seneca or Varro—in his own peculiar pronunciation, monosyllabically elaborated, or Anglicized, into something like *verse verse*. By an imposing manner, and the help of these distorted syllables, he climbed (but that was little) to the highest parochial honours which St. Andrew's has to bestow.

He is dead—and thus much I thought due to his memory, both for my first orders (little wondrous talismans!—slight keys, and insignificant to outward sight, but opening to me more than Arabian paradises!) and moreover, that by his testamentary beneficence I came into possession of the only landed property which I could ever call my own—situate near the road-way village of pleasant Puckeridge, in Hertfordshire. When I journeyed down to take possession, and planted foot on my own ground, the stately habits of the donor descended upon me, and I strode (shall I confess the vanity?) with larger paces over my allotment of three-quarters of an acre, with its commodious mansion in the midst, with the feeling of an English freeholder that all betwixt sky and centre was my own. The estate has passed into more prudent hands, and nothing but an agrarian can restore it.

In those days were pit orders. Beshrew the uncomfortable manager who abolished them!—with one of these we went. I remember the waiting at the door—not that which is left—but between that and an inner door in shelter —O when shall I be such an expectant again!—with the cry of nonpareils, an indispensable play-house accompaniment in those days. As near as I can recollect, the fashionable pronunciation of the theatrical fruiteresses then was, 'Chase some oranges, chase some numparels, chase a bill of the play;'—chase *pro* chuse. But when we got in, and I beheld the green curtain that veiled a heaven to my imagination, which was soon to be disclosed—the breathless anticipations I endured! I had seen something like it in the plate prefixed to Troilus and Cressida, in Rowe's Shakespeare— the tent scene with Diomede—and a sight of that plate can always bring back in a measure the feeling of that evening.— The boxes at that time, full of well-dressed women of quality, projected over the pit; and the pilasters reaching down were adorned with a glistering substance (I know not what) under glass (as it seemed), resembling—a homely fancy—but I judged it to be sugar-candy—yet, to my raised imagination, divested of its homelier qualities, it appeared a glorified candy!—The orchestra lights at length arose, those 'fair Auroras!' Once the bell sounded. It was to ring out yet once again—and, incapable of the anticipation, I reposed my shut eyes in a sort of resignation upon the maternal lap. It rang the second time. The curtain drew up—I was not past six years old—and the play was Artaxerxes!

I had dabbled a little in the Universal History—the ancient part of it—and here was the court of Persia. It was being admitted to a sight of the past. I took no proper interest in the action going on, for I understood not its import—but I heard the word Darius, and I was in the midst of Daniel. All feeling was absorbed in vision. Gorgeous vests, gardens, palaces, princesses, passed before me. I knew not players. I was in Persepolis for the time; and the burning idol of their devotion almost converted me into a worshipper. I was awe-struck, and believed those significations to be something more than elemental fires. It was all enchantment and a dream. No such pleasure has since visited me but in dreams.—Harlequin's Invasion followed; where, I remember, the transformation of the magistrates into reverend beldams seemed to me a piece of grave historic justice, and the tailor carrying his own head to be as sober a verity as the legend of St. Denys.

The next play to which I was taken was the Lady of the Manor, of which, with the exception of some scenery, very faint traces are left in my memory. It was followed by a pantomime, called Lun's Ghost—a satiric touch, I apprehend, upon Rich, not long since dead—but to my apprehension (too sincere for satire), Lun was as remote a piece of antiquity as Lud—the father of a line of Harlequins—transmitting his dagger of lath (the wooden sceptre) through countless ages. I saw the primeval Motley come from his silent tomb in a ghastly vest of white patch-work, like the apparition of a dead rainbow. So Harlequins (thought I) look when they are dead.

My third play followed in quick succession. It was the Way of the World. I think I must have sat at it as grave as a judge; for, I remember, the hysteric affectations of good Lady Wishfort affected me like some solemn tragic passion. Robinson Crusoe followed; in which Crusoe, man Friday, and the parrot, were as good and authentic as in the story.— The clownery and pantaloonery of these pantomimes have clean passed out of my head. I believe, I no more laughed at them, than at the same age I should have been disposed to laugh at the grotesque Gothic heads (seeming to me then replete with devout meaning) that gape, and grin, in stone around the inside of the old Round Church (my church) of the Templars.

I saw these plays in the season 1781–2, when I was from

six to seven years old. After the intervention of six or seven other years (for at school all play-going was inhibited) I again entered the doors of a theatre. That old Artaxerxes evening had never done ringing in my fancy. I expected the same feelings to come again with the same occasion. But we differ from ourselves less at sixty and sixteen, than the latter does from six. In that interval what had I not lost! At the first period I knew nothing, understood nothing, discriminated nothing. I felt all, loved all, wondered all—

> Was nourished, I could not tell how—

I had left the temple a devotee, and was returned a rationalist. The same things were there materially; but the emblem, the reference, was gone!—The green curtain was no longer a veil, drawn between two worlds, the unfolding of which was to bring back past ages, to present 'a royal ghost,'—but a certain quantity of green baize, which was to separate the audience for a given time from certain of their fellow-men who were to come forward and pretend those parts. The lights—the orchestra lights—came up a clumsy machinery. The first ring, and the second ring, was now but a trick of the prompter's bell—which had been, like the note of the cuckoo, a phantom of a voice, no hand seen or guessed at which ministered to its warning. The actors were men and women painted. I thought the fault was in them; but it was in myself, and the alteration which those many centuries—of six short twelve-months—had wrought in me.— Perhaps it was fortunate for me that the play of the evening was but an indifferent comedy, as it gave me time to crop some unreasonable expectations, which might have interfered with the genuine emotions with which I was soon after enabled to enter upon the first appearance to me of Mrs. Siddons in Isabella. Comparison and retrospection soon yielded to the present attraction of the scene; and the theatre became to me, upon a new stock, the most delightful of recreations.

XLIV

THE LANDLORD'S DEBT

THE landlord appeared at all times glad to see me and insisted that I should sit within the bar, where, leaving his other guests to be attended to by a niece of his who officiated as his housekeeper, he would sit beside me and talk of matters concerning 'the ring,' indulging himself with a cigar and a glass of sherry, which he told me was his favourite wine, whilst I drank my ale.

'I loves the conversation of all you coves of the ring,' said he once, 'which is natural, seeing as how I have fought in a ring myself. Ah, there is nothing like the ring; I wish I was not rather too old to go again into it. I often think I should like to have another rally—one more rally, and then —but there's a time for all things—youth will be served, every dog has his day, and mine has been a fine one—let me be content. After beating Tom of Hopton there was not much more to be done in the way of reputation; I have long sat in my bar the wonder and glory of this here neighbourhood. I'm content, as far as reputation goes; I only wish money would come in a little faster; however, the next main of cocks will bring me in something handsome—comes off next Wednesday at ——, have ventured ten five-pound notes—shouldn't say ventured either—run no risk at all, because why? I knows my birds.'

About ten days after this harangue, I called again at about three o'clock one afternoon. The landlord was seated on a bench by a table in the common room, which was entirely empty; he was neither smoking nor drinking, but sat with his arms folded and his head hanging down over his breast. At the sound of my step he looked up. 'Ah,' said he, 'I am glad you are come, I was just thinking about you.' 'Thank you,' said I; 'it was very kind of you, especially at a time like this, when your mind must be full of your good fortune. Allow me to congratulate you on the sums of money you won by the main of cocks at ——. I hope you brought it all safe home.' 'Safe home!' said the landlord; 'I brought myself safe home, and that was all; came home without a shilling, regularly done, cleaned out.' 'I am sorry for that,' said I; 'but after you had won the money you ought to have been satisfied, and not risked it again. How did you lose it? I hope not by the pea and thimble.' 'Pea and thimble!' said the landlord; 'not I; those confounded cocks left me nothing to lose by the pea and thimble.' 'Dear me!' said I, 'I thought that you knew your birds.' 'Well, so I did,' said the landlord, 'I knew the birds to be good birds, and so they proved, and would have won if better birds had not been brought against them, of which I knew nothing, and so, do you see, I am done, regularly done.' 'Well,' said I, 'don't be cast down; there is one thing of which the cocks by their misfortune cannot deprive you—your reputation; make the most of that, give up cock-fighting, and be content with the custom of your house, of which you will always have plenty, as long as you are the wonder and glory of the neighbourhood.'

The landlord struck the table before him violently with his fist. 'Confound my reputation!' said he. 'No reputation that I have will be satisfaction to my brewer for the seventy pounds I owe him. Reputation won't pass for the current coin of this here realm; and let me tell you, that if it a'n't backed by some of it it a'n't a bit better than rotten cabbage, as I have found. Only three weeks since I was, as I told you, the wonder and glory of the neighbourhood; and people used to come and look at me and worship me, but as soon as it began to be whispered about that I owed money to the brewer they presently left off all that kind of thing; and now, during the last three days, since the tale of my misfortune with the cocks has got wind, almost everybody has left off coming to the house, and the few who does merely comes to insult and flout me. It was only last night that fellow Hunter called me an old fool in my own kitchen here. He wouldn't have called me a fool a fortnight ago; 'twas I called him fool then, and last night he called me old fool; what do you think of that? the man that beat Tom of Hopton to be called, not only a fool, but an old fool; and I hadn't heart, with one blow of this here fist into his face, to send his head ringing against the wall, for when a man's pocket is low, do you see, his heart a'n't much higher; but it is of no use talking, something must be done. I was thinking of you just as you came in, for you are just the person that can help me.'

'If you mean,' said I, 'to ask me to lend you the money which you want, it will be to no purpose, as I have very little of my own, just enough for my own occasions. It is true, if you desired it, I would be your intercessor with the person to whom you owe the money, though I should hardly imagine that anything I could say——' 'You are right there,' said the landlord, 'much the brewer would care for anything you could say on my behalf—your going would be the very way to do me up entirely. A pretty opinion he would have of the state of my affairs if I were to send him such a 'cessor as you; and as for your lending me money, don't think I was ever fool enough to suppose either that you had any, or if you had, that you would be fool enough to lend me any. No, no, the coves of the ring knows better. I have been in the ring myself, and knows what fighting a cove is; and though I was fool enough to back those birds, I was never quite fool enough to lend anybody money. What I am about to propose is something very different from going to my landlord, or lending any capital—something which, though it will put money into my pocket, will likewise put something handsome into your own. I want to get up a fight in this here neighbourhood, which would be sure to bring plenty of people to my house, for a week before and after it takes place; and as people can't come without drinking, I think I could, during one fortnight, get off for the brewer all the sour and unsaleable liquids he now has, which people wouldn't drink at any other time, and by that means, do you see, liquidate my debt; then, by means of betting, making first all right, do you see, I have no doubt that I could put something handsome into my pocket and yours, for I should wish you to be the fighting man, as I think I can depend upon you.' 'You really must excuse me,' said I; 'I have no wish to figure as a pugilist; besides, there is such a difference in our ages. You may be the stronger man of the two, and perhaps the hardest hitter, but I am in much better condition, am more active on my legs, so that I am almost sure I should have the advantage; for, as you very properly observed, "Youth will be served."' 'Oh, I didn't mean to fight,' said the landlord; 'I think I could beat you if I were to train a little; but in the fight I propose I looks more to the main chance than anything else. I question whether half so many people could be brought together if you were to fight with me as the person I have in view, or whether there would be half such opportunities for betting; for I am a man, do you see. The person I wants you to fight with is not a man, but the young woman you keeps company with.'

'The young woman I keep company with!' said I. 'Pray what do you mean?' ...

'What I wants, is to get up a fight between a man and a woman. There never has yet been such a thing in the ring, and the mere noise of the matter would bring thousands of people together, quite enough to drink out—for the thing should be close to my house—all the brewer's stock of liquids, both good and bad.' 'But,' said I, 'you were the other day boasting of the respectability of your house. Do you think that a fight between a man and a woman close to your establishment would add to its respectability?' 'Confound the respectability of my house,' said the landlord; 'will the respectability of my house pay the brewer, or keep the roof over my head? No, no! when respectability won't keep a man, do you see, the best thing is to let it go and wander. Only let me have my own way, and both the brewer, myself, and every one of us, will be satisfied. And then the betting—what a deal we may make by the betting!—and that we shall have all to ourselves, you, I, and the young woman; the brewer will have no hand in that. I can manage to raise ten pounds; and if, by flashing that about, I don't manage to make a hundred, call me horse.' 'But suppose,' said I, 'the party should lose on whom you sport your money, even as the birds did?' 'We must first make all right,' said the landlord, 'as I told you before.

The birds were irrational beings, and therefore couldn't come to an understanding with the others, as you and the young woman can. The birds fought fair; but I intend you and the young woman should fight cross.' 'What do you mean by cross?' said I. 'Come, come,' said the landlord, 'don't attempt to gammon me. You in the ring, and pretend not to know what fighting cross is! That won't do, my fine fellow; but as no one is near us, I will speak out. I intend that you and the young woman should understand one another and agree beforehand which should be beat; and if you take my advice you will determine between you that the young woman shall be beat, as I am sure that the odds will run high upon her, her character as a fist woman being spread far and wide, so that all the flats who think it will be all right, will back her, as I myself would, if I thought it would be a fair thing.' 'Then,' said I, 'you would not have us fight fair.' 'By no means,' said the landlord, 'because why? I conceives that a cross is a certainty to those who are in it, whereas by the fair thing one may lose all he has.' 'But,' said I, 'you said the other day that you liked the fair thing.' 'That was by way of gammon,' said the landlord; 'just, do you see, as a Parliament cove might say, speechifying from a barrel to a set of flats, whom he means to sell. Come, what do you think of the plan?'

'It is a very ingenious one,' said I.

'A'n't it,' said the landlord. 'The folks in this neighbourhood are beginning to call me old fool; but if they don't call me something else, when they sees me friends with the brewer, and money in my pocket, my name is not Catchpole. Come, drink your ale, and go home to the young gentlewoman.'

'I am going,' said I, rising from my seat, after finishing the remainder of the ale.

'Do you think she'll have any objection?' said the landlord.

'To do what?' said I.

'Why, to fight cross.'

'Yes, I do,' said I.

'But you will do your best to persuade her?'

'No, I will not,' said I.
'Are you fool enough to wish to fight fair?'
'No,' said I, 'I am wise enough to wish not to fight at all.'
'And how's my brewer to be paid?' said the landlord.
'I really don't know,' said I.
'I'll change my religion,' said the landlord.

XLV

THREE SONGS FROM LOVELACE

TO LUCASTA. GOING TO THE WARRES

TELL me not, (sweet,) I am unkinde,
    That from the nunnerie
    Of thy chaste breast and quiet minde
To warre and armes I flie.

True: a new Mistress now I chase,
    The first foe in the field,
And with a stronger faith embrace
    A sword, a horse, a shield.

Yet this inconstancy is such,
    As you too shall adore;
I could not love thee, dear, so much,
    Lov'd I not Honour more.

TO ALTHEA. FROM PRISON

When love with unconfinèd wings
    Hovers within my gates:
And my divine *Althea* brings
    To whisper at the grates;
When I lye tangled in her haire,
    And fettered to her eye,
The birds, that wanton in the aire,
    Know no such liberty.

When flowing cups run swiftly round
    With no allaying *Thames*,
Our carelesse heads with roses bound,
    Our hearts with loyal flames;
When thirsty griefe in wine we steepe,
    When healths and draughts go free,
Fishes, that tipple in the deepe,
    Know no such libertie.

When (like committed linnets) I
    With shriller throat shall sing
The sweetnes, mercy, majesty,
    And glories of my King.
When I shall voyce aloud, how good
    He is, how great should be,
Inlargèd winds, that curle the flood,
    Know no such liberty.

Stone walls doe not a prison make,
    Nor iron bars a cage;
Mindes innocent and quiet take
    That for an hermitage:
If I have freedome in my love,
    And in my soule am free,
Angels alone that sore above
    Enjoy such liberty.

THE GRASSHOPPER
TO MY NOBLE FRIEND, MR. CHARLES COTTON

Oh thou, that swing'st upon the waving eare
    Of some well-fillèd oaten beard,
Drunk ev'ry night with a delicious teare
    Dropt thee from Heav'n, where now th'art reard.

The joyes of earth and ayre are thine intire,
    That with thy feet and wings doth hop and flye;
And when thy poppy workes, thou dost retire
    To thy carv'd acorn-bed to lye.

Up with the day, the Sun thou welcomst then,
　Sportst in the guilt plats of his beames,
And all these merry dayes mak'st merry men,
　Thy selfe, and melancholy streames.

But ah, the sickle! golden eares are cropt;
　Ceres and *Bacchus* bid good night;
Sharpe frosty fingers all your flowrs have topt,
　And what sithes spar'd, winds shave off quite.

Poore verdant foole! and now green ice, thy joys
　Large and as lasting as thy peirch of grasse,
Bid us lay in 'gainst winter raine, and poize
　Their flouds with an o'erflowing glasse.

Thou best of men and friends! we will create
　A genuine summer in each other's breast;
And spite of this cold Time and frozen Fate,
　Thaw us a warm seate to our rest.

Our sacred harthes shall burne eternally
　As vestal flames; the North-wind, he
Shall strike his frost-stretch'd winges, dissolve and flye
　This Ætna in epitome.

Dropping December shall come weeping in,
　Bewayle th' usurping of his raigne;
But when in show'rs of old Greeke[1] we beginne,
　Shall crie, he hath his crowne againe!

Night as cleare Hesper shall our tapers whip
　From the light casements, where we play,
And the dark hagge from her black mantle strip,
　And sticke there everlasting day.

Thus richer than untempted kings are we,
　That asking nothing, nothing need:
Though lord of all what seas imbrace, yet he
　That wants himselfe, is poore indeed.

[1] Greek Wine.

XLVI

LONDON OF THE STUARTS

ALMOST all the noble families of England had long migrated beyond the walls. The district where most of their town houses stood lies between the city and the regions which are now considered as fashionable. A few great men still retained their hereditary hotels in the Strand. The stately dwellings on the south and west of Lincoln's Inn Fields, the Piazza of Covent Garden, Southampton Square, which is now called Bloomsbury Square, and King's Square in Soho Fields, which is now called Soho Square, were among the favourite spots. Foreign princes were carried to see Bloomsbury Square, as one of the wonders of England. Soho Square, which had just been built, was to our ancestors a subject of pride with which their posterity will hardly sympathize. Monmouth Square had been the name while the fortunes of the Duke of Monmouth flourished; and on the southern side towered his mansion. The front, though ungraceful, was lofty and richly adorned. The walls of the principal apartments were finely sculptured with fruit, foliage, and armorial bearings, and were hung with embroidered satin. Every trace of this magnificence has long disappeared; and no aristocratical mansion is to be found in that once aristocratical quarter. . . .

Nearer to the Court, on a space called St. James's Fields, had just been built St. James's Square and Jermyn Street. St. James's Church had recently been opened for the accommodation of the inhabitants of this new quarter. Golden Square, which was in the next generation inhabited by lords and ministers of state, had not yet been begun. Indeed the only dwellings to be seen on the north of Piccadilly were three or four isolated and almost rural mansions, of which the most celebrated was the costly pile erected by Clarendon, and nicknamed Dunkirk House. It had been purchased after its founder's downfall by the Duke of Albemarle. The

Clarendon Hotel and Albemarle Street still preserve the memory of the site.

He who then rambled to what is now the gayest and most crowded part of Regent Street found himself in a solitude, and was sometimes so fortunate as to have a shot at a woodcock. On the north the Oxford road ran between hedges. Three or four hundred yards to the south were the garden walls of a few great houses which were considered as quite out of town. On the west was a meadow renowned for a spring from which, long afterwards, Conduit Street was named. On the east was a field not to be passed without a shudder by any Londoner of that age. There, as in a place far from the haunts of men, had been dug, twenty years before, when the great plague was raging, a pit into which the dead carts had nightly shot corpses by scores. It was popularly believed that the earth was deeply tainted with infection, and could not be disturbed without imminent risk to human life. No foundations were laid there till two generations had passed without any return of the pestilence, and till the ghastly spot had long been surrounded by buildings.

We should greatly err if we were to suppose that any of the streets and squares then bore the same aspect as at present. The great majority of the houses, indeed, have, since that time, been wholly, or in great part, rebuilt.. If the most fashionable parts of the capital could be placed before us such as they then were, we should be disgusted by their squalid appearance, and poisoned by their noisome atmosphere.

In Covent Garden a filthy and noisy market was held close to the dwellings of the great. Fruit women screamed, carters fought, cabbage stalks and rotten apples accumulated in heaps at the thresholds of the Countess of Berkshire and of the Bishop of Durham.

The centre of Lincoln's Inn Fields was an open space where the rabble congregated every evening, within a few yards of Cardigan House and Winchester House, to hear mountebanks harangue, to see bears dance, and to set dogs at oxen. Rubbish was shot in every part of the area. Horses were exercised there. The beggars were as noisy and importunate as in the worst governed cities of the Continent. A Lincoln's Inn mumper was a proverb. The whole fraternity knew the arms and liveries of every charitably disposed grandee in the neighbourhood, and, as soon as his lordship's coach and six appeared, came hopping and crawling in crowds to persecute him. . . .

When such was the state of the region inhabited by the most luxurious portion of society, we may easily believe that the great body of the population suffered what would now be considered as insupportable grievances. The pavement was detestable; all foreigners cried shame upon it. The drainage was so bad that in rainy weather the gutters soon became torrents. Several facetious poets have commemorated the fury with which these black rivulets roared down Snow Hill and Ludgate Hill, bearing to Fleet Ditch a vast tribute of animal and vegetable filth from the stalls of butchers and greengrocers. This flood was profusely thrown to right and left by coaches and carts. To keep as far from the carriage road as possible was therefore the wish of every pedestrian. The mild and timid gave the wall. The bold and athletic took it. If two roisterers met, they cocked their hats in each other's faces, and pushed each other about till the weaker was shoved towards the kennel. If he was a mere bully he sneaked off, muttering that he should find a time. If he was pugnacious, the encounter probably ended in a duel behind Montague House.

The houses were not numbered. There would indeed have been little advantage in numbering them; for of the coachmen, chairmen, porters, and errand boys of London, a very small proportion could read. It was necessary to use marks which the most ignorant could understand. The shops were therefore distinguished by painted or sculptured signs, which gave a gay and grotesque aspect to the streets. The walk from Charing Cross to Whitechapel lay through an endless succession of Saracens' Heads, Royal Oaks, Blue Bears, and Golden Lambs, which disappeared when they were no longer required for the direction of the common people.

When the evening closed in, the difficulty and danger of walking about London became serious indeed. The garret windows were opened, and pails were emptied, with little regard to those who were passing below. Falls, bruises, and broken bones were of constant occurrence. For, till the last year of the reign of Charles the Second, most of the streets were left in profound darkness. Thieves and robbers plied their trade with impunity: yet they were hardly so terrible to peaceable citizens as another class of ruffians. It was a favourite amusement of dissolute young gentlemen to swagger by night about the town, breaking windows, upsetting sedans, beating quiet men, and offering rude caresses to pretty women. Several dynasties of these tyrants had, since the Restoration, domineered over the streets. The Muns and Tityre Tus had given place to the Hectors, and the Hectors had been recently succeeded by the Scourers. At a later period arose the Nicker, the Hawcubite, and the yet more dreaded name of Mohawk. The machinery for keeping the peace was utterly contemptible. There was an Act of Common Council which provided that more than a thousand watchmen should be constantly on the alert in the city, from sunset to sunrise, and that every inhabitant should take his turn of duty. But this Act was negligently executed. Few of those who were summoned left their homes; and those few generally found it more agreeable to tipple in alehouses than to pace the streets.

It ought to be noticed that, in the last year of the reign of Charles the Second, began a great change in the police of London, a change which has perhaps added as much to the happiness of the body of the people as revolutions of much greater fame. An ingenious projector, named Edward Heming, obtained letters patent conveying to him, for a term of years, the exclusive right of lighting up London. He undertook, for a moderate consideration, to place a light before every tenth door, on moonless nights, from Michaelmas to Lady Day, and from six to twelve of the clock. Those who now see the capital all the year round, from dusk to dawn, blazing with a splendour beside which the illuminations for La Hogue and Blenheim would have looked pale, may perhaps smile to think of Heming's lanterns, which glimmered feebly before one house in ten during a small part of one night in three. But such was not the feeling of his contemporaries. His scheme was enthusiastically applauded, and furiously attacked. The friends of improvement extolled him as the greatest of all the benefactors of his city. What, they asked, were the boasted inventions of Archimedes, when compared with the achievement of the man who had turned the nocturnal shades into noon day? In spite of these eloquent eulogies the cause of darkness was not left undefended. There were fools in that age who opposed the introduction of what was called the new light as strenuously as fools in our age have opposed the introduction of vaccination and railroads, as strenuously as the fools of an age anterior to the dawn of history doubtless opposed the introduction of the plough and of alphabetical writing. Many years after the date of Heming's patent there were extensive districts in which no lamp was seen.

We may easily imagine what, in such times, must have been the state of the quarters of London which were peopled by the outcasts of society. Among those quarters one had attained a scandalous pre-eminence. On the confines of the City and the Temple had been founded, in the thirteenth century, a House of Carmelite Friars, distinguished by their white hoods. The precinct of this house had, before the Reformation, been a sanctuary for criminals, and still retained the privilege of protecting debtors from arrest. Insolvents consequently were to be found in every dwelling, from cellar to garret. Of these a large proportion were knaves and libertines, and were followed to their asylum by women more abandoned than themselves. The civil power was unable to keep order in a district swarming with such inhabitants; and thus Whitefriars became the favourite resort of all who wished to be emancipated from the restraints of the law. Though the immunities legally belonging to the place extended only to cases of debt, cheats, false witnesses, forgers, and highwaymen found refuge there. For amidst a rabble so desperate no peace officer's life was in safety. At the cry of 'Rescue,' bullies with swords and cudgels, and termagant hags with spits and broomsticks, poured forth by hundreds; and the intruder was fortunate if he escaped back into Fleet Street, hustled, stripped, and pumped upon. Even the warrant of the Chief Justice of England could not be executed without the help of a company of musketeers. Such relics of the barbarism of the darkest ages were to be found within a short walk of the chambers where Somers was studying history and law, of the chapel where Tillotson was preaching, of the coffee house where Dryden was passing judgment on poems and plays, and of the hall where the Royal Society was examining the astronomical system of Isaac Newton.

XLVII

HOME-COMING UP THE CHANNEL

A WEEK afterwards the *Narcissus* entered the chops of the Channel. Under white wings she skimmed low over the blue sea like a great tired bird speeding to its nest. The clouds raced with her mastheads; they rose astern enormous and white, soared to the zenith, flew past, and falling down the wide curve of the sky seemed to dash headlong into the sea—the clouds swifter than the ship, more free, but without a home. The coast to welcome her stepped out of space into the sunshine. The lofty headlands trod masterfully into the sea; the wide bays smiled in the light; the shadows of homeless clouds ran along the sunny plains, leaped over valleys, without a check darted up the hills, rolled down the slopes; and the sunshine pursued them with patches of running brightness. On the brows of dark cliffs white lighthouses shone in pillars of light. The Channel glittered like a blue mantle shot with gold and starred by the silver of the capping seas. The *Narcissus* rushed past the headlands and the bays. Outward-bound vessels crossed her track, lying over, and with their masts stripped for a slogging fight with the hard sou'wester. And, inshore, a string of smoking steamboats waddled, hugging the coast, like migrating and amphibious monsters, distrustful of the restless waves.

At night the headlands retreated, the bays advanced into one unbroken line of gloom. The lights of the earth mingled with the lights of heaven; and above the tossing lanterns of a trawling fleet a great lighthouse shone steadily, such as an enormous riding light burning above a vessel of fabulous dimensions. Below its steady glow, the coast, stretching away straight and black, resembled the high side of an indestructible craft riding motionless upon the immortal and unresting sea. The dark land lay alone in the midst of waters, like a mighty ship bestarred with vigilant lights—a ship carrying the burden of millions of lives—a ship freighted with dross and with jewels, with gold and with steel. She towered up immense and strong, guarding priceless traditions and untold suffering, sheltering glorious memories and base forgetfulness, ignoble virtues and splendid transgressions. A great ship! For ages had the ocean battered in vain her enduring sides; she was there when the world was vaster and darker, when the sea was great and mysterious, and ready to surrender the prize of fame to audacious men. A ship mother of fleets and nations! The great flagship of the race; stronger than the storms! and anchored in the open sea.

The *Narcissus*, heeling over to off-shore gusts, rounded the South Foreland, passed through the Downs, and, in tow, entered the river. Shorn of the glory of her white wings, she wound obediently after the tug through the maze of invisible channels. As she passed them the red-painted light-vessels, swung at their moorings, seemed for an instant to sail with great speed in the rush of tide, and the next moment were left hopelessly behind. The big buoys on the tails of banks slipped past her sides very low, and, dropping in her wake, tugged at their chains like fierce watch dogs. The reach narrowed; from both sides the land approached the ship. She went steadily up the river. On the riverside slopes the houses appeared in groups—seemed to stream down the declivities at a run to see her pass, and, checked by the mud of the foreshore, crowded on the banks. Further on, the tall factory chimneys appeared in insolent bands and watched her go by, like a straggling crowd of slim giants, swaggering and upright under the black plummets of smoke, cavalierly aslant. She swept round the bends; an impure breeze shrieked a welcome between her stripped spars; and the land, closing in, stepped between the ship and the sea.

A low cloud hung before her—a great opalescent and tremulous cloud, that seemed to rise from the steaming brows of millions of men. Long drifts of smoky vapours soiled it with livid trails; it throbbed to the beat of millions of hearts, and from it came an immense and lamentable murmur—the murmur of millions of lips praying, cursing, sighing, jeering —the undying murmur of folly, regret, and hope exhaled by the crowds of the anxious earth. The *Narcissus* entered the cloud; the shadows deepened; on all sides there was the clang of iron, the sound of mighty blows, shrieks, yells. Black barges drifted stealthily on the murky stream. A mad jumble of begrimed walls loomed up vaguely in the smoke, bewildering and mournful, like a vision of disaster. The tugs, panting furiously, backed and filled in the stream, to hold the ship steady at the dock-gates; from her bows two lines went through the air whistling, and struck at the land viciously, like a pair of snakes. A bridge broke in two before her, as if by enchantment; big hydraulic capstans began to turn all by themselves, as though animated by a mysterious and unholy spell. She moved through a narrow lane of water between two low walls of granite, and men with check-ropes in their hands kept pace with her, walking on the broad flagstones. A group waited impatiently on each side of the vanished bridge: rough heavy men in caps; sallow-faced men in high hats; two bareheaded women; ragged children, fascinated, and with wide eyes. A cart coming at a jerky trot pulled up sharply. One of the women screamed at the silent ship—'Hallo, Jack!' without looking at any one in particular and all hands looked at her from the forecastle head.—'Stand clear! Stand clear of that rope!' cried the dockmen, bending over stone posts. The crowd murmured, stamped where they stood.—'Let go your quarter-checks! Let go!' sang out a ruddy-faced old man on the quay. The ropes splashed heavily falling in the water, and the *Narcissus* entered the dock.

The stony shores ran away right and left in straight lines, enclosing a sombre and rectangular pool. Brick walls rose high above the water—soulless walls, staring through hundreds of windows as troubled and dull as the eyes of over-fed brutes. At their base monstrous iron cranes crouched, with chains hanging from their long necks, balancing cruel-looking hooks over the decks of lifeless ships. A noise of wheels rolling over stones, the thump of heavy things falling, the racket of feverish winches, the grinding of strained chains, floated on the air. Between high buildings the dust of all the continents soared in short flights; and a penetrating smell of perfumes and dirt, of spices and hides, of things costly and of things filthy, pervaded the space, made for it an atmosphere precious and disgusting. The *Narcissus* came gently into her berth; the shadows of soulless walls fell upon her, the dust of all the continents leaped upon her deck, and a swarm of strange men, clambering up her sides, took possession of her in the name of the sordid earth. She had ceased to live.

XLVIII

THE LOTOS-EATERS

"COURAGE!' he said, and pointed toward the land,
'This mounting wave will roll us shoreward soon.'
In the afternoon they came unto a land
In which it seemed always afternoon.
All round the coast the languid air did swoon,
Breathing like one that hath a weary dream.
Full-faced above the valley stood the moon;
And like a downward smoke, the slender stream
Along the cliff to fall and pause and fall did seem.

A land of streams! some, like a downward smoke,
Slow-dropping veils of thinnest lawn, did go;
And some thro' wavering lights and shadows broke,
Rolling a slumbrous sheet of foam below.
They saw the gleaming river seaward flow
From the inner land: far off, three mountain-tops,
Three silent pinnacles of aged snow,
Stood sunset-flush'd: and, dew'd with showery drops,
Up-clomb the shadowy pine above the woven copse.

The charmed sunset linger'd low adown
In the red West: thro' mountain clefts the dale
Was seen far inland, and the yellow down
Border'd with palm, and many a winding vale
And meadow, set with slender galingale;
A land where all things always seem'd the same!
And round about the keel with faces pale,
Dark faces pale against that rosy flame,
The mild-eyed melancholy Lotos-eaters came.
Branches they bore of that enchanted stem,
Laden with flower and fruit, whereof they gave
To each, but whoso did receive of them,
And taste, to him the gushing of the wave
Far far away did seem to mourn and rave
On alien shores; and if his fellow spake,
His voice was thin, as voices from the grave;
And deep asleep he seem'd, yet all awake,
And music in his ears his beating heart did make.

They sat them down upon the yellow sand,
Between the sun and moon upon the shore;
And sweet it was to dream of Fatherland,
Of child, and wife, and slave; but evermore
Most weary seem'd the sea, weary the oar,
Weary the wandering fields of barren foam.
Then some one said, 'We will return no more';
And all at once they sang, 'Our island home
Is far beyond the wave; we will no longer roam.'

CHORIC SONG

I

There is sweet music here that softer falls
Than petals from blown roses on the grass,
Or night-dews on still waters between walls
Of shadowy granite, in a gleaming pass;
Music that gentlier on the spirit lies,
Than tir'd eyelids upon tir'd eyes;
Music that brings sweet sleep down from the blissful skies.
Here are cool mosses deep,
And thro' the moss the ivies creep,
And in the stream the long-leaved flowers weep,
And from the craggy ledge the poppy hangs in sleep.

II

Why are we weigh'd upon with heaviness,
And utterly consumed with sharp distress,
While all things else have rest from weariness?
All things have rest: why should we toil alone,
We only toil, who are the first of things,
And make perpetual moan,
Still from one sorrow to another thrown:
Nor ever fold our wings,
And cease from wanderings,
Nor steep our brows in slumber's holy balm;
Nor harken what the inner spirit sings,
'There is no joy but calm!'
Why should we only toil, the roof and crown of things?

III

Lo! in the middle of the wood,
The folded leaf is woo'd from out the bud
With winds upon the branch, and there
Grows green and broad, and takes no care,
Sun-steep'd at noon, and in the moon

Nightly dew-fed; and turning yellow
Falls, and floats adown the air.
Lo! sweeten'd with the summer light,
The full-juiced apple, waxing over-mellow,
Drops in a silent autumn night.
All its allotted length of days,
The flower ripens in its place,
Ripens and fades, and falls, and hath no toil,
Fast-rooted in the fruitful soil.

IV

Hateful is the dark-blue sky,
Vaulted o'er the dark-blue sea.
Death is the end of life; ah, why
Should life all labour be?
Let us alone. Time driveth onward fast,
And in a little while our lips are dumb.
Let us alone. What is it that will last?
All things are taken from us, and become
Portions and parcels of the dreadful Past.
Let us alone. What pleasure can we have
To war with evil? Is there any peace
In ever climbing up the climbing wave?
All things have rest, and ripen toward the grave
In silence; ripen, fall, and cease:
Give us long rest or death, dark death, or dreamful ease.

V

How sweet it were, hearing the downward stream,
With half-shut eyes ever to seem
Falling asleep in a half-dream!
To dream and dream, like yonder amber light,
Which will not leave the myrrh-bush on the height;
To hear each other's whisper'd speech;
Eating the Lotos day by day,
To watch the crisping ripples on the beach,
And tender curving lines of creamy spray;

To lend our hearts and spirits wholly
To the influence of mild-minded melancholy;
To muse and brood and live again in memory,
With those old faces of our infancy
Heap'd over with a mound of grass,
Two handfuls of white dust, shut in an urn of brass!

VI

Dear is the memory of our wedded lives,
And dear the last embraces of our wives
And their warm tears: but all hath suffer'd change:
For surely now our household hearths are cold:
Our sons inherit us: our looks are strange:
And we should come like ghosts to trouble joy.
Or else the island princes over-bold
Have eat our substance, and the minstrel sings
Before them of the ten years' war in Troy
And our great deeds, as half-forgotten things.
Is there confusion in the little isle?
Let what is broken so remain.
The Gods are hard to reconcile:
'Tis hard to settle order once again.
There *is* confusion worse than death,
Trouble on trouble, pain on pain,
Long labour unto aged breath,
Sore task to hearts worn out by many wars
And eyes grown dim with gazing on the pilot-stars.

VII

But, propt on beds of amaranth and moly,
How sweet (while warm airs lull us, blowing lowly)
With half-dropt eyelid still,
Beneath a heaven dark and holy,
To watch the long bright river drawing slowly
His waters from the purple hill—

To hear the dewy echoes calling
From cave to cave thro' the thick-twined vine—
To watch the emerald-colour'd water falling
Thro' many a wov'n acanthus-wreath divine!
Only to hear and see the far-off sparkling brine,
Only to hear were sweet, stretch'd out beneath the pine.

VIII

The Lotos blooms below the barren peak:
The Lotos blows by every winding creek:
All day the wind breathes low with mellower tone:
Thro' every hollow cave and alley lone
Round and round the spicy downs the yellow Lotos-dust is blown.
We have had enough of action, and of motion we,
Roll'd to starboard, roll'd to larboard, when the surge was seething free,
Where the wallowing monster spouted his foam-fountains in the sea.
Let us swear an oath, and keep it with an equal mind,
In the hollow Lotos-land to live and lie reclined
On the hills like Gods together, careless of mankind.
For they lie beside their nectar, and the bolts are hurl'd
Far below them in the valleys, and the clouds are lightly curl'd
Round their golden houses, girdled with the gleaming world:
Where they smile in secret, looking over wasted lands,
Blight and famine, plague and earthquake, roaring deeps and fiery sands,
Clanging fights, and flaming towns, and sinking ships, and praying hands.
But they smile, they find a music centred in a doleful song
Steaming up, a lamentation and an ancient tale of wrong,
Like a tale of little meaning tho' the words are strong;
Chanted from an ill-used race of men that cleave the soil,
Sow the seed, and reap the harvest with enduring toil,
Storing yearly little dues of wheat, and wine and oil;

Till they perish and they suffer—some, 'tis whisper'd—
   down in hell
Suffer endless anguish, others in Elysian valleys dwell,
Resting weary limbs at last on beds of asphodel.
Surely, surely, slumber is more sweet than toil, the shore
Than labour in the deep mid-ocean, wind and wave and
   oar;
Oh rest ye, brother mariners, we will not wander more.

XLIX

THE DEATH OF THE RED FOX

AS I was so sitting and thinking, a sound of men and horses came to me through the wood; and presently after, at a turning of the road, I saw four travellers come into view. The way was in this part so rough and narrow that they came single and led their horses by the reins. The first was a great, red-headed gentleman, of an imperious and flushed face, who carried his hat in his hand and fanned himself, for he was in a breathing heat. The second, by his decent black garb and white wig, I correctly took to be a lawyer. The third was a servant, and wore some part of his clothes in tartan, which showed that his master was of a Highland family, and either an outlaw or else in singular good odour with the Government, since the wearing of tartan was against the Act. If I had been better versed in these things, I would have known the tartan to be of the Argyle (or Campbell) colours. . . . As for the fourth, who brought up the tail, I had seen his like before, and knew him at once to be a sheriff's officer. I had no sooner seen these people coming than I made up my mind (for no reason that I can tell) to go through with my adventure; and when the first came alongside of me, I rose up from the bracken and asked him the way to Aucharn.

He stopped and looked at me, as I thought, a little oddly; and then, turning to the lawyer, 'Mungo,' said he, 'there's many a man would think this more of a warning than two pyats. Here am I on my road to Duror on the job ye ken; and here is a young lad starts up out of the bracken, and speers if I am on the way to Aucharn.' . . .

'If ye had asked me the way to the door of James Stewart on any other day but this, I would have set ye right and bidden ye God speed. But to-day—eh, Mungo?' And he turned again to look at the lawyer.

But just as he turned there came the shot of a firelock from higher up the hill; and with the very sound of it Glenure fell upon the road.

'Oh, I am dead!' he cried, several times over.

The lawyer had caught him up and held him in his arms, the servant standing over and clasping his hands. And now the wounded man looked from one to another with scared eyes, and there was a change in his voice that went to the heart.

'Take care of yourselves,' says he. 'I am dead.'

He tried to open his clothes as if to look for the wound, but his fingers slipped on the buttons. With that he gave a great sigh, his head rolled on his shoulder, and he passed away. The lawyer said never a word, but his face was as sharp as a pen and as white as the dead man's; the servant broke out into a great noise of crying and weeping, like a child; and I, on my side, stood staring at them in a kind of horror. The sheriff's officer had run back at the first sound of the shot, to hasten the coming of the soldiers. At last the lawyer laid down the dead man in his blood upon the road, and got to his own feet with a kind of stagger. I believe it was his movement that brought me to my senses; for he had no sooner done so than I began to scramble up the hill, crying out, 'The murderer! the murderer!' So little a time had elapsed, that when I got to the top of the first steepness, and could see some part of the open mountain, the murderer was still moving away at no great distance. He was a big man, in a black coat, with metal buttons, and carried a long fowling-piece.

'Here!' I cried. 'I see him!'

At that the murderer gave a little, quick look over his shoulder, and began to run. The next moment he was lost in a fringe of birches; then he came out again on the upper side, where I could see him climbing like a jackanapes, for that part was again very steep; and then he dipped behind a shoulder, and I saw him no more. All this time I had been running on my side, and had got a good way up, when a voice cried upon me to stand. I was at the edge of the upper wood, and so now, when I halted and looked back, I saw all the open part of the hill below me. The lawyer and the sheriff's officer were standing just above the road, crying and waving on me to come back; and on their left, the redcoats, musket in hand, were beginning to struggle singly out of the lower wood.

'Why should I come back?' I cried. 'Come you on!'

'Ten pounds if ye take that lad!' cried the lawyer. 'He's an accomplice. He was posted here to hold us in talk.'

At that word ... my heart came in my mouth with quite a new kind of terror. Indeed, it is one thing to stand the danger of your life, and quite another to run the peril of both life and character. The thing, besides, had come so suddenly, like thunder out of a clear sky, that I was all amazed and helpless. The soldiers began to spread, some of them to run, and others to put up their pieces and cover me; and still I stood.

'Jouk in here among the trees,' said a voice, close by.

Indeed, I scarce knew what I was doing, but I obeyed; and as I did so, I heard the firelocks bang and the balls whistle in the birches. Just inside the shelter of the trees I found Alan Breck standing, with a fishing-rod. He gave me no salutation; indeed it was no time for civilities; only 'Come!' says he, and set off running along the side of the mountain towards Balachulish; and I, like a sheep, to follow him. Now we ran among the birches; now stooping behind low humps upon the mountain side; now crawling on all fours among the heather. The pace was deadly; my heart seemed bursting against my ribs; and I had neither time to think nor breath to speak with. Only I remember seeing with wonder, that Alan every now and then would straighten himself to his full height and look back; and every time he did so, there came a great far-away cheering and crying of the soldiers. Quarter of an hour later, Alan stopped, clapped down flat in the heather, and turned to me.

'Now,' said he, 'it's earnest. Do as I do for your life.'

And at the same speed, but now with infinitely more precaution, we traced back again across the mountain side by the same way that we had come, only perhaps higher; till at last Alan threw himself down in the upper wood of Lettermore, where I had found him at the first, and lay, with his face in the bracken, panting like a dog. My own sides so ached, my head so swam, my tongue so hung out of my mouth with heat and dryness, that I lay beside him like one dead. Alan was the first to come round. He rose, went to the border of the wood, peered out a little, and then returned and sat down.

'Well,' said he, 'yon was a hot burst, David.'

I said nothing, nor so much as lifted my face. . . .

'Are ye still wearied?' he asked again.

'No,' said I, still with my face in the bracken; 'no, I am not wearied now, and I can speak. You and me must twine,' I said. 'I liked you very well, Alan; but your ways are not mine, and they're not God's: and the short and the long of it is just that we must twine.'

'I will hardly twine from ye, David, without some kind of reason for the same,' said Alan, mighty gravely. 'If ye ken anything against my reputation it's the least thing that ye should do, for old acquaintance sake, to let me hear the name of it; and if ye have only taken a distaste to my society, it will be proper for me to judge if I'm insulted.'

'Alan,' said I, 'what is the sense of this? Ye ken very well yon Campbell-man lies in his blood upon the road.'

He was silent for a little. . . .

'Do you mean you had no hand in it?' cried I, sitting up.

'I will tell you first of all, Mr. Balfour of Shaws, as one friend to another,' said Alan, 'that if I were going to kill a gentleman, it would not be in my own country, to bring trouble on my clan; and I would not go wanting sword and gun, and with a long fishing-rod upon my back.'

'Well,' said I, 'that's true!'

'And now,' continued Alan, taking out his dirk and laying his hand upon it in a certain manner, 'I swear upon the Holy Iron I had neither art nor part, act nor thought in it.'

'I thank God for that!' cried I, and offered him my hand. He did not appear to see it.

'And here is a great deal of work about a Campbell!' said he. 'They are not so scarce, that I ken!'

'At least,' said I, 'you cannot justly blame me, for you know very well what you told me in the brig. But the temptation and the act are different, I thank God again for that. We may all be tempted; but to take a life in cold blood, Alan!' And I could say no more for the moment. 'And do you know who did it?' I added. 'Do you know that man in the black coat?'

'I have nae clear mind about his coat,' said Alan, cunningly; 'but it sticks in my head that it was blue.'

'Blue or black, did ye know him?' said I.

'I couldnae just conscientiously swear to him,' says Alan. 'He gaed very close by me, to be sure, but it's a strange thing that I should just have been tying my brogues.'

'Can you swear that you don't know him, Alan?' I cried, half angered, half in a mind to laugh at his evasions.

'Not yet,' says he; 'but I've a grand memory for forgetting, David.'

'And yet there was one thing I saw clearly,' said I; 'and that was, that you exposed yourself and me to draw the soldiers.'

'It's very likely,' said Alan; 'and so would any gentleman. You and me were innocent of that transaction.'

'The better reason, since we were falsely suspected, that we should get clear,' I cried. 'The innocent should surely come before the guilty.'

'Why, David,' said he, 'the innocent have aye a chance to get assoiled in court; but for the lad that shot the bullet,

I think the best place for him will be the heather. Them that havenae dipped their hands in any little difficulty, should be very mindful of the case of them that have. And that is the good Christianity.'

L

SIR JOHN MOORE

THUS ended the career of Sir John Moore, a man whose uncommon capacity was sustained by the purest virtue, and governed by a disinterested patriotism more in keeping with the primitive than the luxurious age of a great nation. His tall graceful person, his dark searching eyes, strongly defined forehead, and singularly expressive mouth, indicated a noble disposition and a refined understanding. The lofty sentiments of honour habitual to his mind, were adorned by a subtle playful wit, which gave him in conversation an ascendancy he always preserved by the decisive vigour of his actions. He maintained the right with a vehemence bordering upon fierceness, and every important transaction in which he was engaged increased his reputation for talent, and confirmed his character as a stern enemy to vice, a steadfast friend to merit, a just and faithful servant of his country. The honest loved him, the dishonest feared him. For while he lived he did not shun, but scorned and spurned the base, and with characteristic propriety they spurned at him when he was dead.

A soldier from his earliest youth, Moore thirsted for the honours of his profession. He knew himself worthy to lead a British army, and hailed the fortune which placed him at the head of the troops destined for Spain. As the stream of time passed the inspiring hopes of triumph disappeared, but the austerer glory of suffering remained, and with a firm heart he accepted that gift of a severe fate. Confident in the strength of his genius, he disregarded the clamours of presumptuous ignorance. Opposing sound military views to the foolish projects so insolently thrust upon him by the ambassador, he conducted his long and arduous retreat with sagacity, intelligence, and fortitude; no insult disturbed, no falsehood deceived him, no remonstrance shook his determination; fortune frowned without subduing his constancy; death struck, but the spirit of the man remained unbroken when his shattered body scarcely afforded it a habitation. Having done all that was just towards others, he remembered what was due to himself. Neither the shock of the mortal blow, nor the lingering hours of acute pain which preceded his dissolution, could quell the pride of his gallant heart, or lower the dignified feeling with which, conscious of merit, he at the last moment asserted his right to the gratitude of the country he had served so truly.

If glory be a distinction, for such a man death is not a leveller!

There is a small battery of the old town which fronts the east, and whose wall is washed by the waters of the bay. It is a sweet spot, and the prospect which opens from it is extensive. The battery itself may be about eighty yards square; some young trees are springing up about it, and it is rather a favourite resort of the people of Corunna.

In the centre of this battery stands the tomb of Moore, built by the chivalrous French, in commemoration of the fall of their heroic antagonist. It is oblong, and surmounted by a slab, and on either side bears one of the simple and sublime epitaphs for which our rivals are celebrated, and which stand in such powerful contrast with the bloated and bombastic inscriptions which deform the walls of Westminster Abbey:—

'JOHN MOORE,
LEADER OF THE ENGLISH ARMIES,
SLAIN IN BATTLE,
1809.'

The tomb itself is of marble, and around it is a quadrangular wall, breast-high, of rough Gallegan granite; close to each corner rises from the earth the breech of an immense brass cannon, intended to keep the wall compact and close. These outer erections are, however, not the work of the French, but of the English government.

Yes, there lies the hero, almost within sight of the glorious hill where he turned upon his pursuers like a lion at bay and terminated his career. Many acquire immortality without seeking it, and die before its first ray has gilded their name; of these was Moore. The harassed general, flying through Castile with his dispirited troops before a fierce and terrible enemy, little dreamed that he was on the point of attaining that for which many a better, greater, though certainly not braver man, had sighed in vain. His very misfortunes were the means which secured him immortal fame; his disastrous route, bloody death, and finally his tomb on a foreign strand, far from kin and friends. There is scarcely a Spaniard but has heard of this tomb, and speaks of it with a strange kind of awe. Immense treasures are said to have been buried with the heretic general, though for what purpose no one pretends to guess. The demons of the clouds, if we may trust the Gallegans, followed the English in their flight, and assailed them with water-spouts as they toiled up the steep winding paths of Fuencebadon, whilst legends the most wild are related of the manner in which the stout soldier fell. Yes, even in Spain, immortality has already crowned the head of Moore,—Spain, the land of oblivion, where the Guadalete, the ancient Lethe, flows.

THE BURIAL OF SIR JOHN MOORE

Not a drum was heard, not a funeral note,
    As his corpse to the rampart we hurried;
Not a soldier discharged his farewell shot
    O'er the grave where our hero we buried.

We buried him darkly at dead of night,
    The sods with our bayonets turning;
By the struggling moonbeam's misty light
    And the lantern dimly burning.

No useless coffin enclosed his breast,
  Not in sheet nor in shroud we wound him;
But he lay like a warrior taking his rest
  With his martial cloak around him.

Few and short were the prayers we said,
  And we spoke not a word of sorrow;
But we steadfastly gazed on the face that was dead,
  And we bitterly thought of the morrow.

We thought, as we hollow'd his narrow bed
  And smoothed down his lonely pillow,
That the foe and the stranger would tread o'er his head,
  And we far away on the billow!

Lightly they'll talk of the spirit that's gone
  And o'er his cold ashes upbraid him,—
But little he'll reck, if they let him sleep on
  In the grave where a Briton has laid him.

But half of our heavy task was done
  When the clock struck the hour for retiring;
And we heard the distant and random gun
  That the foe was sullenly firing.

Slowly and sadly we laid him down,
  From the field of his fame fresh and gory;
We carved not a line, and we raised not a stone—
  But we left him alone with his glory.

LI

ENGLISH-GROWN TOBACCO

PETTIGREW asked me to come to his house one evening and test some tobacco that had been grown in his brother's Devonshire garden. I had so far had no opportunity of judging for myself whether this attempt to grow tobacco on English soil was to succeed. Very complimentary was Pettigrew's assertion that he had restrained himself from trying the tobacco until we could test it in company.

At the dinner-table while Mrs. Pettigrew was present we managed to talk for a time of other matters; but the tobacco was on our minds, and I was glad to see that, despite her raillery, my hostess had a genuine interest in the coming experiment. She drew an amusing picture, no doubt a little exaggerated, of her husband's difficulty in refraining from testing the tobacco until my arrival, declaring that every time she entered the smoking-room she found him staring at it. Pettigrew took this in good part, and informed me that she had carried the tobacco several times into the drawing-room to show it proudly to her friends. He was very delighted, he said, that I was to remain over-night, as that would give us a long evening to test the tobacco thoroughly. A neighbour of his had also been experimenting; and Pettigrew, who has a considerable sense of humour, told me a diverting story about this gentleman and his friends having passed judgment on home-grown tobacco after smoking one pipe of it! We were laughing over the ridiculously unsatisfactory character of this test (so called) when we adjourned to the smoking-room. Before we did so Mrs. Pettigrew bade me good-night. She had also left strict orders with the servants that we were on no account to be disturbed.

As soon as we were comfortably seated in our smoking-chairs, which takes longer than some people think, Pettigrew offered me a Cabana. I would have preferred to begin at once with the tobacco; but of course he was my host, and I put myself entirely in his hands. I noticed that, from the moment his wife left us, he was a little excited, talking more than is his wont. He seemed to think that he was not doing his duty as a host if the conversation flagged for a moment, and what was still more curious, he spoke of everything except his garden-tobacco. I emphasize this here at starting, lest any one should think that I was in any way responsible for the manner in which our experiment was conducted. If fault there was, it lies at Pettigrew's door. I remember distinctly asking him—not in a half-hearted way but boldly—to produce his tobacco. I did this at an early hour of the proceedings, immediately after I had lit a second cigar. The reason I took that cigar will be obvious to every gentleman who smokes. Had I declined it, Pettigrew might have thought that I disliked the brand, which would have been painful to him. However, he did not at once bring out the tobacco; indeed, his precise words, I remember, were that we had lots of time. As his guest I could not press him further.

Pettigrew smokes more quickly than I do, and he had reached the end of his second cigar when there was still five minutes of mine left. It distresses me to have to say what followed. He hastily lit a third cigar, and then, unlocking a cupboard, produced about two ounces of his garden-tobacco. His object was only too plain. Having just begun a third cigar he could not be expected to try the tobacco at present, but there was nothing to prevent my trying it. I regarded Pettigrew rather contemptuously, and then I looked with much interest at the tobacco. It was of an inky colour. When I looked up I caught Pettigrew's eye on me. He withdrew it hurriedly; but soon afterwards I saw him looking in the same sly way again. There was a rather painful silence for a time, and then he asked me if I had anything to say. I replied firmly that I was looking forward to trying the tobacco with very great interest. By this time my cigar was reduced to a stump; but, for reasons that Pettigrew misunderstood, I continued to smoke it. Somehow, our chairs had got out of position now, and we were sitting with our backs to each other. I felt that Pettigrew was looking at me covertly over his shoulder, and took a side glance to make sure of this. Our eyes met, and I bit my lips. If there is one thing I loathe, it is to be looked at in this shame-faced manner.

I continued to smoke the stump of my cigar until it scorched my under-lip, and at intervals Pettigrew said, without looking round, that my cigar seemed everlasting. I treated his innuendo with contempt; but at last I had to let the cigar-end go. Not to make a fuss I dropped it very quietly; but Pettigrew must have been listening for the sound. He wheeled round at once, and pushed the garden-tobacco toward me. Never, perhaps, have I thought so little of him as at that moment. My indignation probably showed in my face, for he drew back, saying that he thought I 'wanted to try it.' Now I had never said that I did not want to try it. The reader has seen that I went to Pettigrew's house solely with the object of trying the tobacco. Had Pettigrew, then, any ground for insinuating that I did not mean to try it? Restraining my passion I lit a third cigar, and then put the question to him bluntly. Did he, or did he not, mean to try that tobacco? I dare say I was a little brusque; but it must be remembered that I had come all the way from the Inn at considerable inconvenience to give the tobacco a thorough trial.

As is the way with men of Pettigrew's type, when you corner them, he attempted to put the blame on me. 'Why had I not tried the tobacco,' he asked, 'instead of taking a third cigar?' For reply, I asked bitingly whether that was not his third cigar. He admitted it was; but said that he smoked more quickly than I did, as if that put his behaviour in a more favourable light. I smoked my third cigar very slowly, not because I wanted to put off the experiment; for, as every one must have noted, I was most anxious to try it, but just to see what would happen. When Pettigrew had finished his cigar—and I thought he would never be done with it—he gazed at the garden-tobacco for a time, and then took a pipe from the mantelpiece. He held it first in one hand, then in the other, and then he brightened up and said that he would clean his pipes. This he did very slowly. When he had cleaned all his pipes he again looked at the garden-tobacco, which I pushed toward him. He glared at me as if I had not been doing a friendly thing, and then said, in an apologetic manner, that he would smoke a pipe until my cigar was finished. I said 'All right' cordially, thinking that he now meant to begin the experiment; but conceive my feelings when he produced a jar of the Arcadia Mixture. He filled his pipe with this and proceeded to light it, looking at me defiantly. His excuse about waiting till I had finished was too pitiful to take notice of. I finished my cigar in a few minutes, and now was the time when I would have liked to begin the experiment. As Pettigrew's guest, however, I could not take that liberty, though he impudently pushed the garden-tobacco towards me. I produced my pipe, my intention being only to half fill it with Arcadia, so that Pettigrew and I might finish our pipes at the same time. Custom, however, got the better of me, and inadvertently I filled my pipe, only noticing this when it was too late to remedy the mistake. Pettigrew thus finished before me; and though I advised him to begin on the garden-tobacco without waiting for me, he insisted on smoking half a pipeful of Arcadia, just to keep me company. It was an extraordinary thing that, try as we might, we could not finish our pipes at the same time.

About 2 a.m. Pettigrew said something about going to bed; and I arose and put down my pipe. We stood looking at the fireplace for a time, and he expressed regret that I had to leave so early in the morning. Then he put out two of the lights, and after that we both looked at the garden-tobacco. He seemed to have a sudden idea; for rather briskly he tied the tobacco up into a neat paper parcel and handed it to me, saying that I would perhaps give it a trial at the Inn. I took it without a word, but opening my hand suddenly I let it fall. My first impulse was to pick it up; but then it struck me that Pettigrew had not noticed what had happened, and that, were he to see me pick it up, he might think that I had not taken sufficient care of it. So I let it lie, and, bidding him good-night, went off to bed. I was at the foot of the stair when I thought that, after all, I should like the tobacco, so I returned. I could not see the package anywhere, but something was fizzing up the chimney, and Pettigrew had the tongs in his hand. He muttered something about his wife taking up wrong notions. Next morning that lady was very satirical about our having smoked the whole two ounces.

LII

POEMS FROM BLAKE

INTRODUCTION

PIPING down the valleys wild,
    Piping songs of pleasant glee,
    On a cloud I saw a child,
And he laughing said to me:

'Pipe a song about a Lamb!'
    So I piped with merry cheer.
'Piper, pipe that song again;'
    So I piped: he wept to hear.

'Drop thy pipe, thy happy pipe;
    Sing thy songs of happy cheer:'
So I sang the same again,
    While he wept with joy to hear.

'Piper, sit thee down and write
    In a book, that all may read.'
So he vanish'd from my sight,
    And I pluck'd a hollow reed,

And I made a rural pen,
    And I stain'd the water clear,
And I wrote my happy songs
    Every child may joy to hear.

NURSE'S SONG

When the voices of children are heard on the green
    And whisp'rings are in the dale,
The days of my youth rise fresh in my mind,
    My face turns green and pale.

Then come home, my children, the sun is gone down,
  And the dews of night arise;
Your spring and your day are wasted in play,
  And your winter and night in disguise.

THE LAND OF DREAMS

Awake, awake, my little boy!
Thou wast thy mother's only joy;
Why dost thou weep in thy gentle sleep?
Awake! thy father does thee keep.

'O, what land is the Land of Dreams?
What are its mountains, and what are its streams?
O father! I saw my mother there,
Among the lilies by waters fair.

'Among the lambs, clothèd in white,
She walk'd with her Thomas in sweet delight.
I wept for joy, like a dove I mourn,
O! when shall I again return?'

Dear child, I also by pleasant streams
Have wander'd all night in the Land of Dreams;
But tho' calm and warm the waters wide,
I could not get to the other side.

'Father, O Father! what do we here
In this land of unbelief and fear?
The Land of Dreams is better far,
Above the light of the morning star.'

THE TIGER

Tiger! Tiger! burning bright
In the forests of the night,
What immortal hand or eye
Could frame thy fearful symmetry?

In what distant deeps or skies
Burnt the fire of thine eyes?
On what wings dare He aspire?
What the hand dare seize the fire?
And what shoulder, and what art,
Could twist the sinews of thy heart?
And when thy heart began to beat,
What dread hand? and what dread feet?
What the hammer? what the chain?
In what furnace was thy brain?
What the anvil? what dread grasp
Dare its deadly terrors clasp?
When the stars threw down their spears,
And water'd heaven with their tears,
Did He smile His work to see?
Did He who made the Lamb make thee?
Tiger! Tiger! burning bright
In the forests of the night,
What immortal hand or eye
Dare frame thy fearful symmetry?

THE LITTLE VAGABOND

Dear mother, dear mother, the church is cold,
But the ale-house is healthy and pleasant and warm;
Besides I can tell where I am used well,
Such usage in Heaven will never do well.
But if at the church they would give us some ale,
And a pleasant fire our souls to regale,
We'd sing and we'd pray all the livelong day,
Nor ever once wish from the church to stray.
Then the parson might preach, and drink, and sing,
And we'd be as happy as birds in the spring;
And modest dame Lurch, who is always at church,
Would not have bandy children, nor fasting, nor birch.
And God, like a father, rejoicing to see
His children as pleasant and happy as He,
Would have no more quarrel with the devil or the barrel,
But kiss him, and give him both drink and apparel.

AH! SUN-FLOWER

Ah, Sun-flower! weary of time,
   Who countest the steps of the sun;
Seeking after that sweet golden clime,
   Where the traveller's journey is done;
Where the youth pined away with desire,
   And the pale virgin shrouded in snow,
Arise from their graves, and aspire
   Where my Sun-flower wishes to go.

THE CLOD AND THE PEBBLE

'Love seeketh not itself to please,
   Nor for itself hath any care,
But for another gives its ease,
   And builds a Heaven in Hell's despair.'

So sung a little Clod of clay,
   Trodden with the cattle's feet,
But a Pebble of the brook
   Warbled out these metres meet:

'Love seeketh only self to please,
   To bind another to its delight,
Joys in another's loss of ease,
   And builds a Hell in Heaven's despite.'

AUGURIES OF INNOCENCE

To see a world in a grain of sand,
   And a heaven in a wild flower,
Hold infinity in the palm of your hand,
   And eternity in an hour.

A robin redbreast in a cage
Puts all Heaven in a rage.
A dove-house fill'd with doves and pigeons
Shudders Hell thro' all its regions.
A dog starv'd at his master's gate
Predicts the ruin of the state,

A horse misused upon the road
Calls to Heaven for human blood.
Each outcry of the hunted hare
A fibre from the brain does tear.
A skylark wounded in the wing,
A cherubim does cease to sing.
The game-cock clipped and arm'd for fight
Does the rising sun affright.
Every wolf's and lion's howl
Raises from Hell a human soul.
The wild deer, wand'ring here and there,
Keeps the human soul from care.
The lamb misus'd breeds public strife,
And yet forgives the butcher's knife.
He who shall hurt the little wren
Shall never be belov'd by men.
He who the ox to wrath has mov'd
Shall never be by woman lov'd.
The wanton boy that kills the fly
Shall feel the spider's enmity.
He who torments the chafer's sprite
Weaves a bower in endless night.
The caterpillar on the leaf
Repeats to thee thy mother's grief.
Kill not the moth nor butterfly,
For the last judgment draweth nigh.
He who shall train the horse to war
Shall never pass the polar bar.
The beggar's dog and widow's cat
Feed them and thou wilt grow fat.

The bat that flits at close of eve
Has left the brain that won't believe.
The owl that calls upon the night
Speaks the unbeliever's fright.
The gnat that sings his summer's song
Poison gets from Slander's tongue.
The poison of the snake and newt
Is the sweat of Envy's foot.

The poison of the honey-bee
Is the artist's jealousy.
A truth that's told with bad intent
Beats all the lies you can invent.

Joy and woe are woven fine,
A clothing for the soul divine;
Under every grief and pine
Runs a joy with silken twine.
It is right it should be so;
Man was made for joy and woe;
And, when this we rightly know,
Thro' the world we safely go.
The babe is more than swaddling-bands;
Throughout all these human lands
Tools were made, and born were hands,
Every farmer understands.
Every tear from every eye
Becomes a babe in eternity;
This is caught by females bright,
And return'd to its own delight.
The bleat, the bark, bellow, and roar,
Are waves that beat on Heaven's shore.
The babe that weeps the rod beneath
Writes revenge in realms of death.
He who mocks the infant's faith
Shall be mock'd in age and death.
He who shall teach the child to doubt
The rotting grave shall ne'er get out.
He who respects the infant's faith
Triumphs over Hell and Death.
The child's toys and the old man's reasons
Are the fruits of the two seasons.
The questioner, who sits so sly,
Shall never know how to reply.
He who replies to words of doubt
Doth put the light of knowledge out.
A riddle, or the cricket's cry,
Is to doubt a fit reply.

> The emmet's inch and eagle's mile
> Make lame Philosophy to smile.
> He who doubts from what he sees
> Will ne'er believe, do what you please.
> If the sun and moon should doubt,
> They'd immediately go out.

LIII

THE SOLITARY FARMER

BUT now I began to exercise myself with new thoughts: I daily read the word of God, and applied all the comforts of it to my present state. One morning, being very sad, I opened the Bible upon these words, 'I will never, never leave thee, nor forsake thee.' Immediately it occurred that these words were to me; why else should they be directed in such a manner, just at the moment when I was mourning over my condition, as one forsaken of God and man? 'Well, then,' said I, 'if God does not forsake me, of what ill consequence can it be, or what matters it, though the world should all forsake me, seeing on the other hand, if I had all the world, and should lose the favour and blessing of God, there would be no comparison in the loss?'

From this moment, I began to conclude in my mind, that it was possible for me to be more happy in this forsaken, solitary condition, than it was probable I should ever have been in any other particular state in the world; and with this thought I was going to give thanks to God for bringing me to this place. I know not what it was, but something shocked my mind at that thought, and I durst not speak the words. 'How canst thou become such a hypocrite,' said I, even audibly, 'to pretend to be thankful for a condition, which, however thou mayest endeavour to be contented with, thou wouldst rather pray heartily to be delivered from?' So I stopped there; but though I could not say I thanked God for being there, yet I sincerely gave thanks to God for opening my eyes, by whatever afflicting providences, to see the former condition of my life, and to mourn for my wickedness, and repent. I never opened the Bible, or shut it, but my very soul within me blessed God for directing my friend in England, without any order of mine, to pack it up among my goods, and for assisting me afterwards to save it out of the wreck of the ship.

Thus, and in this disposition of mind, I began my third year; and though I have not given the reader the trouble of so particular an account of my works this year as the first; yet in general it may be observed, that I was very seldom idle, but having regularly divided my time according to the several daily employments that were before me, such as, first, my duty to God, and the reading the Scriptures, which I constantly set apart some time for, thrice every day; secondly, the going abroad with my gun for food, which generally took me up three hours in every morning, when it did not rain; thirdly, the ordering, cutting, preserving, and cooking, what I had killed or caught for my supply: these took up great part of the day. Also, it is to be considered, that in the middle of the day, when the sun was in the zenith, the violence of the heat was too great to stir out; so that about four hours in the evening was all the time I could be supposed to work in, with this exception, that sometimes I changed my hours of hunting and working, and went to work in the morning, and abroad with my gun in the afternoon.

To this short time allowed for labour, I desire may be added the exceeding laboriousness of my work; the many hours which for want of tools, want of help, and want of skill, everything I did took up out of my time. For example, I was full two and forty days in making a board for a long shelf, which I wanted in my cave; whereas, two sawyers, with their tools and a saw-pit, would have cut six of them out of the same tree in half a day.

My case was this: it was to be a large tree which was to be cut down, because my board was to be a broad one. This tree I was three days in cutting down, and two more cutting off the boughs, and reducing it to a log, or piece of timber. With inexpressible hacking and hewing, I reduced both the sides of it into chips till it began to be light enough to move; then I turned it, and made one side of it smooth and flat as a board from end to end; then, turning that side downward, cut the other side till it brought the plank to be about three inches thick, and smooth on both sides. Any one may judge the labour of my hands in such a piece of work; but labour and patience carried me through that, and many other things. I only observe this in particular, to show the reason why so much of my time went away with so little work, viz. that what might be a little to be done with help and tools, was a vast labour and required a prodigious time to do alone, and by hand. But notwithstanding this, with patience and labour I got through everything that my circumstances made necessary to me to do, as will appear by what follows.

I was now, in the months of November and December, expecting my crop of barley and rice. The ground I had manured and dug up for them was not great; for, as I observed, my seed of each was not above the quantity of half a peck, for I had lost one whole crop by sowing in the dry season. But now my crop promised very well, when on a sudden I found I was in danger of losing it all again by enemies of several sorts, which it was scarcely possible to keep from it; as, first the goats, and wild creatures which I called hares, who, tasting the sweetness of the blade, lay in it night and day, as soon as it came up, and eat it so close, that it could get no time to shoot up into stalk.

This I saw no remedy for but by making an inclosure about it with a hedge; which I did with a great deal of toil, and the more, because it required speed. However, as my arable land was but small, suited to my crop, I got it totally well fenced in about three weeks' time; and shooting some of the creatures in the daytime, I set my dog to guard it in the night, tying him up to a stake at the gate, where he would stand and bark all night long; so in a little time, the enemies forsook the place, and the corn grew very strong and well, and began to ripen apace.

But as the beasts ruined me before, while my corn was in the blade, so the birds were as likely to ruin me now, when it was in the ear; for, going along by the place to see how it throve, I saw my little crop surrounded with fowls, of I know not how many sorts, who stood, as it were, watching till I should be gone. I immediately let fly among them, for I always had my gun with me. I had no sooner shot, but there rose up a little cloud of fowls, which I had not seen at all, from among the corn itself.

This touched me sensibly, for I foresaw that in a few days they would devour all my hopes; that I should be starved, and never be able to raise a crop at all; and what to do I could not tell; however, I resolved not to lose my corn, if possible, though I should watch it night and day. In the first place I went among it, to see what damage was already done, and found they had spoiled a good deal of it; but that as it was yet too green for them, the loss was not so great but that the remainder was likely to be a good crop, if it could be saved.

I stayed by it to load my gun, and then coming away, I could easily see the thieves sitting upon all the trees about me, as if they only waited till I was gone away, and the event proved it to be so; for as I walked off, as if I was gone, I was no sooner out of their sight, than they dropped down one by one into the corn again. I was so provoked, that I could not have patience to stay till more came on, knowing that every grain that they ate now was, as it might be said, a peck-loaf to me in the consequence; but coming up to the hedge, I fired again, and killed three of them. This was what I wished for; so I took them up, and served them as we serve notorious thieves in England—hanged them in chains, for a terror to others. It is impossible to imagine that this should have such an effect as it had, for the fowls would not only not come at the corn, but, in short, they forsook all that part of the island, and I could never see a bird near the place as long as my scarecrows hung there. This I was very glad of, you may be sure, and about the latter end of December, which was our second harvest of the year, I reaped my corn.

I was sadly put to it for a scythe or sickle to cut it down, and all I could do was to make one, as well as I could, out of one of the broadswords, or cutlasses, which I saved among the arms out of the ship. However, as my first crop was but small, I had no great difficulty to cut it down; in short, I reaped it in my way, for I cut nothing off but the ears, and carried it away in a great basket which I had made, and so rubbed it out with my hands; and at the end of all my harvesting, I found that out of my half-peck of seed I had near two bushels of rice, and about two bushels and a half of barley; that is to say, by my guess, for I had no measure at that time.

However, this was a great encouragement to me, and I foresaw that, in time, it would please God to supply me with bread. And yet here I was perplexed again, for I neither knew how to grind or make meal of my corn, or indeed, how to clean it and part it; nor, if made into meal, how to make bread of it; and if how to make it, yet I knew not how to bake it. These things being added to my desire of having a good quantity for store, and to secure a constant supply, I resolved not to taste any of this crop, but to preserve it all for seed against the next season; and, in the meantime, to employ all my study and hours of working to accomplish this great work of providing myself with corn and bread.

LIV

THE BATTLE AT RAMOTH-GILEAD

AND they continued three years without war between Syria and Israel. And it came to pass in the third year, that Jehoshaphat the king of Judah came down to the king of Israel. And the king of Israel said unto his servants, Know ye that Ramoth in Gilead is our's, and we be still, and take it not out of the hand of the king of Syria? And he said unto Jehoshaphat, Wilt thou go with me to battle to Ramoth-gilead? And Jehoshaphat said to the king of Israel, I am as thou art, my people as thy people, my horses as thy horses. And Jehoshaphat said unto the king of Israel, Enquire, I pray thee, at the word of the Lord to-day. Then the king of Israel gathered the prophets together, about four hundred men, and said unto them, Shall I go against Ramoth-gilead to battle, or shall I forbear? And they said, Go up; for the Lord shall deliver it into the hand of the king. And Jehoshaphat said, Is there not here a prophet of the LORD besides, that we might enquire of him? And the king of Israel said unto Jehoshaphat, There is yet one man, Micaiah the son of Imlah, by whom we may enquire of the LORD: but I hate him; for he doth not prophesy good concerning me, but evil. And Jehoshaphat said, Let not the king say so. Then the king of Israel called an officer, and said, Hasten hither Micaiah the son of Imlah. And the king of Israel and Jehoshaphat the king of Judah sat each on his throne, having put on their robes, in a void place in the entrance of the gate of Samaria; and all the prophets prophesied before them. And Zedekiah the son of Chenaanah made him horns of iron: and he said, Thus saith the LORD, With these shalt thou push the Syrians until thou have consumed them. And all the prophets prophesied so, saying, Go up to Ramoth-gilead, and prosper: for the LORD shall deliver it into the king's hand.

And the messenger that was gone to call Micaiah spake unto him, saying, Behold now, the words of the prophets declare good unto the king with one mouth: let thy word, I pray thee, be like the word of one of them, and speak that which is good. And Micaiah said, As the LORD liveth, what the LORD saith unto me, that will I speak. So he came to the king. And the king said unto him, Micaiah, shall we go against Ramoth-gilead to battle, or shall we forbear? And he answered him, Go, and prosper: for the LORD shall deliver it into the hand of the king. And the king said unto him, How many times shall I adjure thee that thou tell me nothing but that which is true in the name of the LORD? And he said, I saw all Israel scattered upon the hills, as sheep that have not a shepherd: and the LORD said, These have no master: let them return every man to his house in peace. And the king of Israel said unto Jehoshaphat, Did I not tell thee that he would prophesy no good concerning me, but evil? And he said, Hear thou therefore the word of the

LORD: I saw the LORD sitting on his throne, and all the host of heaven standing by him on his right hand and on his left. And the LORD said, Who shall persuade Ahab, that he may go up and fall at Ramoth-gilead? And one said on this manner, and another said on that manner. And there came forth a spirit, and stood before the LORD, and said, I will persuade him. And the LORD said unto him, Wherewith? And he said, I will go forth, and I will be a lying spirit in the mouth of all his prophets. And he said, Thou shalt persuade him, and prevail also: go forth, and do so. Now therefore, behold, the LORD hath put a lying spirit in the mouth of all these thy prophets, and the LORD hath spoken evil concerning thee. But Zedekiah the son of Chenaanah went near, and smote Micaiah on the cheek, and said, Which way went the Spirit of the LORD from me to speak unto thee? And Micaiah said, Behold, thou shalt see in that day, when thou shalt go into an inner chamber to hide thyself. And the king of Israel said, Take Micaiah, and carry him back unto Amon the governor of the city, and to Joash the king's son; And say, Thus saith the king, Put this fellow in the prison, and feed him with bread of affliction and with water of affliction, until I come in peace. And Micaiah said, If thou return at all in peace, the LORD hath not spoken by me. And he said, Hearken, O people, every one of you.

So the king of Israel and Jehoshaphat the king of Judah went up to Ramoth-gilead. And the king of Israel said unto Jehoshaphat, I will disguise myself, and enter into the battle; but put thou on thy robes. And the king of Israel disguised himself, and went into the battle. But the king of Syria commanded his thirty and two captains that had rule over his chariots, saying, Fight neither with small nor great, save only with the king of Israel. And it came to pass, when the captains of the chariots saw Jehoshaphat, that they said, Surely it is the king of Israel. And they turned aside to fight against him: and Jehoshaphat cried out. And it came to pass, when the captains of the chariots perceived that it was not the king of Israel, that they turned back from pursuing him. And a certain man drew a bow at a venture, and smote the king of Israel between the joints of the harness: wherefore he said unto the driver of his chariot, Turn thine hand, and carry me out of the host; for I am wounded. And the battle increased that day: and the king was stayed up in his chariot against the Syrians, and died at even: and the blood ran out of the wound into the midst of the chariot. And there went a proclamation throughout the host about the going down of the sun, saying, Every man to his city, and every man to his own country. So the king died, and was brought to Samaria; and they buried the king in Samaria. And one washed the chariot in the pool of Samaria; and the dogs licked up his blood; and they washed his armour; according unto the word of the LORD which he spake. Now the rest of the acts of Ahab, and all that he did, and the ivory house which he made, and all the cities that he built, are they not written in the book of the chronicles of the kings of Israel? So Ahab slept with his fathers.

LV

THE BOW STREET RUNNER AND THE ROMANY CHAL

'DID you never hear of the poisoned plum pudding?'
'Never.'
'Then I will tell you about it. It happened about six years ago, a few months after she had quitted us—she had gone first among her own people, as she called them; but there was another small party of Romans, with whom she soon became very intimate. It so happened that this small party got into trouble; whether it was about a horse or an ass, or passing bad money, no matter to you and me, who had no hand in the business; three or four of them were taken and lodged in —— Castle, and amongst them was a woman; but the sherengro, or principal man of the party, and who it seems had most hand in the affair, was still at large. All of

a sudden a rumour was spread abroad that the woman was about to play false, and to peach the rest. Said the principal man, when he heard it, "If she does, I am nashkado." Mrs. Hearne was then on a visit to the party, and when she heard the principal man take on so, she said: "But I suppose you know what to do?" "I do not," said he. "Then hir mi devlis," said she, "you are a fool. But leave the matter to me, I know how to dispose of her in Roman fashion." Why she wanted to interfere in the matter, brother, I don't know, unless it was from pure brimstoneness of disposition—she had no hand in the matter which had brought the party into trouble, she was only on a visit, and it had happened before she came; but she was always ready to give dangerous advice. Well, brother, the principal man listened to what she had to say, and let her do what she would; and she made a pudding, a very nice one, no doubt—for, besides plums, she put in drows and all the Roman condiments that she knew of; and she gave it to the principal man, and the principal man put it into a basket and directed it to the woman in —— Castle, and the woman in the castle took it and——'

'Ate of it,' said I, 'just like my case?'

'Quite different, brother; she took it, it is true, but instead of giving way to her appetite as you might have done, she put it before the rest whom she was going to impeach—perhaps she wished to see how they liked it before she tasted it herself—and all the rest were poisoned, and one died, and there was a precious outcry, and the woman cried loudest of all; and she said: "It was my death was sought for; I know the man, and I'll be revenged," and then the Poknees spoke to her and said, "Where can we find him?" and she said, "I am awake to his motions; three weeks from hence, the night before the full moon, at such and such an hour, he will pass down such a lane with such a man."'

'Well,' said I, 'and what did the Poknees do?'

'Do, brother, sent for a plastramengro from Bow Street, quite secretly, and told him what the woman had said; and the night before the full moon, the plastramengro went to the place which the juwa had pointed out, all alone, brother;

and, in order that he might not be too late, he went two hours before his time. I know the place well, brother, where the plastramengro placed himself behind a thick holly tree, at the end of a lane, where a gate leads into various fields, through which there is a path for carts and horses. The lane is called the dark lane by the Gorgios, being much shaded by trees; so the plastramengro placed himself in the dark lane behind the holly tree; it was a cold February night, dreary, though; the wind blew in gusts, and the moon had not yet risen, and the plastramengro waited behind a tree till he was tired, and thought he might as well sit down; so he sat down and was not long in falling to sleep, and there he slept for some hours; and when he awoke, the moon had risen, and was shining bright, so that there was a kind of moonlight even in the dark lane; and the plastramengro pulled out his watch, and contrived to make out that it was just two hours beyond the time when the men should have passed by. Brother, I do not know what the plastramengro thought of himself, but I know, brother, what I should have thought of myself in his situation. I should have thought, brother, that I was a drowsy scoppelo, and that I had let the fellow pass by whilst I was sleeping behind a bush. As it turned out, however, his going to sleep did no harm, but quite the contrary; just as he was going away, he heard a gate slam in the direction of the fields, and then he heard the low stumping of horses, as if on soft ground, for the path in those fields is generally soft, and at that time it had been lately ploughed up. Well, brother, presently he saw two men on horseback coming towards the lane through the field behind the gate; the man who rode foremost was a tall, big fellow, the very man he was in quest of: the other was a smaller chap, not so small either, but a light, wiry fellow, and a proper master of his hands when he sees occasion for using them. Well, brother, the foremost man came to the gate, reached at the hank, undid it, and rode through, holding it open for the other. Before, however, the other could follow into the lane, out bolted the plastramengro from behind the tree, kicked the gate to with his foot, and, seizing the big man on horseback, "You are my prisoner," said he. I am of opinion, brother, that the plastramengro, notwithstanding he went to sleep, must have been a regular fine fellow.'

'I am entirely of your opinion,' said I; 'but what happened then?'

'Why, brother, the Romany chal, after he had somewhat recovered from his surprise, for it is rather uncomfortable to be laid hold of at night-time, and told you are a prisoner; more especially when you happen to have two or three things on your mind, which, if proved against you, would carry you to the nashky. The Romany chal, I say, clubbed his whip, and aimed a blow at the plastramengro, which, if it had hit him on the skull, as was intended, would very likely have cracked it. The plastramengro, however, received it partly on his staff, so that it did him no particular damage. Whereupon seeing what kind of customer he had to deal with, he dropped his staff, and seized the chal with both his hands, who forthwith spurred his horse, hoping by doing so, either to break away from him, or fling him down; but it would not do—the plastramengro held on like a bulldog, so that the Romany chal, to escape being hauled to the ground, suddenly flung himself off the saddle, and then happened in that lane, close by the gate, such a struggle between those two—the chal and the runner—as I suppose will never happen again. But you must have heard of it; every one has heard of it; every one has heard of the fight between the Bow Street engro and the Romany chal.'

'I never heard of it till now.'

'All England rung of it, brother. There never was a better match than between those two. The runner was somewhat the stronger of the two—all these engroes are strong fellows—and a great deal cooler, for all of that sort are wondrous cool people—he had, however, to do with one who knew full well how to take his own part. The chal fought the engro, brother, in the old Roman fashion. He bit, he kicked, and screamed like a wild cat of Benygant; casting foam from his mouth, and fire from his eyes. Sometimes he was beneath the engro's legs, and sometimes he was upon his shoulders. What the engro found the most difficult was to get a firm hold of the chal, for no sooner did he seize the chal by any part of his wearing apparel, than the chal either tore himself away, or contrived to slip out of it; so that in a little time the chal was three parts naked; and as for holding him by the body, it was out of the question, for he was as slippery as an eel. At last the engro seized the chal by the Belcher's handkerchief, which he wore in a knot round his neck, and do whatever the chal could, he could not free himself; and when the engro saw that, it gave him fresh heart, no doubt; "It's of no use," said he; "you had better give in; hold out your hands for the darbies, or I will throttle you."'

'And what did the other fellow do, who came with the chal?' said I.

'I sat still on my horse, brother.'

'You?' said I. 'Were you the man?'

'I was he, brother.'

'And why did you not help your comrade?'

'I have fought in the ring, brother.'

'And what had fighting in the ring to do with fighting in the lane?'

'You mean not fighting. A great deal, brother; it taugh me to prize fair play. When I fought Staffordshire Dick, t'other side of London, I was alone, brother. Not a Romany chal to back me, and he had all his brother pals about him; but they gave me fair play, brother; and I beat Staffordshire Dick, which I couldn't have done had they put one finger on his side the scale; for he was as good a man as myself, or nearly so. Now, brother, had I but bent a finger in favour of the Romany chal the plastramengro would never have come alive out of the lane; but I did not, for I thought to myself fair play is a precious stone; so you see, brother——'

'That you are quite right, Mr. Petulengro; I see that clearly.'

LVI

THE ELECTION AT EATANSWILL

'WELL, Sam,' said Mr. Pickwick, as his valet appeared at his bed-room door, just as he was concluding his toilet; 'all alive to-day, I suppose?'

'Reg'lar game, sir,' replied Mr. Weller; 'our people's a collecting down at the Town Arms, and they're a hollering themselves hoarse already.'

'Ah,' said Mr. Pickwick, 'do they seem devoted to their party, Sam?'

'Never see such dewotion in my life, sir.'

'Energetic, eh?' said Mr. Pickwick.

'Uncommon,' replied Sam; 'I never see men eat and drink so much afore. I wonder they a'nt afeer'd o' bustin.'

'That's the mistaken kindness of the gentry here,' said Mr. Pickwick.

'Wery likely,' replied Sam, briefly.

'Fine, fresh, hearty fellows they seem,' said Mr. Pickwick, glancing from the window.

'Wery fresh,' replied Sam; 'me, and the two waiters at the Peacock, has been a pumpin' over the independent woters as supped there last night.'

'Pumping over independent voters!' exclaimed Mr. Pickwick.

'Yes,' said his attendant, 'every man slept vere he fell down; we dragged 'em out, one by one, this mornin', and put 'em under the pump, and they're in reg'lar fine order, now. Shillin' a head the committee paid for that 'ere job.'

'Can such things be!' exclaimed the astonished Mr. Pickwick.

'Lord bless your heart, sir,' said Sam, 'why where was you half baptized?—that's nothin', that a'nt.'

'Nothing?' said Mr. Pickwick.

'Nothin' at all, sir,' replied his attendant. 'The night afore the last day o' the last election here, the opposite party bribed the barmaid at the Town Arms, to hocus the brandy and water of fourteen unpolled electors as was a stopping in the house.'

'What do you mean by "hocussing" brandy and water?' inquired Mr. Pickwick.

'Puttin' laud'num in it,' replied Sam. 'Blessed if she didn't send 'em all to sleep till twelve hours arter the election was over. They took one man up to the booth, in a truck, fast asleep, by way of experiment, but it was no go—they wouldn't poll him; so they brought him back, and put him to bed again.'

'Strange practices, these,' said Mr. Pickwick; half speaking to himself and half addressing Sam.

'Not half so strange as a miraculous circumstance as happened to my own father, at an election time, in this werry place, sir,' replied Sam.

'What was that?' inquired Mr. Pickwick.

'Why he drove a coach down here once,' said Sam; "lection time came on, and he was engaged by vun party to bring down woters from London. Night afore he was a going to drive up, committee on t'other side sends for him quietly, and away he goes vith the messenger, who shows him in;— large room—lots of gen'l'm'n—heaps of papers, pens and ink, and all that 'ere. "Ah, Mr. Weller," says the gen'l'm'n in the chair, "glad to see you, sir; how are you?"—"Werry well, thank'ee, sir," says my father; "I hope *you're* pretty middlin," says he.—"Pretty well, thank'ee, sir," says the gen'l'm'n; "sit down, Mr. Weller—pray sit down, sir." So my father sits down, and he and the gen'l'm'n looks werry hard at each other. "You don't remember me?" says the gen'l'm'n.—"Can't say I do," says my father.—"Oh, I know you," says the gen'l'm'n; "know'd you when you was a boy," says he.—"Well, I don't remember you," says my father.—"That's very odd," says the gen'l'm'n.—"Werry," says my father.—"You must have a bad mem'ry, Mr. Weller," says the gen'l'm'n.—"Well, it is a wery bad 'un," says my father.—"I thought so," says the gen'l'm'n. So then they pours him out a glass of wine, and gammons him about his driving, and gets him into a reg'lar good humour, and at last shoves a twenty pound note in his hand. "It's a werry bad road between this and London," says the gen'l'm'n.— "Here and there it *is* a heavy road," says my father.—"'Specially near the canal, I think," says the gen'l'm'n.—"Nasty bit that 'ere," says my father.—"Well, Mr. Weller," says the gen'l'm'n, "you're a werry good whip, and can do what you like with your horses, we know. We're all werry fond o' you, Mr. Weller, so in case you *should* have an accident when you're a bringing these here woters down, and *should* tip 'em over into the canal vithout hurtin' of 'em, this is for yourself," says he.—"Gen'l'm'n, you're werry kind," says my father, "and I'll drink your health in another glass of wine," says he; which he did, and then buttons up the money, and bows himself out. You wouldn't believe, sir,' continued Sam, with a look of inexpressible impudence at his master, 'that on the wery day as he came down with them woters, his coach *was* upset on that 'ere wery spot, and ev'ry man on 'em was turned into the canal.'

'And got out again?' inquired Mr. Pickwick, hastily.

'Why,' replied Sam, very slowly, 'I rather think one old gen'l'm'n was missin'; I know his hat was found, but I a'n't quite certain whether his head was in it or not. But what I look at, is the hex-traordinary, and wonderful coincidence, that arter what that gen'l'm'n said, my father's coach should be upset in that wery place, and on that wery day!'

'It is, no doubt, a very extraordinary circumstance indeed,' said Mr. Pickwick. 'But brush my hat, Sam, for I hear Mr. Winkle calling me to breakfast.'

* * * * *

'Whiffin, proclaim silence,' said the mayor, with an air of pomp befitting his lofty station. In obedience to this command the crier performed another concerto on the bell, whereupon a gentleman in the crowd called out 'muffins'; which occasioned another laugh.

'Gentlemen,' said the Mayor, at as loud a pitch as he could

possibly force his voice to, 'Gentlemen. Brother electors of the Borough of Eatanswill. We are met here to-day for the purpose of choosing a representative in the room of our late——'

Here the Mayor was interrupted by a voice in the crowd.

'Suc-cess to the Mayor!' cried the voice, 'and may he never desert the nail and sarspan business, as he got his money by.'

This allusion to the professional pursuits of the orator was received with a storm of delight which, with a bell-accompaniment, rendered the remainder of his speech inaudible, with the exception of the concluding sentence, in which he thanked the meeting for the patient attention with which they had heard him throughout,—an expression of gratitude which elicited another burst of mirth, of about a quarter of an hour's duration.

Next, a tall thin gentleman, in a very stiff white neckerchief, after being repeatedly desired by the crowd to 'send a boy home, to ask whether he hadn't left his woice under the pillow,' begged to nominate a fit and proper person to represent them in Parliament. And when he said it was Horatio Fizkin, Esquire, of Fizkin Lodge, near Eatanswill, the Fizkinites applauded, and the Slumkeyites groaned, so long, and so loudly, that both he and the seconder might have sung comic songs in lieu of speaking, without anybody's being a bit the wiser.

The friends of Horatio Fizkin, Esquire, having had their innings, a little choleric, pink-faced man stood forward to propose another fit and proper person to represent the electors of Eatanswill in Parliament; and very swimmingly the pink-faced gentleman would have gone on, if he had not been rather too choleric to entertain a sufficient perception of the fun of the crowd. But after a very few sentences of figurative eloquence, the pink-faced gentleman got from denouncing those who interrupted him in the mob, to exchanging defiances with the gentlemen on the hustings; whereupon arose an uproar which reduced him to the necessity of expressing his feelings by serious pantomime, which he did, and then left the stage to his seconder, who delivered a written speech of half an hour's length, and wouldn't be stopped, because he had sent it all to the *Eatanswill Gazette*, and the *Eatanswill Gazette* had already printed it, every word.

LVII

SONGS FROM PEACOCK

THE WAR-SONG OF DINAS VAWR

THE mountain sheep are sweeter,
    But the valley sheep are fatter;
    We therefore deemed it meeter
To carry off the latter.
We made an expedition;
    We met a host, and quelled it;
We forced a strong position,
    And killed the men who held it.

On Dyfed's richest valley,
    Where herds of kine were browsing,
We made a mighty sally,
    To furnish our carousing.
Fierce warriors rushed to meet us;
    We met them, and o'erthrew them:
They struggled hard to beat us;
    But we conquered them, and slew them.

As we drove our prize at leisure,
    The king marched forth to catch us:
His rage surpassed all measure,
    But his people could not match us.
He fled to his hall-pillars;
    And, ere our force we led off,
Some sacked his house and cellars,
    While others cut his head off.

We there, in strife bewild'ring,
  Spilt blood enough to swim in:
We orphaned many children,
  And widowed many women.
The eagles and the ravens
  We glutted with our foemen;
The heroes and the cravens,
  The spearmen and the bowmen.

We brought away from battle,
  And much their land bemoaned them,
Two thousand head of cattle,
  And the head of him who owned them:
Ednyfed, king of Dyfed,
  His head was borne before us;
His wine and beasts supplied our feasts,
  And his overthrow, our chorus.

Though I be now a grey, grey friar,
  Yet I was once a hale young knight:
The cry of my dogs was the only choir
  In which my spirit did take delight.
Little I recked of matin bell,
  But drowned its toll with my clanging horn:
And the only beads I loved to tell
  Were the beads of dew on the spangled thorn.

An archer keen I was withal,
  As ever did lean on greenwood tree;
And could make the fleetest roebuck fall,
  A good three hundred yards from me.
Though changeful time, with hand severe,
  Has made me now these joys forgo,
Yet my heart bounds whene'er I hear
  Yoicks! hark away! and tally ho!

THE MEN OF GOTHAM

Seamen three! What men be ye?
   Gotham's three wise men we be.
Whither in your bowl so free?
   To rake the moon from out the sea.
The bowl goes trim. The moon doth shine.
And our ballast is old wine;
And your ballast is old wine.

Who art thou, so fast adrift?
   I am he they call Old Care.
Here on board we will thee lift.
   No: I may not enter there.
Wherefore so? 'Tis Jove's decree,
In a bowl Care may not be;
In a bowl Care may not be.

Fear ye not the waves that roll?
   No: in charmed bowl we swim.
What the charm that floats the bowl?
   Water may not pass the brim.
The bowl goes trim. The moon doth shine.
And our ballast is old wine;
And your ballast is old wine.

THE GRAVE OF LOVE

I dug, beneath the cypress shade,
   What well might seem an elfin's grave;
And every pledge in earth I laid,
   That erst thy false affection gave.

I pressed them down the sod beneath;
   I placed one mossy stone above;
And twined the rose's faded wreath
   Around the sepulchre of love.

Frail as thy love, the flowers were dead
    Ere yet the evening sun was set;
But years shall see the cypress spread,
    Immutable as my regret.

THE POOL OF THE DIVING FRIAR

Gwenwynwyn withdrew from the feasts of his hall;
He slept very little, he prayed not at all;
He pondered, and wandered, and studied alone;
And sought, night and day, the philosopher's stone.

He found it at length, and he made its first proof
By turning to gold all the lead of his roof:
Then he bought some magnanimous heroes, all fire,
Who lived but to smite and be smitten for hire.

With these, on the plains like a torrent he broke;
He filled the whole country with flame and with smoke;
He killed all the swine, and he broached all the wine;
He drove off the sheep, and the beeves, and the kine;

He took castles and towns; he cut short limbs and lives;
He made orphans and widows of children and wives:
This course many years he triumphantly ran,
And did mischief enough to be called a great man.

When, at last, he had gained all for which he had striven,
He bethought him of buying a passport to heaven;
Good and great as he was, yet he did not well know
How soon, or which way, his great spirit might go.

He sought the grey friars, who, beside a wild stream,
Refected their frames on a primitive scheme;
The gravest and wisest Gwenwynwyn found out,
All lonely and ghostly, and angling for trout.

Below the white dash of a mighty cascade,
Where a pool of the stream a deep resting-place made,
And rock-rooted oaks stretched their branches on high,
The friar stood musing, and throwing his fly.

To him said Gwenwynwyn, 'Hold, father, here's store,
For the good of the church, and the good of the poor;'
Then he gave him the stone; but, ere more he could speak,
Wrath came on the friar, so holy and meek:

He had stretched forth his hand to receive the red gold,
And he thought himself mocked by Gwenwynwyn the Bold;
And in scorn of the gift, and in rage at the giver,
He jerked it immediately into the river.

Gwenwynwyn, aghast, not a syllable spake;
The philosopher's stone made a duck and a drake:
Two systems of circles a moment were seen,
And the stream smoothed them off, as they never had been.

Gwenwynwyn regained, and uplifted, his voice:
'Oh friar, grey friar, full rash was thy choice;
The stone, the good stone, which away thou hast thrown,
Was the stone of all stones, the philosopher's stone!'

The friar looked pale, when his error he knew;
The friar looked red, and the friar looked blue;
And heels over head, from the point of a rock,
He plunged, without stopping to pull off his frock.

He dived very deep, but he dived all in vain,
The prize he had slighted he found not again:
Many times did the friar his diving renew,
And deeper and deeper the river still grew.

Gwenwynwyn gazed long, of his senses in doubt,
To see the grey friar a diver so stout:
Then sadly and slowly his castle he sought,
And left the friar diving, like dabchick distraught.

Gwenwynwyn fell sick with alarm and despite,
Died, and went to the devil the very same night:
The magnanimous heroes he held in his pay
Sacked his castle, and marched with the plunder away.

No knell on the silence of midnight was rolled,
For the flight of the soul of Gwenwynwyn the Bold:
The brethren, unfee'd, let the mighty ghost pass,
Without praying a prayer, or intoning a mass.

The friar haunted ever beside the dark stream;
The philosopher's stone was his thought and his dream;
And day after day, ever head under heels,
He dived all the time he could spare from his meals.

He dived, and he dived, to the end of his days,
As the peasant oft witnessed with fear and amaze:
The mad friar's diving-place long was their theme,
And no plummet can fathom that pool of the stream.

And still, when light clouds on the midnight winds ride,
If by moonlight you stray on the lone river-side,
The ghost of the friar may be seen diving there,
With head in the water and heels in the air.

LVIII

GILBERT WHITE ON BIRDS

A GOOD ornithologist should be able to distinguish birds by their air as well as by their colours and shape; on the ground as well as on the wing; and in the bush as well as in the hand. For, though it must not be said that every *species* of bird has a manner peculiar to itself, yet there is somewhat in most *genera* at least that at first sight discriminates them, and enables a judicious observer to pronounce upon them with some certainty. . . . Thus *kites* and *buzzards* sail round in circles with wings expanded and motionless; and it is from their gliding manner that the former are still called in the north of *England gleads*, from the *Saxon* verb *glidan*, to glide. The *kestrel*, or *windhover*, has a peculiar mode of hanging in the air in one place, his wings all the while being briskly agitated. *Hen-harrier* fly low over heaths or fields of corn, and beat the ground regularly like a pointer or setting-dog. *Owls* move in a buoyant manner, as if lighter than the air; they seem to want ballast. There is a peculiarity belonging to *ravens* that must draw the attention even of the most incurious— they spend all their leisure time in striking and cuffing each other on the wing in a kind of playful skirmish; and, when they move from one place to another, frequently turn on their backs with a loud croak, and seem to be falling to the ground. When this odd gesture betides them, they are scratching themselves with one foot, and thus lose the centre of gravity. *Rooks* sometimes dive and tumble in a frolicksome manner; *crows* and *daws* swagger in their walk; *woodpeckers* fly *volatu undoso*, opening and closing their wings at every stroke, and so are always rising or falling in curves.

All of this genus use their tails, which incline downward, as a support, while they run up trees. *Parrots*, like all other hooked-clawed birds, walk awkwardly, and make use of their bill as a third foot, climbing and descending with ridiculous caution. All the *gallinæ* parade and walk gracefully, and run nimbly; but fly with difficulty, with an impetuous whirring, and in a straight line. *Magpies* and *jays* flutter with powerless wings, and make no dispatch; *herons* seem incumbered with too much sail for their light bodies, but these vast hollow wings are necessary in carrying burdens, such as large fishes and the like; *pigeons*, and particularly the sort called *smiters*, have a way of clashing their wings the one against the other over their backs with a loud snap; another variety, called *tumblers*, turn themselves over in the air. Some birds have movements peculiar to the season of love; thus *ring-doves*, though strong and rapid at other times, yet in the spring hang about on the wing in a toying and playful manner; thus the *cock-snipe*, while breeding, forgetting his former flight, fans the air like the *wind-hover*; and the *green-finch* in particular, exhibits such languishing and faultering gestures as to appear like a wounded and dying bird; the *kingfisher* darts along like an arrow; *fern-owls*, or *goat-suckers*, glance in the dusk over the tops of trees like a meteor; *starlings* as it were swim along, while *missel-thrushes* use a wild and desultory flight; *swallows* sweep over the surface of the ground and water, and distinguish themselves by rapid turns and quick evolutions; *swifts* dash round in circles; and the *bank-martin* moves with frequent vacillations like a butterfly. Most of the small birds fly by jerks, rising and falling as they advance. Most small birds hop; but *wagtails* and *larks* walk, moving their legs alternately. *Skylarks* rise and fall perpendicularly as they sing; *wood-larks* hang poised in the air; and *titlarks* rise and fall in large curves, singing in their descent. The *white-throat* uses odd jerks and gesticulations over the tops of hedges and bushes. All the *duck-kind* waddle; *divers* and *auks* walk as if fettered, and stand erect on their tails: these are the *compedes* of *Linnæus*. *Geese* and *cranes*, and most wild fowls, move in figured flights, often changing their position. . . . *Dabchicks*, *moor-hens*, and *coots*, fly erect, with their legs hanging down, and hardly make any dispatch; the reason is plain, their wings are placed too forward out of the true centre of gravity; as the legs of *auks* and *divers* are situated too backward.

From the motion of birds, the transition is natural enough to their notes and language, of which I shall say something. Not that I would pretend to understand their language like the *vizier*; who, by the recital of a conversation which passed between two owls reclaimed a sultan, before, delighting in conquest and devastation; but I would be thought only to mean that many of the winged tribes have various sounds and voices adapted to express their various passions, wants, and feelings; such as anger, fear, love, hatred, hunger, and the like. All species are not equally eloquent; some are copious and fluent as it were in their utterance, while others are confined to a few important sounds: no bird, like the fish kind, is quite mute, though some are rather silent. The language of birds is very ancient, and, like other ancient modes of speech, very elliptical; little is said, but much is meant and understood.

The notes of the eagle kind are shrill and piercing; and about the season of nidification much diversified, as I have been often assured by a curious observer of Nature, who long resided at *Gibraltar*, where eagles abound. The notes of our *hawks* much resemble those of the king of birds. *Owls* have very expressive notes; they hoot in a fine vocal sound, much resembling the *vox humana*, and reducible by a pitch-pipe to a musical key. This note seems to express complacency and rivalry among the males: they use also a quick call and an horrible scream; and can snore and hiss when they mean to menace. *Ravens*, besides their loud croak, can exert a deep and solemn note that makes the woods to echo; the amorous sound of a *crow* is strange and ridiculous; *rooks*, in the breeding season, attempt sometimes in the gaiety of their hearts to sing, but with no great success; the *parrot*-kind have many modulations of voice, as appears by their aptitude to learn human sounds; *doves* coo in an amorous and mournful manner, and are emblems of despairing lovers; the *woodpecker* sets up a sort of loud and hearty laugh; the *fern-owl*, or *goat-sucker*, from the dusk till day-break, serenades his mate with the clattering of castanets. All the tuneful *passeres* express their complacency by sweet modulations, and a variety of melody. The *swallow*, as has been observed in a former letter, by a shrill alarm bespeaks the attention of the other *hirundines*, and bids them be aware that the hawk is at hand. Aquatic and gregarious birds, especially the nocturnal, that shift their quarters in the dark, are very noisy and loquacious; as cranes, wild-geese, wild-ducks, and the like: their perpetual clamour prevents them from dispersing and losing their companions.

In so extensive a subject sketches and outlines are as much as can be expected; for it would be endless to instance in all the infinite variety of the feathered nation. We shall therefore confine the remainder of this letter to the few domestic fowls of our yard, which are most known, and therefore best understood. And first the *peacock*, with his gorgeous train, demands our attention; but, like most of the gaudy birds, his notes are grating and shocking to the ear: the yelling of cats, and the braying of an ass, are not more disgustful. The voice of the *goose* is trumpet-like, and clanking; and once saved the Capitol at *Rome*, as grave historians assert: the hiss, also, of the *gander*, is formidable and full of menace, and 'protective of his young.' Among *ducks* the sexual distinction of voice is remarkable; for, while the *quack* of the female is loud and sonorous, the voice of the *drake* is inward and harsh, and feeble, and scarce discernible. The cock *turkey* struts and gobbles to his mistress in a most uncouth manner; he hath also a pert and petulant note when he attacks his adversary. When a hen *turkey* leads forth her young brood she keeps a watchful eye; and if a bird of prey appear, though ever so high in the air, the careful mother announces the enemy with a little inward moan, and watches him with a steady and attentive look; but, if he approach, her note becomes earnest and alarming, and her outcries are redoubled.

No inhabitants of a yard seem possessed of such a variety of expression and so copious a language as common poultry. Take a chicken of four or five days old, and hold it up to a window where there are flies, and it will immediately seize its prey, with little twitterings of complacency; but if you tender it a wasp or a bee, at once it's note becomes harsh, and expressive of disapprobation and a sense of danger. When a pullet is ready to lay she intimates the event by a joyous and easy soft note. Of all the occurrences of their life that of *laying* seems to be the most important; for no sooner has a hen disburdened herself, than she rushes forth with a clamorous kind of joy, which the cock and the rest of his mistresses immediately adopt. The tumult is not confined to the family concerned, but catches from yard to yard, and spreads to every homestead within hearing, till at last the whole village is in an uproar. As soon as a hen becomes a mother her new relation demands a new language: she then runs clucking and screaming about, and seems agitated as if possessed. The father of the flock has also a considerable vocabulary; if he finds food, he calls a favourite concubine to partake; and if a bird of prey passes over, with a warning voice he bids his family beware. The gallant **chanticleer** has, at command, his amorous phrases and his terms of defiance. But the sound by which he is best known is his *crowing*: by this he has been distinguished in all ages as the countryman's clock or larum, as the watchman that proclaims the divisions of the night. Thus the poet elegantly styles him:

> '——the crested cock, whose clarion sounds
> The silent hours.'

A neighbouring gentleman one summer had lost most of his chickens by a sparrow-hawk, that came gliding down between a faggot pile and the end of his house to the place where the coops stood. The owner, inwardly vexed to see his flock thus diminished, hung a setting net adroitly between the pile and the house, into which the caitiff dashed, and was entangled. Resentment suggested the law of retaliation; he therefore clipped the hawk's wings, cut off his talons, and, fixing a cork on his bill, threw him down among the brood-hens. Imagination cannot paint the scene that ensued; the expressions that fear, rage, and revenge inspired were new, or at least such as had been unnoticed before: the exasperated matrons upbraided, they execrated, they insulted, they triumphed. In a word, they never desisted from buffeting their adversary till they had torn him in an hundred pieces.

LIX

FROM 'ADONAIS'

PEACE, peace! he is not dead, he doth not sleep—
He hath awakened from the dream of life—
'Tis we, who lost in stormy visions, keep
With phantoms an unprofitable strife,
And in mad trance, strike with our spirit's knife
Invulnerable nothings.—*We* decay
Like corpses in a charnel; fear and grief
Convulse us and consume us day by day,
And cold hopes swarm like worms within our living clay.

He has outsoared the shadow of our night;
Envy and calumny and hate and pain,
And that unrest which men miscall delight,
Can touch him not and torture not again;
From the contagion of the world's slow stain
He is secure, and now can never mourn
A heart grown cold, a head grown gray in vain;
Nor, when the spirit's self has ceased to burn,
With sparkless ashes load an unlamented urn.

He lives, he wakes—'tis Death is dead, not he;
Mourn not for Adonais.—Thou young Dawn,
Turn all thy dew to splendour, for from thee
The spirit thou lamentest is not gone;
Ye caverns and ye forests, cease to moan!
Cease, ye faint flowers and fountains, and thou Air,
Which like a mourning veil thy scarf hadst thrown
O'er the abandoned Earth, now leave it bare
Even to the joyous stars which smile on its despair!

He is made one with Nature: there is heard
His voice in all her music, from the moan
Of thunder, to the song of night's sweet bird;
He is a presence to be felt and known
In darkness and in light, from herb and stone,
Spreading itself where'er that Power may move
Which has withdrawn his being to its own;
Which wields the world with never-wearied love,
Sustains it from beneath, and kindles it above.

He is a portion of the loveliness
Which once he made more lovely: he doth bear
His part, while the one Spirit's plastic stress
Sweeps through the dull dense world, compelling there,
All new successions to the forms they wear;
Torturing th' unwilling dross that checks its flight
To its own likeness, as each mass may bear;
And bursting in its beauty and its might
From trees and beasts and men into the Heaven's light.

The splendours of the firmament of time
May be eclipsed, but are extinguished not;
Like stars to their appointed height they climb,
And death is a low mist which cannot blot
The brightness it may veil. When lofty thought
Lifts a young heart above its mortal lair,
And love and life contend in it, for what
Shall be its earthly doom, the dead live there
And move like winds of light on dark and stormy air.

The inheritors of unfulfilled renown
Rose from their thrones, built beyond mortal thought,
Far in the Unapparent. Chatterton
Rose pale,—his solemn agony had not
Yet faded from him; Sidney, as he fought
And as he fell and as he lived and loved
Sublimely mild, a Spirit without spot,
Arose; and Lucan, by his death approved:
Oblivion as they rose shrank like a thing reproved.

And many more, whose names on Earth are dark,
But whose transmitted effluence cannot die
So long as fire outlives the parent spark,
Rose, robed in dazzling immortality.
'Thou art become as one of us,' they cry,
'It was for thee yon kingless sphere has long
Swung blind in unascended majesty,
Silent alone amid an Heaven of Song.
Assume thy wingèd throne, thou Vesper of our throng!'

Who mourns for Adonais? Oh, come forth,
Fond wretch! and know thyself and him aright.
Clasp with thy panting soul the pendulous Earth;
As from a centre, dart thy spirit's light
Beyond all worlds, until its spacious might
Satiate the void circumference: then shrink
Even to a point within our day and night;
And keep thy heart light lest it make thee sink
When hope has kindled hope, and lured thee to the brink.

FROM 'ADONAIS'

Or go to Rome, which is the sepulchre,
Oh, not of him, but of our joy: 'tis nought
That ages, empires, and religions there
Lie buried in the ravage they have wrought;
For such as he can lend,—they borrow not
Glory from those who made the world their prey;
And he is gathered to the kings of thought
Who waged contention with their time's decay,
And of the past are all that cannot pass away.

Go thou to Rome,—at once the Paradise,
The grave, the city, and the wilderness;
And where its wrecks like shattered mountains rise,
And flowering weeds, and fragrant copses dress
The bones of Desolation's nakedness
Pass, till the spirit of the spot shall lead
Thy footsteps to a slope of green access
Where, like an infant's smile, over the dead
A light of laughing flowers along the grass is spread;

And gray walls moulder round, on which dull Time
Feeds, like slow fire upon a hoary brand;
And one keen pyramid with wedge sublime,
Pavilioning the dust of him who planned
This refuge for his memory, doth stand
Like flame transformed to marble; and beneath,
A field is spread, on which a newer band
Have pitched in Heaven's smile their camp of death,
Welcoming him we lose with scarce extinguished breath.

Here pause: these graves are all too young as yet
To have outgrown the sorrow which consigned
Its charge to each; and if the seal is set,
Here, on one fountain of a mourning mind,
Break it not thou! too surely shalt thou find
Thine own well full, if thou returnest home,
Of tears and gall. From the world's bitter wind
Seek shelter in the shadow of the tomb.
What Adonais is, why fear we to become?

The One remains, the many change and pass;
Heaven's light forever shines, Earth's shadows fly;
Life, like a domé of many-coloured glass,
Stains the white radiance of Eternity,
Until Death tramples it to fragments.—Die,
If thou wouldst be with that which thou dost seek!
Follow where all is fled!—Rome's azure sky,
Flowers, ruins, statues, music, words, are weak
The glory they transfuse with fitting truth to speak.

Why linger, why turn back, why shrink, my Heart?
Thy hopes are gone before: from all things here
They have departed; thou shouldst now depart!
A light is passed from the revolving year,
And man, and woman; and what still is dear
Attracts to crush, repels to make thee wither.
The soft sky smiles,—the low wind whispers near;
'Tis Adonais calls! oh, hasten thither,
No more let Life divide what Death can join together.

That Light whose smile kindles the Universe,
That Beauty in which all things work and move,
That Benediction which the eclipsing Curse
Of birth can quench not, that sustaining Love
Which through the web of being blindly wove
By man and beast and earth and air and sea,
Burns bright or dim, as each are mirrors of
The fire for which all thirst; now beams on me,
Consuming the last clouds of cold mortality.

The breath whose might I have invoked in song
Descends on me; my spirit's bark is driven,
Far from the shore, far from the trembling throng
Whose sails were never to the tempest given;
The massy earth and spherèd skies are riven!
I am borne darkly, fearfully, afar;
Whilst, burning through the inmost veil of Heaven,
The soul of Adonais, like a star,
Beacons from the abode where the Eternal are.

LX

MRS. BATTLE'S OPINIONS ON WHIST

'A CLEAR fire, a clean hearth, and the rigour of the game.' This was the celebrated *wish* of old Sarah Battle (now with God) who, next to her devotions, loved a good game at whist. She was none of your lukewarm gamesters, your half and half players, who have no objection to take a hand, if you want one to make up a rubber; who affirm that they have no pleasure in winning; that they like to win one game, and lose another; that they can while away an hour very agreeably at a card-table, but are indifferent whether they play or no; and will desire an adversary, who has slipt a wrong card, to take it up and play another. These insufferable triflers are the curse of a table. One of these flies will spoil a whole pot. Of such it may be said, that they do not play at cards, but only play at playing at them.

Sarah Battle was none of that breed. She detested them, as I do, from her heart and soul; and would not, save upon a striking emergency, willingly seat herself at the same table with them. She loved a thorough-paced partner, a determined enemy. She took, and gave, no concessions. She hated favours. She never made a revoke, nor ever passed it over in her adversary without exacting the utmost forfeiture. She fought a good fight: cut and thrust. She held not her good sword (her cards) 'like a dancer.' She sate bolt upright; and neither showed you her cards, nor desired to see yours. All people have their blind side—their superstitions; and I have heard her declare, under the rose, that Hearts was her favourite suit.

I never in my life—and I knew Sarah Battle many of the best years of it—saw her take out her snuff-box when it was her turn to play; or snuff a candle in the middle of a game; or ring for a servant, till it was fairly over. She never introduced, or connived at, miscellaneous conversation during its process. As she emphatically observed, cards were cards:

and if I ever saw unmingled distaste in her fine last-century countenance, it was at the airs of a young gentleman of a literary turn, who had been with difficulty persuaded to take a hand; and who, in his excess of candour, declared, that he thought there was no harm in unbending the mind now and then, after serious studies, in recreations of that kind! She could not bear to have her noble occupation, to which she wound up her faculties, considered in that light. It was her business, her duty, the thing she came into the world to do,—and she did it. She unbent her mind afterwards—over a book.

* * * * *

Quadrille, she has often told me, was her first love; but whist had engaged her maturer esteem. The former, she said, was showy and specious, and likely to allure young persons. The uncertainty and quick shifting of partners—a thing which the constancy of whist abhors;—the dazzling supremacy and regal investiture of Spadille—absurd, as she justly observed, in the pure aristocracy of whist, where his crown and garter give him no proper power above his brother-nobility of the Aces;—the giddy vanity, so taking to the inexperienced, of playing alone:—above all, the overpowering attractions of a *Sans Prendre Vole*,—to the triumph of which there is certainly nothing parallel or approaching, in the contingencies of whist;—all these, she would say, make quadrille a game of captivation to the young and enthusiastic. But whist was the *solider* game: that was her word. It was a long meal; not, like quadrille, a feast of snatches. One or two rubbers might co-extend in duration with an evening. They gave time to form rooted friendships, to cultivate steady enmities. She despised the chance-started, capricious, and ever fluctuating alliances of the other. The skirmishes of quadrille, she would say, reminded her of the petty ephemeral embroilments of the little Italian states, depicted by Machiavel; perpetually changing postures and connexions; bitter foes to-day, sugared darlings to-morrow; kissing and scratching in a breath;—but the wars of whist were comparable to the long, steady, deep-rooted, rational, antipathies of the great French and English nations.

* * * * *

Piquet she held the best game at the cards for two persons, though she would ridicule the pedantry of the terms—such as pique—repique—the capot—they savoured (she thought) of affectation. But games for two, or even three, she never greatly cared for. She loved the quadrate, or square. She would argue thus:—Cards are warfare: the ends are gain, with glory. But cards are war, in disguise of a sport: when single adversaries encounter, the ends proposed are too palpable. By themselves, it is too close a fight; with spectators, it is not much bettered. No looker on can be interested, except for a bet, and then it is a mere affair of money; he cares not for your luck *sympathetically*, or for your play.— Three are still worse; a mere naked war of every man against every man, as in cribbage, without league or alliance; or a rotation of petty and contradictory interests, a succession of heartless leagues, and not much more hearty infractions of them, as in tradrille.—But in square games (*she meant whist*) all that is possible to be attained in card-playing is accomplished. There are the incentives of profit with honour, common to every species—though the *latter* can be but very imperfectly enjoyed in those other games, where the spectator is only feebly a participator. But the parties in whist are spectators and principals too. They are a theatre to themselves, and a looker-on is not wanted. He is rather worse than nothing, and an impertinence. Whist abhors neutrality, or interests beyond its sphere. You glory in some surprising stroke of skill or fortune, not because a cold—or even an interested—by-stander witnesses it, but because your *partner* sympathizes in the contingency. You win for two. You triumph for two. Two are exalted. Two again are mortified; which divides their disgrace, as the conjunction doubles (by taking off the invidiousness) your glories. Two losing to two are better reconciled, than one to one in that close butchery. The hostile feeling is weakened by multiplying the channels. War becomes a civil game.—By such reasonings as these the old lady was accustomed to defend her favourite pastime.

No inducement could ever prevail upon her to play at any game, where chance entered into the composition, *for nothing*. Chance, she would argue—and here again, admire the subtlety of her conclusion!—chance is nothing, but where something else depends upon it. It is obvious, that cannot be *glory*. What rational cause of exultation could it give to a man to turn up size ace a hundred times together by himself? or before spectators, where no stake was depending?—Make a lottery of a hundred thousand tickets with but one fortunate number—and what possible principle of our nature, except stupid wonderment, could it gratify to gain that number as many times successively, without a prize? —Therefore she disliked the mixture of chance in backgammon, where it was not played for money. She called it foolish, and those people idiots, who were taken with a lucky hit under such circumstances. Games of pure skill were as little to her fancy. Played for a stake, they were a mere system of over-reaching. Played for glory, they were a mere setting of one man's wit,—his memory, or combination-faculty rather—against another's; like a mock-engagement at a review, bloodless and profitless.—She could not conceive a *game* wanting the sprightly infusion of chance, —the handsome excuses of good fortune. Two people playing at chess in a corner of a room, whilst whist was stirring in the centre, would inspire her with insufferable horror and ennui. Those well-cut similitudes of Castles, and Knights, the *imagery* of the board, she would argue, (and I think in this case justly) were entirely misplaced and senseless. Those hard head-contests can in no instance ally with the fancy. They reject form and colour. A pencil and dry slate (she used to say) were the proper arena for such combatants.

To those puny objectors against cards, as nurturing the bad passions, she would retort, that man is a gaming animal. He must be always trying to get the better in something or other:—that this passion can scarcely be more safely expended than upon a game at cards: that cards are a temporary illusion; in truth, a mere drama; for we do but *play* at being mightily concerned, where a few idle shillings are at stake, yet, during the illusion, we *are* as mightily concerned as those whose stake is crowns and kingdoms. They are a sort of dream-fighting; much ado; great battling, and little bloodshed; mighty means for disproportioned ends; quite as diverting, and a great deal more innoxious, than many of those more serious *games* of life, which men play, without esteeming them to be such.

LXI

THE GLORIES OF OUR BLOOD AND STATE

THE glories of our blood and state
 Are shadows, not substantial things;
 There is no armour against fate:
Death lays his icy hand on kings.
  Sceptre and crown
  Must tumble down,
 And in the dust be equal made
With the poor crooked scythe and spade.

Some men with swords may reap the field,
 And plant fresh laurels where they kill;
But their strong nerves at last must yield,
 They tame but one another still;
  Early or late
  They stoop to fate,
 And must give up their murmuring breath,
When they, pale captives, creep to death.

The garlands wither on your brow;
 Then boast no more your mighty deeds;
Upon death's purple altar, now,
 See where the victor-victim bleeds!

　　　　　Your heads must come
　　　　　To the cold tomb;
　　　　Only the actions of the just
　　　　Smell sweet and blossom in their dust.

THE VISION OF BELSHAZZAR

Belshazzar the king made a great feast to a thousand of his lords, and drank wine before the thousand. Belshazzar, whiles he tasted the wine, commanded to bring the golden and silver vessels which his father Nebuchadnezzar had taken out of the temple which was in Jerusalem; that the king, and his princes, his wives, and his concubines, might drink therein. Then they brought the golden vessels that were taken out of the temple of the house of God which was at Jerusalem; and the king, and his princes, his wives, and his concubines, drank in them. They drank wine, and praised the gods of gold, and of silver, of brass, of iron, of wood, and of stone.

In the same hour came forth fingers of a man's hand, and wrote over against the candlestick upon the plaister of the wall of the king's palace: and the king saw the part of the hand that wrote. Then the king's countenance was changed, and his thoughts troubled him, so that the joints of his loins were loosed, and his knees smote one against another. The king cried aloud to bring in the astrologers, the Chaldeans, and the soothsayers. And the king spake, and said to the wise men of Babylon, Whosoever shall read this writing, and shew me the interpretation thereof, shall be clothed with scarlet, and have a chain of gold about his neck, and shall be the third ruler in the kingdom. Then came in all the king's wise men: but they could not read the writing, nor make known to the king the interpretation thereof. Then was king Belshazzar greatly troubled, and his countenance was changed in him, and his lords were astonied.

Now the queen, by reason of the words of the king and his lords, came into the banquet house: and the queen spake and said, O king, live for ever: let not thy thoughts trouble thee, nor let thy countenance be changed: there is a man in thy kingdom, in whom is the spirit of the holy gods; and in the days of thy father light and understanding and wisdom, like the wisdom of the gods, was found in him; whom the king Nebuchadnezzar, thy father, the king, I say, thy father, made master of the magicians, astrologers, Chaldeans, and soothsayers; forasmuch as an excellent spirit, and knowledge, and understanding, interpreting of dreams, and shewing of hard sentences, and dissolving of doubts, were found in the same Daniel, whom the king named Belteshazzar: now let Daniel be called, and he will shew the interpretation.

Then was Daniel brought in before the king. And the king spake and said unto Daniel, Art thou that Daniel, which art of the children of the captivity of Judah, whom the king my father brought out of Jewry? I have even heard of thee, that the spirit of the gods is in thee, and that light and understanding and excellent wisdom is found in thee. And now the wise men, the astrologers, have been brought in before me, that they should read this writing, and make known unto me the interpretation thereof: but they could not show the interpretation of the thing: and I have heard of thee, that thou canst make interpretations, and dissolve doubts: now if thou canst read the writing, and make known to me the interpretation thereof, thou shalt be clothed with scarlet, and have a chain of gold about thy neck, and shalt be the third ruler in the kingdom.

Then Daniel answered and said before the king, Let thy gifts be to thyself, and give thy rewards to another; yet I will read the writing unto the king, and make known to him the interpretation. O thou king, the most high God gave Nebuchadnezzar thy father a kingdom, and majesty, and glory, and honour: and for the majesty that he gave him, all people, nations, and languages, trembled and feared before him: whom he would he slew; and whom he would he kept alive; and whom he would he set up; and whom he would he put down. But when his heart was lifted up, and his mind hardened in pride, he was deposed from his kingly throne, and they took his glory from him: and he was driven from the sons of men; and his heart was made like the beasts, and his dwelling was with the wild asses: they fed him with grass like oxen, and his body was wet with the dew of heaven; till he knew that the most high God ruled in the kingdom of men, and that he appointeth over it whomsoever he will. And thou his son, O Belshazzar, hast not humbled thine heart, though thou knewest all this; but hast lifted up thyself against the Lord of heaven; and they have brought the vessels of his house before thee, and thou, and thy lords, thy wives, and thy concubines, have drunk wine in them; and thou hast praised the gods of silver, and gold, of brass, iron, wood, and stone, which see not, nor hear, nor know: and the God in whose hand thy breath is, and whose are all thy ways, hast thou not glorified: then was the part of the hand sent from him: and this writing was written. And this is the writing that was written, MENE, MENE, TEKEL, UPHARSIN. This is the interpretation of the thing: MENE; God hath numbered thy kingdom, and finished it. TEKEL; Thou art weighed in the balances, and art found wanting. PERES; Thy kingdom is divided, and given to the Medes and Persians.

Then commanded Belshazzar, and they clothed Daniel with scarlet, and put a chain of gold about his neck, and made a proclamation concerning him, that he should be the third ruler of the kingdom.

In that night was Belshazzar the king of the Chaldeans slain.

LXII

THE SECOND LINE OF DEFENCE

THE CAPTAIN OF VOLUNTEERS

OF all the brave captains that ever were seen,
   Appointed to fight by a king or a queen;
   By a queen or a king appointed to fight,
Sure never a captain was like this brave knight.

He pull'd off his slippers and wrapper of silk,
And foaming as furious as whisk-pared milk,
Says he to his lady, My lady, I'll go,
My company calls me; you must not say no.

With eyes all in tears, says my lady, says she,
O cruel Sir Dilberry, do not kill me!
For I never will leave thee, but cling round thy middle,
And die in the arms of Sir Dilberry Diddle.

Says Diddle again to his lady, My dear,
(And with a white handkerchief wip'd off a tear)
The hottest of actions will only be farce,
For sure thou art Venus! Says she, Thou art Mars!

Awhile they stood simp'ring, like master and miss,
And Cupid thought he would have given one kiss;
'Twas what she expected, admits no dispute;
But he touch'd his own finger, and blew a salute.

By a place I can't mention, not knowing its name,
At the head of his company Dilberry came;
And the drums to the window call ev'ry eye,
To see the defence of the nation pass by.

Old bible-fac'd women, through spectacles dim,
With hemming and coughing, cry'd, Lord, it is him!
While boys and the girls, who more clearly could see
Cry'd, Yonder's Sir Dilberry Diddle—that's he.

Of all the fair ladies that came to the show,
Sir Diddle's fair lady stood first in the row;
O charming, says she, how he looks all in red!
How he turns out his toes! how he holds up his head

Do but see his cockade, and behold his dear gun,
Which shines like a looking-glass held in the sun!
O see thyself now, thou'rt so martially smart,
And look as you lookt when you conquer'd my heart.

The sweet sounding notes of Sir Dilberry Diddle,
More ravish'd his ears than the sound of a fiddle;
And as it grew faint, that he heard it no more,
He soften'd the word of command to—encore.

The battle now over, without any blows,
The heroes unarm and strip off their clothes;
The captain refresh'd with a sip of rose-water,
Hands his dear to the coach, bows, and then steps in after.

John's orders were special to drive very slow,
For fevers oft follow fatigue, we all know;
But prudently cautious, in Venus's lap,
His head under apron, brave Mars took a nap.

He dream'd, fame reports, that he cut all the throats
Of the French as they landed in flat-bottom'd boats;
In his sleep if such dreadful destruction he makes,
What havoc, ye gods! shall we have when he wakes?

SUNDAY MORNING DRILL

On drawing near, they saw through the boughs of a clump of intervening trees, still leafless, but bursting into buds of amber hue, a glittering which seemed to be reflected from points of steel. In a few moments they heard above the tender chiming of the church bells the loud voice of a man giving words of command, at which all the metallic points suddenly shifted like the bristles of a porcupine, and glistened anew.

' 'Tis the drilling,' said Loveday. 'They drill now between the services, you know, because they can't get the men together so readily in the week. It makes me feel that I ought to be doing more than I am!'

When they had passed round the belt of trees, the company of recruits became visible, consisting of the able-bodied inhabitants of the hamlets thereabout, more or less known to Bob and Anne. They were assembled on the green plot outside the churchyard-gate, dressed in their common clothes, and the sergeant who had been putting them through their drill was . . . now engaged in untying a canvas money-bag, from which he drew forth a handful of shillings, giving one to each man in payment for his attendance.

'Men, I dismissed ye too soon—parade, parade again, I say,' he cried. 'My watch is fast, I find. There's another twenty minutes afore the worship of God commences. Now all of you that ha'n't got firelocks, fall in at the lower end. Eyes right and dress!'

As every man was anxious to see how the rest stood, those at the end of the line pressed forward for that purpose, till the line assumed the form of a bow.

'Look at ye now! Why, you are all a crooking in! Dress, dress!'

They dressed forthwith; but impelled by the same motive they soon resumed their former figure, and so they were despairingly permitted to remain.

'Now, I hope you'll have a little patience,' said the sergeant, as he stood in the centre of the arc, 'and pay strict attention to the word of command, just exactly as I give it out to ye; and if I should go wrong, I shall be much obliged to any friend who'll put me right again, for I have only been in the army three weeks myself, and we are all liable to mistakes.'

'So we be, so we be,' said the line heartily.

' 'Tention, the whole, then. Poise fawlocks! Very well done!'

'Please, what must we do that haven't got no firelocks!' said the lower end of the line in a helpless voice.

'Now, was ever such a question! Why, you must do nothing at all, but think *how* you'd poise 'em *if* you had 'em.

You middle men, that are armed with hurdle-sticks and cabbage-stumps just to make-believe, must of course use 'em as if they were the real thing. Now then, cock fawlocks! Present! Fire! (Pretend to, I mean, and the same time throw yer imagination into the field o' battle.) Very good—very good indeed; except that some of you were a *little* too soon, and the rest a *little* too late.'

'Please, sergeant, can I fall out, as I am master-player in the choir, and my bass-viol strings won't stand at this time o' year, unless they be screwed up a little before the passon comes in?'

'How can you think of such trifles as churchgoing at such a time as this, when your own native country is on the point of invasion?' said the sergeant sternly. 'And, as you know, the drill ends three minutes afore church begins, and that's the law, and it wants a quarter of an hour yet. Now, at the word *Prime*, shake the powder (supposing you've got it) into the priming-pan, three last fingers behind the rammer; then shut your pans, drawing your right arm nimble-like towards your body. I ought to have told ye before this, that at *Hand your katridge*, seize it and bring it with a quick motion to your mouth, bite the top well off, and don't swaller so much of the powder as to make ye hawk and spet instead of attending to your drill. What's that man a-saying of in the rear rank?'

'Please, sir, 'tis Anthony Cripplestraw, wanting to know how he's to bite off his katridge, when he haven't a tooth left in 's head?'

'Man! Why, what's your genius for war? Hold it up to your right-hand man's mouth, to be sure, and let him nip it off for ye. Well, what have you to say, Private Tremlett? Don't ye understand English?'

'Ask yer pardon, sergeant; but what must we infantry of the awkward squad do if Boney comes afore we get our firelocks?'

'Take a pike, like the rest of the incapables. You'll find a store of them ready in the corner of the church tower. Now then—Shoulder—r—r—r——'

'There, they be tinging in the passon!' exclaimed David, Miller Loveday's man, who also formed one of the company, as the bells changed from chiming all three together to a quick beating of one. The whole line drew a breath of relief, threw down their arms, and began running off.

'Well, then, I must dismiss ye,' said the sergeant. 'Come back—come back! Next drill is Tuesday afternoon at four. And, mind, if your masters won't let ye leave work soon enough, tell me, and I'll write a line to Gover'ment! 'Tention! To the right—left wheel, I mean—no, no—right wheel. Mar—r—r—rch!'

Some wheeled to the right and some to the left, and some obliging men, including Cripplestraw, tried to wheel both ways.

'Stop, stop; try again! 'Cruits and comrades, unfortunately when I'm in a hurry I can never remember my right hand from my left, and never could as a boy. You must excuse me, please. Practice makes perfect, as the saying is; and, much as I've learnt since I 'listed, we always find something new. Now then, right wheel! march! halt! Stand at ease! dismiss! I think that's the order o't, but I'll look in the Gover'ment book afore Tuesday.'

LXIII

THE RED ENSIGN

NOTHING under canvas could be expected to make a port on such an idle night of dreamy splendour and spiritual stillness. We would have to glide idly to and fro, keeping our station within the appointed bearings, and, unless a fresh breeze sprang up with the dawn, we would land before sunrise on a small islet that, within two miles of us, shone like a lump of frozen moonlight, to 'break a crust and take a pull at the wine bottle.' I was familiar with the procedure. The stout boat emptied of her crowd would nestle her buoyant, capable side against the very rock

—such is the perfectly smooth amenity of the classic sea when in a gentle mood. The crust broken, and the mouthful of wine swallowed—it was literally no more than that with this abstemious race—the pilots would pass the time stamping their feet on the slabs of sea-salted stone and blowing into their nipped fingers. One or two misanthropists would sit apart perched on boulders like man-like sea-fowl of solitary habits; the sociably disposed would gossip scandalously in little gesticulating knots; and there would be perpetually one or another of my hosts taking aim at the empty horizon with the long, brass tube of the telescope, a heavy, murderous-looking piece of collective property, everlastingly changing hands with brandishing and levelling movements. Then about noon (it was a short turn of duty—the long turn lasted twenty-four hours) another boatful of pilots would relieve us—and we should steer for the old Phœnician port, dominated, watched over from the ridge of a dust-grey arid hill by the red-and-white-striped pile of the Notre Dame de la Garde.

All this came to pass as I had foreseen in the fullness of my very recent experience. But also something not foreseen by me did happen, something which causes me to remember my last outing with the pilots. It was on this occasion that my hand touched, for the first time, the side of an English ship.

No fresh breeze had come with the dawn, only the steady little draught got a more keen edge on it as the eastern sky became bright and glassy with a clean, colourless light. It was while we were all ashore on the islet that a steamer was picked up by the telescope, a black speck like an insect posed on the hard edge of the offing. She emerged rapidly to her water-line and came on steadily, a slim hull with a long streak of smoke slanting away from the rising sun. We embarked in a hurry, and headed the boat out for our prey, but we hardly moved three miles an hour.

She was a big, high-class cargo-steamer of a type that is to be met on the sea no more, black hull with low white superstructures powerfully rigged with three masts and a lot of yards on the fore; two hands at her enormous wheel—steam steering-gear was not a matter of course in these days—and with them on the bridge three others, bulky in thick blue jackets, ruddy-faced, muffled up, with peaked caps—I suppose all her officers. There are ships I have met more than once and known well by sight whose names I have forgotten; but the name of that ship seen once so many years ago in the clear flush of a cold pale sunrise I have not forgotten. How could I—the first English ship on whose side I ever laid my hand! The name—I read it letter by letter on the bow—was *James Westoll*. Not very romantic you will say. The name of a very considerable, well-known and universally respected North-country shipowner, I believe. James Westoll! What better name could an honourable hard-working ship have? To me the very grouping of the letters is alive with the romantic feeling of her reality as I saw her floating motionless, and borrowing an ideal grace from the austere purity of the light.

We were then very near her and, on a sudden impulse, I volunteered to pull bow in the dinghy which shoved off at once to put the pilot on board while our boat, fanned by the faint air which had attended us all through the night, went on gliding gently past the black glistening length of the ship. A few strokes brought us alongside, and it was then that, for the very first time in my life, I heard myself addressed in English—the speech of my secret choice, of my future, of long friendships, of the deepest affections, of hours of toil and hours of ease, and of solitary hours too, of books read, of thoughts pursued, of remembered emotions—of my very dreams! And if (after being thus fashioned by it in that part of me which cannot decay) I dare not claim it aloud as my own, then, at any rate the speech of my children. Thus small events grow memorable by the passage of time. As to the quality of the address itself I cannot say it was very striking. Too short for eloquence and devoid of all charm of tone, it consisted precisely of the three words 'Look out there,' growled out huskily above my head.

It proceeded from a big fat fellow (he had an obtrusive, hairy double chin) in a blue woollen shirt and roomy breeches pulled up very high, even to the level of his breast-bone, by a pair of braces quite exposed to public view. As where he stood there was no bulwark but only a rail and stanchions I was able to take in at a glance the whole of his voluminous person from his feet to the high crown of his soft black hat, which sat like an absurd flanged cone on his big head. The grotesque and massive aspect of that deck hand (I suppose he was that—very likely the lamp-trimmer) surprised me very much. My course of reading, of dreaming and longing for the sea had not prepared me for a sea-brother of that sort. I never met again a figure in the least like his except in the illustrations to Mr. W. W. Jacobs' most entertaining tales of barges and coasters; but the inspired talent of Mr. Jacobs for poking endless fun at poor, innocent sailors in a prose which, however extravagant in its felicitous invention, is always artistically adjusted to observed truth, was not yet. Perhaps Mr. Jacobs himself was not yet. I fancy that, at most, if he had made his nurse laugh it was about all he had achieved at that early date.

Therefore, I repeat, other disabilities apart, I could not have been prepared for the sight of that husky old porpoise. The object of his concise address was to call my attention to a rope which he incontinently flung down for me to catch. I caught it, though it was not really necessary, the ship having no way on her by that time. Then everything went on very swiftly. The dinghy came with a slight bump against the steamer's side, the pilot, grabbing the rope ladder, had scrambled half-way up before I knew that our task of boarding was done; the harsh, muffled clanging of the engine-room telegraph struck my ear through the iron plate; my companion in the dinghy was urging me to 'shove off—push hard'; and when I bore against the smooth flank of the first English ship I ever touched in my life, I felt it already throbbing under my open palm.

Her head swung a little to the west, pointing towards the miniature lighthouse of the Jolliette breakwater, far away there, hardly distinguishable against the land. The dinghy danced a squashy, splashy jig in the wash of the wake, and turning in my seat I followed the *James Westoll* with my eyes. Before she had gone in a quarter of a mile she hoisted her flag as the harbour regulations prescribe for arriving and departing ships. I saw it suddenly flicker and stream out on the flagstaff. The Red Ensign! In the pellucid, colourless atmosphere bathing the drab and grey masses of that southern land, the livid islets, the sea of pale glassy blue under the pale glassy sky of that cold sunrise, it was as far as the eye could reach the only spot of ardent colour—flame-like, intense, and presently as minute as the tiny red spark the concentrated reflection of a great fire kindles in the clear heart of a globe of crystal. The Red Ensign—the symbolic, protecting warm bit of bunting flung wide upon the seas, and destined for so many years to be the only roof over my head.

HOME THOUGHTS, FROM THE SEA

Nobly, nobly Cape Saint Vincent to the North-west died
    away;
Sunset ran, one glorious blood-red, reeking into Cadiz Bay;
Bluish 'mid the burning water, full in face Trafalgar lay;
In the dimmest North-east distance dawned Gibraltar grand
    and gray;
'Here and here did England help me: how can I help Eng-
    land?'—say,
Whoso turns as I, this evening, turn to God to praise and
    pray,
While Jove's planet rises yonder, silent over Africa.

LXIV

A MAN AND A GOOSE

IT happened that among the numerous letters I received from readers of *Birds and Man* on its first appearance there was one which particularly interested me, from an old gentleman, a retired schoolmaster in the cathedral city of Wells. He was a delightful letter-writer, but by-and-bye our correspondence ceased and I heard no more of him for three or four years. Then I was at Wells, spending a few days looking up and inquiring after old friends in the place, and remembering my pleasant letter-writer I went to call on him. During our conversation he told me that the chapter which had impressed him most in my book was the one on the goose, especially all that related to the lofty dignified bearing of the bird, its independent spirit and fearlessness of its human masters, in which it differs so greatly from all other domestic birds. He knew it well; he had been feelingly persuaded of that proud spirit in the bird, and had greatly desired to tell me of an adventure he had met with; but the incident reflected so unfavourably on himself, as a humane and fair-minded or sportsmanlike person, that he had refrained. However, now that I had come to see him he would make a clean breast of it.

It happened that in January some winters ago, there was a very great fall of snow in England, especially in the south and west. The snow fell without intermission all day and all night, and on the following morning Wells appeared half buried in it. He was then living with a daughter who kept house for him in a cottage standing in its own grounds on the outskirts of the town. On attempting to leave the house he found they were shut in by the snow, which had banked itself against the walls to the height of the eaves. Half an hour's vigorous spade work enabled him to get out from the kitchen door into the open, and the sun in a blue sky shining on a dazzling white and silent world. But no milkman was going his rounds, and there would be no baker nor butcher nor any other tradesman to call for orders. And there were no provisions in the house! But the milk for breakfast was the first thing needed, and so with a jug in his hand he went bravely out to try and make his way to the milk shop which was not far off.

A wall and hedge bounded his front garden on one side, and this was now entirely covered by an immense snowdrift, sloping up to a height of about seven feet. It was only when he paused to look at this vast snow heap in his garden that he caught sight of a goose, a very big snow-white bird without a grey spot in its plumage, standing within a few yards of him, about four feet from the ground. Its entire snowy whiteness with snow for a background had prevented him from seeing it until he looked directly at it. He stood still gazing in astonishment and admiration at this noble bird, standing so motionless with its head raised high that it was like the figure of a goose carved out of some crystalline white stone and set up at that spot on the glittering snowdrift. But it was no statue; it had living eyes which without the least turning of the head watched him and every motion he made. Then all at once the thought came into his head that here was something, very good succulent food in fact, sent, he almost thought providentially, to provision his house; for how easy it would be for him as he passed the bird to throw himself suddenly upon and capture it! It had belonged to some one, no doubt, but that great snowstorm and the furious north-east wind had blown it far far from its native place, and it was lost to its owner for ever. Practically it was now a wild bird free for him to take without any qualms and to nourish himself on its flesh while the snow siege lasted. Standing there, jug in hand, he thought it out, and then took a few steps towards the bird in order to see if there was any sign of suspicion in it; but there was none, only he could see that the goose without turning its head was all the time regarding him out of the corner of one eye. Finally he came to the conclusion that his best plan was to go for the milk and on his return to set the jug down by the gate when coming in, then to walk in a careless, unconcerned manner towards the door, taking no notice of the goose until he got abreast of it, and then turn suddenly and hurl himself upon it. Nothing could be easier; so away he went and in about twenty minutes was back again with the milk, to find the bird in the same place standing as before motionless in the same attitude. It was not disturbed at his coming in at the gate, nor did it show the slightest disposition to move when he walked towards it in his studied careless manner. Then, when within three yards of it, came the supreme moment, and wheeling suddenly round he hurled himself with violence upon his victim, throwing out his arms to capture it, and so great was the impulse he had given himself that he was buried to the ankles in the drift. But before going into it, in that brief moment, the fraction of a second, he saw what happened; just as his hands were about to touch it the wings opened and the bird was lifted from its stand and out of his reach as if by a miracle. In the drift he was like a drowning man, swallowing snow into his lungs for water. For a few dreadful moments he thought it was all over with him; then he succeeded in struggling out and stood trembling and gasping and choking, blinded with snow. By-and-bye he recovered and had a look round, and lo! there stood his goose on the summit of the snow bank about three yards from the spot where it had been! It was standing as before, perfectly motionless, its long neck and head raised, and was still in appearance the snow-white figure of a carved bird, only it was more conspicuous and impressive now, being outlined against the blue sky, and as before it was regarding him out of the corner of one eye. He had never, he said, felt so ashamed of himself in his life! If the bird had screamed and fled from him it would not have been so bad, but there it had chosen to remain, as if despising his attempt at harming it too much even to feel resentment. A most uncanny bird! it seemed to him that it had divined his intention from the first and had been prepared for his every movement; and now it appeared to him to be saying mentally: 'Have you got no more plans to capture me in your clever brain, or have you quite given it up?'

Yes, he had quite, quite given it up!

And then the goose, seeing there were no more plans, quietly unfolded its wings and rose from the snowdrift and flew away over the town and the cathedral away on the further side, and towards the snow-covered Mendips; he standing there watching it until it was lost to sight in the pale sky.

LXV

CLOUD AND STORM ON MONT BLANC

OUR porters, with one exception, reached the Pierre l'Echelle as soon as ourselves; and here having refreshed themselves, and the due exchange of loads having been made, we advanced upon the glacier, which we crossed until we came nearly opposite to the base of the Grands Mulets. The existence of one wide crevasse, which was deemed impassable, had this year introduced the practice of assailing the rocks at their base, and climbing them to the cabin, an operation which Balmat wished to avoid. At Chamouni, therefore, he had made inquiries regarding the width of the chasm; and acting on his advice I had had a ladder constructed in two pieces, which, united together by iron attachments, was supposed to be of sufficient length to span the fissure. On reaching the latter, the pieces were united, and the ladder thrown across; but the bridge was so frail and shaky at the place of junction, and the chasm so deep, that Balmat pronounced the passage impracticable.

The porters were all grouped beside the crevasse when this announcement was made, and, like hounds in search of the scent, the group instantly broke up, seeking in all directions for a means of passage. The talk was incessant and animating; attention was now called in one direction, anon in another, the men meanwhile throwing themselves into the most picturesque groups and attitudes. All eyes at length were directed upon a fissure which was spanned at one point by an arch of snow, certainly under two feet deep at the crown. A stout rope was tied round the waist of one of our porters, and he was sent forward to test the bridge. He approached it cautiously, treading down the snow to give it compactness, and thus make his footing sure as he advanced; bringing regelation into play, he gave the mass the necessary continuity, and crossed in safety. The rope was subsequently stretched over the *pont*, and each of us causing his right hand to slide along it, followed without accident. Soon afterwards, however, we met with a second and very formidable crevasse, to cross which we had but half of our ladder, which was applied as follows:—The side of the fissure on which we stood was lower than the opposite one; over the edge of the latter projected a cornice of snow, and a ledge of the same material jutted from the wall of the crevasse a little below us. The ladder was placed from ledge to cornice, both of its ends being supported by snow. I could hardly believe that so frail a bearing could possibly support a man's weight; but a porter was tied as before, and sent up the ladder, while we followed protected by the rope. We were afterwards tied together, and thus advanced in an orderly line to the Grands Mulets.

The cabin was wet and disagreeable, but the sunbeams fell upon the brown rocks outside, and thither Mr. Wills and myself repaired to watch the changes of the atmosphere. I took possession of the flat summit of a prism of rock, where, lying upon my back, I watched the clouds forming, and melting, and massing themselves together, and tearing themselves like wool asunder in the air above. It was nature's language addressed to the intellect; these clouds were visible symbols which enabled us to understand what was going on in the invisible air. Here unseen currents met, possessing different temperatures, mixing their contents both of humidity and motion, producing a mean temperature unable to hold their moisture in a state of vapour. The water-particles, obeying their mutual attractions, closed up, and a visible cloud suddenly shook itself out, where a moment before we had the pure blue of heaven. Some of the clouds were wafted by the air towards atmospheric regions already saturated with moisture, and along their frontal borders new cloudlets ever piled themselves, while the hinder portions, invaded by a drier or a warmer air, were dissipated; thus the cloud advanced, with gain in front and loss behind, its permanence depending on the balance between them. The day waned, and the sunbeams began to assume the colouring due to their passage through the horizontal air. The glorious light, ever deepening in colour, was poured bounteously over crags, and snows, and clouds, and suffused with gold and crimson the atmosphere itself.

I had never seen anything grander than the sunset on that day. Clouds with their central portions densely black, denying all passage to the beams which smote them, floated westward, while the fiery fringes which bordered them were rendered doubly vivid by contrast with the adjacent gloom. The smaller and more attenuated clouds were intensely illuminated throughout. Across other inky masses were drawn zigzag bars of radiance which resembled streaks of lightning. The firmament between the clouds faded from a blood-red through orange and daffodil into an exquisite green, which spread like a sea of glory through which those magnificent argosies slowly sailed. Some of the clouds were drawn in straight chords across the arch of heaven, these being doubtless the sections of layers of cloud whose horizontal dimensions were hidden from us. The cumuli around and near the sun himself could not be gazed upon, until, as the day declined, they gradually lost their effulgence and became tolerable to the eyes. All was calm—but there was a wildness in the sky like that of anger, which boded evil passions on the part of the atmosphere. The sun at length sank behind the hills, but for some time afterwards carmine clouds swung themselves on high, and cast their ruddy hues upon the mountain snows. Duskier and colder waxed the west, colder and sharper the breeze of evening upon the Grands Mulets, and as twilight deepened towards night, and the stars commenced to twinkle through the chilled air, we retired from the scene.

The anticipated storm at length gave notice of its coming. The sea-waves, as observed by Aristotle, sometimes reach the shore before the wind which produces them is felt; and here the tempest sent out its precursors, which broke in detached shocks upon the cabin before the real storm arrived. Billows of air, in ever quicker succession, rolled over us with a long surging sound, rising and falling as crest succeeded trough and trough succeeded crest. And as the pulses of a vibrating body, when their succession is quick enough, blend to a continuous note, so these fitful gusts linked themselves finally to a storm which made its own wild music among the crags. Grandly it swelled, carrying the imagination out of doors, to the clouds and darkness, to the loosened avalanches and whirling snow upon the mountain heads. Moored to the rock on two sides, the cabin stood firm, and its manifest security allowed the mind the undisturbed enjoyment of the atmospheric war. We were powerfully shaken, but had no fear of being uprooted; and a certain grandeur of the heart rose responsive to the grandeur of the storm. Mounting higher and higher, it at length reached its maximum strength, from which it lowered fitfully, until at length, with a melancholy wail, it bade our rock farewell.

A little before half-past one we issued from the cabin. The night being without a moon, we carried three lanterns. The heavens were crowded with stars, among which, however, angry masses of cloud here and there still wandered. The storm, too, had left a rearguard behind it; and strong gusts rolled down upon us at intervals, at one time, indeed, so violent as to cause Balmat to express doubts of our being able to reach the summit. With a thick handkerchief bound around my hat and ears I enjoyed the onset of the wind. Once, turning my head to the left, I saw what appeared to me to be a huge mass of stratus cloud, at a great distance, with the stars shining over it. In another instant a precipice of *névé* loomed upon us; we were close to its base, and along its front the annual layers were separated from each other by broad dark bands. Through the gloom it appeared like a cloud, the lines of bedding giving to it the stratus character.

Immediately before lying down on the previous evening I had opened the little window of the cabin to admit some air. In the sky in front of me shone a curious nodule of misty light with a pale train attached to it. In 1853, on the side of the Brocken, I had observed, without previous notice, a comet discovered a few days previously by a former fellow-student; and here was another 'discovery' of the same kind. I inspected the stranger with my telescope, and assured myself that it was a comet. Mr. Wills chanced to be outside at the time, and made the same observation independently. As we now advanced up the mountain its ominous light gleamed behind us, while high up in heaven to our left the planet Jupiter burned like a lamp of intense brightness. The Petit Plateau forms a kind of reservoir for the avalanches of the Dôme du Gouté, and this year the accumulation of frozen débris upon it was enormous. We could see nothing but the ice-blocks on which the light of the lanterns immediately fell; we only knew that they had been discharged from the *séracs*, and that similar masses now rose threatening to our right, and might at any moment leap down upon us. Balmat commanded silence, and urged us to move across the plateau with all possible celerity. The warning of our guide, the wild and rakish appearance of the sky, the spent projectiles at our feet, and the comet with its 'horrid hair' behind, formed a combination eminently calculated to excite the imagination.

And now the sky began to brighten towards dawn, with that deep and calm beauty which suggests the thought of adoration to the human mind. Helped by the contemplation of the brightening east, which seemed to lend lightness to our muscles, we cheerily breasted the steep slope up to the Grand Plateau.

LXVI

A COUNTRYMAN IN LONDON

To Dr. Lewis.

London, May 29, 1771.

DEAR DOCTOR,

London is literally new to me; new in its streets, houses, and even in its situation; as the Irishman said, 'London is now gone out of town.' What I left open fields, producing hay and corn, I now find covered with streets, and squares, and palaces, and churches. I am credibly informed, that in the space of seven years, eleven thousand new houses have been built in one quarter of Westminster, exclusive of what is daily added to other parts of this unwieldy metropolis. Pimlico and Knightsbridge are now almost joined to Chelsea and Kensington; and if this infatuation continues for half a century, I suppose the whole county of Middlesex will be covered with brick.

It must be allowed, indeed, for the credit of the present age, that London and Westminster are much better paved and lighted than they were formerly. The new streets are spacious, regular, and airy; and the houses generally convenient. The bridge at Blackfriars is a noble monument of taste and public spirit—I wonder how they stumbled upon a work of such magnificence and utility. But, notwithstanding these improvements, the capital is become an overgrown monster; which, like a dropsical head, will in time leave the body and extremities without nourishment and support. The absurdity will appear in its full force, when we consider, that one-sixth part of the natives of this whole extensive kingdom is crowded within the bills of mortality. What wonder that our villages are depopulated, and our farms in want of day-labourers? The abolition of small farms is but one cause of the decrease of population. Indeed, the incredible increase of horses and black cattle, to answer the purposes of luxury, requires a prodigious quantity of hay and grass, which are raised and managed without much labour; but a number of hands will always be wanted for the different branches of agriculture, whether the farm be large or small. The tide of luxury has swept all the inhabitants from the open country—the poorest squire, as well as the richest peer, must have his house in town, and make a figure with an extraordinary number of domestics. The plough-boys, cow-herds, and lower hinds, are debauched and seduced by the appearance and discourse of those coxcombs in livery, when they make their summer excursions. They desert their dirt and drudgery, and swarm up to London, in hopes of getting into service, where they can live luxuriously, and wear fine clothes, without being obliged to work; for idleness is natural to man. Great numbers of these, being disappointed in their expectation, become thieves and sharpers; and London being an immense wilderness, in which there is neither watch nor ward of any signification, nor any order or police, affords them lurking-places as well as prey.

There are many causes that contribute to the daily increase of this enormous mass; but they may be all resolved into the grand source of luxury and corruption. About five-and-twenty years ago, very few, even of the most opulent citizens of London, kept any equipage, or even any servants in livery. Their tables produced nothing but plain boiled and roasted, with a bottle of port and a tankard of beer. At present, every trader in any degree of credit, every broker and attorney, maintains a couple of footmen, a coachman, and postillion. He has his town house, and his country house, his coach, and his post-chaise. His wife and daughters appear in the richest stuffs, bespangled with diamonds. They frequent the court, the opera, the theatre, the masquerade. They hold assemblies at their own houses: they make sumptuous entertainments, and treat with the richest wines of Bordeaux, Burgundy, and Champagne. The substantial tradesman, who was wont to pass his evenings at the alehouse for fourpence halfpenny, now spends three shillings at the tavern, while his wife keeps card-tables at home: she must likewise have fine clothes, her chaise, or pad, with country lodgings, and go three times a week to public diversions. Every clerk, apprentice, and even waiter of tavern or coffee-house, maintains a gelding by himself, or in partnership, and assumes the air and apparel of a *petit-maître*. The gayest places of public entertainment are filled with fashionable figures; which, upon inquiry, will be found to be journeymen tailors, serving-men, and Abigails, disguised like their betters.

In short, there is no distinction or subordination left. The different departments of life are jumbled together. The hod-carrier, the low mechanic, the tapster, the publican, the shop-keeper, the pettifogger, the citizen, and courtier, 'all tread upon the kibes of one another': actuated by the demons of profligacy and licentiousness, they are seen everywhere, rambling, riding, rolling, rushing, justling, mixing, bouncing, cracking, and crashing, in one vile ferment of stupidity and corruption. All is tumult and hurry: one would imagine they were impelled by some disorder of the brain, that will not suffer them to be at rest. The foot passengers run along as if they were pursued by bailiffs. The porters and chairmen trot with their burthens. People who keep their own equipages drive through the streets at full speed. Even citizens, physicians, and apothecaries, glide in their chariots like lightning. The hackney coachmen make their horses smoke, and the pavement shakes under them; and I have actually seen a waggon pass through Piccadilly at the hand-gallop. In a word, the whole nation seems to be running out of their wits.

The diversions of the times are not ill suited to the genius of this incongruous monster, called The Public. Give it noise, confusion, glare, and glitter; it has no idea of elegance and propriety. What are the amusements at Ranelagh? One half of the company are following one another's tails, in an eternal circle, like so many blind asses in an olive mill; where they can neither discourse, distinguish, nor be distinguished; while the other half are drinking hot water, under the denomination of tea, till nine or ten o'clock at night, to keep them awake for the rest of the evening. As for the orchestra, the vocal music especially, it is well for the performers that they cannot be heard distinctly. Vauxhall is a composition of baubles, overcharged with paltry ornaments, ill conceived, and poorly executed, without any unity of design or propriety of disposition. It is an unnatural assemblage of objects, fantastically illuminated in broken masses; seemingly contrived to dazzle the eyes and divert the imagination of the vulgar. Here a wooden lion, there a stone statue: in one place a range of things like coffee-house boxes, covered a-top; in another, a parcel of alehouse benches; in a third, a puppet-show representation of a tin cascade; in a fourth, a gloomy cave of a circular form, like a sepulchral vault half lighted; in a fifth, a scanty slip of grass-plat, that would not afford pasture sufficient for an ass's colt. The walks, which nature seems to have intended for solitude, shade, and silence, are filled with crowds of noisy people, sucking up the nocturnal rheums of an aguish climate; and through these gay scenes a few lamps glimmer like so many farthing candles.

When I see a number of well-dressed people, of both sexes, sitting on the covered benches, exposed to the eyes of the mob, and, which is worse, to the cold, raw, night air, devouring sliced beef, and swilling port and punch and cider, I can't help compassionating their temerity, while I despise their want of taste and decorum: but when they course along those damp and gloomy walks, or crowd together upon the wet gravel, without any other cover than the cope of heaven, listening to a song which one half of them cannot possibly hear, how can I help supposing they are actually possessed by a spirit more absurd and pernicious than anything we meet with in the precincts of Bedlam? In all probability, the proprietors of this, and other public gardens of inferior note, in the skirts of the metropolis, are, in some shape, connected with the faculty of physic, and the company of undertakers; for, considering that eagerness in the pursuit of what is called pleasure, which now predominates through every rank and denomination of life, I am persuaded that more gouts, rheumatisms, catarrhs, and consumptions, are caught in these nocturnal pastimes, *sub dio*, than from all the risks and accidents to which a life of toil and danger is exposed.

These, and other observations, which I have made in this excursion, will shorten my stay at London, and send me back with a double relish to my solitude and mountains. . . .

Yours always,
MATT. BRAMBLE.

LXVII

CHRISTMAS IN THE ANTARCTIC

SUNDAY, *December* 25, *Christmas Day* (1910).—Dead reckoning 69° 5′ S., 178° 30′ E. The night before last I had bright hopes that this Christmas Day would see us in open water. The scene is altogether too Christmassy. Ice surrounds us, low nimbus clouds intermittently discharging light snowflakes obscure the sky, here and there small pools of open water throw shafts of black shadow on to the cloud—this black predominates in the direction from whence we have come, elsewhere the white haze of ice blink is pervading.

We are captured. We do practically nothing under sail to push through, and could do little under steam, and at each step forward the possibility of advance seems to lessen.

The wind which has persisted from the west for so long fell light last night, and to-day comes from the N.E. by N., a steady breeze from 2 to 3 in force. Since one must have hope, ours is pinned to the possible effect of a continuance of easterly wind. Again the call is for patience and again patience. Here at least we seem to enjoy full security. The ice is so thin that it could not hurt by pressure—there are no bergs within reasonable distance—indeed the thinness of the ice is one of the most tantalizing conditions. In spite of the unpropitious prospect everyone on board is cheerful and one foresees a merry dinner to-night.

The mess is gaily decorated with our various banners. There was full attendance at the Service this morning and a lusty singing of hymns.

Should we now try to get east or west?

I have been trying to go west because the majority of tracks lie that side and no one has encountered such hard conditions as ours—otherwise there is nothing to point to this direction, and all through the last week the prospect to the west has seemed less promising than in other directions;

in spite of orders to steer to the S.W. when possible it has been impossible to push in that direction.

An event of Christmas was the production of a family by Crean's rabbit. She gave birth to 17, it is said, and Crean has given away 22!

I don't know what will become of the parent or family; at present they are warm and snug enough, tucked away in the fodder under the forecastle.

Midnight.—To-night the air is thick with falling snow; the temperature 28°. It is cold and slushy without.

A merry evening has just concluded. We had an excellent dinner; tomato soup, penguin breast stewed as an entrée, roast beef, plum pudding, and mince pies, asparagus, champagne, port and liqueurs—a festive menu. Dinner began at 6 and ended at 7. For five hours the company has been sitting round the table singing lustily; we haven't much talent, but everyone has contributed more or less, and the choruses are deafening. It is rather a surprising circumstance that such an unmusical party should be so keen on singing. On Christmas night it was kept up till 1 a.m., and no work is done without a chanty. I don't know if you have ever heard sea chanties being sung. The merchant sailors have quite a répertoire, and invariably call on it when getting up anchor or hoisting sails. Often as not they are sung in a flat and throaty style, but the effect when a number of men break into the chorus is generally inspiriting.

The men had dinner at midday—much the same fare, but with beer and some whisky to drink. They seem to have enjoyed themselves much. Evidently the men's deck contains a very merry band.

There are three groups of penguins roosting on the floes quite close to the ship. I made the total number of birds 39. We could easily capture these birds, and so it is evident that food can always be obtained in the pack.

To-night I noticed a skua gull settle on an upturned block of ice at the edge of a floe on which several penguins were preparing for rest. It is a fact that the latter held a noisy confabulation with the skua as subject—then they advanced as a body towards it; within a few paces the foremost penguin halted and turned, and then the others pushed him on towards the skua. One after another they jibbed at being first to approach their enemy, and it was only with much chattering and mutual support that they gradually edged towards him.

They couldn't reach him as he was perched on a block, but when they got quite close the skua, who up to that time had appeared quite unconcerned, flapped away a few yards and settled close on the other side of the group of penguins. The latter turned and repeated their former tactics until the skua finally flapped away altogether. It really was extraordinarily interesting to watch the timorous protesting movements of the penguins. The frame of mind producing every action could be so easily imagined and put into human sentiments.

On the other side of the ship part of another group of penguins were quarrelling for the possession of a small pressure block which offered only the most insecure foothold. The scrambling antics to secure the point of vantage, the ousting of the bird in possession, and the incontinent loss of balance and position as each bird reached the summit of his ambition was almost as entertaining as the episode of the skua. Truly these little creatures afford much amusement.

Monday, December 25, Christmas (1911).—Lunch. Bar. 21·14. Rise 240 feet. The wind was strong last night and this morning; a light snowfall in the night; a good deal of drift, subsiding when we started, but still about a foot high. I thought it might have spoilt the surface, but for the first hour and a half we went along in fine style. Then we started up a rise, and to our annoyance found ourselves amongst crevasses once more—very hard, smooth névé between high ridges at the edge of crevasses, and therefore very difficult to get foothold to pull the sledges. Got our ski sticks out, which improved matters, but had to tack a good deal and several of us went half down. After half-an-hour of this I looked round and found the second sledge halted some way in rear—evidently some one had gone into a crevasse. We saw the rescue work going on, but had to wait half-an-hour for the party to come up, and got mighty cold. It appears that Lashly went down very suddenly, nearly dragging the crew with him. The sledge ran on and jammed the span so that the Alpine rope had to be got out and used to pull Lashly to the surface again. Lashly says the crevasse was 50 feet deep and 8 feet across, in form U, showing that the word 'unfathomable' can rarely be applied. Lashly is 44 to-day and as hard as nails. His fall has not even disturbed his equanimity.

After topping the crevasse ridge we got on a better surface, and came along fairly well, completing over 7 miles (geo.) just before 1 o'clock. We have risen nearly 250 feet this morning; the wind was strong and therefore trying, mainly because it held the sledge; it is a little lighter now.

Night.—Camp No. 47. Bar. 21·18. T.—7°. I am so replete that I can scarcely write. After sundry luxuries, such as chocolate and raisins at lunch, we started off well, but soon got amongst crevasses, huge snowfields, roadways running almost in our direction, and across hidden cracks into which we frequently fell. Passing for two miles or so along between two roadways, we came on a huge pit with raised sides. Is this a submerged mountain peak or a swirl in the stream? Getting clear of crevasses and on a slightly down grade, we came along at a swinging pace—splendid. I marched on till nearly 7.30, when we had covered 15 miles (geo.) ($17\frac{1}{4}$ stat.). I knew that supper was to be a 'tightener,' and indeed it has been—so much that I must leave description till the morning.

Dead reckoning, Lat. 85° 50' S.; Long. 159° 8' 2" E. Bar. 21·22.

Towards the end of the march we seemed to get into better condition; about us the surface rises and falls on the long slopes of vast mounds or undulations—no very definite system in their disposition. We camped halfway up a long slope.

In the middle of the afternoon we got another fine view of the land. The Dominion Range ends abruptly as observed, then come two straits and two other masses of land. Similarly north of the wild mountains is another strait and another mass of land. The various straits are undoubtedly overflows, and the masses of land mark the inner fringe of the exposed coastal mountains, the general direction of which seems about S.S.E., from which it appears that one could be much closer to the Pole on the Barrier by continuing on it to the S.S.E. We ought to know more of this when Evans's observations are plotted.

I must write a word of our supper last night. We had four courses. The first, pemmican, full whack, with slices of horse meat flavoured with onion and curry powder and thickened with biscuit; then an arrowroot, cocoa and biscuit hoosh sweetened; then a plum-pudding; then cocoa with raisins, and finally a dessert of caramels and ginger. After the feast it was difficult to move. Wilson and I couldn't finish our share of plum-pudding. We have all slept splendidly and feel thoroughly warm—such is the effect of full feeding.

LXVIII

THE MELLSTOCK CAROLS

SHORTLY after ten o'clock the singing-boys arrived at the tranter's house, which was invariably the place of meeting, and preparations were made for the start. The older men and musicians wore thick coats, with stiff perpendicular collars, and coloured handkerchiefs wound round and round the neck till the end came to hand, over all which they just showed their ears and noses, like people looking over a wall. The remainder, stalwart ruddy men and boys, were dressed mainly in snow-white smock-frocks, embroidered upon the shoulders and breasts, in ornamental forms of hearts, diamonds, and zig-zags. The cider-mug was emptied for the ninth time, the music-books were arranged, and the pieces finally decided upon. The boys in the meantime put the old horn-lanterns in order, cut candles into short lengths to fit the lanterns; and, a thin fleece of snow having fallen since the early part of the evening, those who had no leggings went to the stable and wound wisps of hay round their ankles to keep the insidious flakes from the interior of their boots. . . .

Old William Dewy, with the violoncello, played the bass; his grandson Dick the treble violin; and Reuben and Michael Mail the tenor and second violins respectively. The singers consisted of four men and seven boys, upon whom devolved the task of carrying and attending to the lanterns, and holding the books open for the players. Directly music was the theme, old William ever and instinctively came to the front.

'Now mind, naibours,' he said, as they all went out one by one at the door, he himself holding it ajar and regarding them with a critical face as they passed, like a shepherd counting out his sheep. 'You two counter-boys, keep your ears open to Michael's fingering, and don't ye go straying into the treble part along o' Dick and his set, as ye did last year; and mind this especially when we be in "Arise, and hail." Billy Chimlen, don't you sing quite so raving mad as you fain would; and, all o' ye, whatever ye do, keep from making a great scuffle on the ground when we go in at people's gates; but go quietly, so as to strik' up all of a sudden, like spirits.' . . .

Just before the clock struck twelve they lighted the lanterns and started. . . . The breeze had gone down, and the rustle of their feet and tones of their speech echoed with an alert rebound from every post, boundary-stone, and ancient wall they passed, even where the distance of the echo's origin was less than a few yards. Beyond their own slight noises nothing was to be heard, save the occasional bark of foxes in the direction of Yalbury Wood, or the brush of a rabbit among the grass now and then, as it scampered out of their way.

Most of the outlying homesteads and hamlets had been visited by about two o'clock; they then passed across the outskirts of a wooded park toward the main village, nobody being at home at the Manor. Pursuing no recognized track, great care was necessary in walking lest their faces should come in contact with the low-hanging boughs of the old lime-trees, which in many spots formed dense overgrowths of interlaced branches.

'Times have changed from the times they used to be,' said Mail, regarding nobody can tell what interesting old panoramas with an inward eye, and letting his outward glance rest on the ground, because it was as convenient a position as any. 'People don't care much about us now!' I've been thinking we must be almost the last left in the county of the old string players? Barrel-organs, and they things next door to 'em that you blow wi' your foot, have come in terribly of late years.'

'Ay!' said Bowman, shaking his head; and old William, on seeing him, did the same thing.

'More's the pity,' replied another. 'Time was—long and merry ago now!—when not one of the varmits was to be heard of; but it served some of the choirs right. They should have stuck to strings as we did, and keep out clar'nets, and don away with serpents. If you'd thrive in musical religion, stick to strings, says I.'

'Strings be safe soul-lifters, as fur as that do go,' said Mr. Spinks.

'Yet there's worse things than serpents,' said Mr. Penny. 'Old things pass away, 'tis true; but a serpent was a good old note: a deep rich note was the serpent.'

'Clar'nets, however, be bad at all times,' said Michael Mail. 'One Christmas—years agone now, years—I went the rounds wi' the Weatherbury choir. 'Twas a hard frosty night, and the keys of all the clar'nets froze—ah, they did freeze!—so that 'twas like drawing a cork every time a key was opened; the players o' 'em had to go into a hedger-and-ditcher's chimley-corner, and thaw their clar'nets every now and then. An icicle o' spet hung down from the end of every man's clar'net a span long; and as to fingers—well, there, if ye'll believe me, we had no fingers at all, to our knowing.'

'I can well bring back to my mind,' said Mr. Penny,

'what I said to poor Joseph Ryme (who took the tribble part in Chalk-Newton Church for two-and-forty year) when they thought of having clar'nets there. "Joseph," I said, says I, "depend upon't, if so be you have them tooting clar'nets you'll spoil the whole set-out. Clar'nets were not made for the service of the Lard; you can see it by looking at 'em'," I said. And what cam o't? Why, souls, the parson set up a barrel-organ on his own account within two years o' the time I spoke, and the old choir went to nothing.'

'As far as look is concerned,' said the tranter, 'I don't for my part see that a fiddle is much nearer heaven than a clar'net. 'Tis further off. There's always a rakish, scampish twist about a fiddle's looks that seems to say the Wicked One had a hand in making o'en while angels be supposed to play clar'nets in heaven, or som'at like 'em, if we may believe picters.'

'Robert Penny, you was in the right,' broke in the eldest Dewy. 'They should ha' stuck to strings. Your brass-man is a rafting dog—well and good; your reed-man is a dab at stirring ye—well and good; your drum-man is a rare bowel-shaker—good again. But I don't care who hears me say it, nothing will spak to your heart wi' the sweetness o' the man of strings!'

'Strings for ever!' said little Jimmy.

'Strings alone would have held their ground against all the new comers in creation.' ('True, true!' said Bowman.) 'But clar'nets was death.' ('Death they was!' said Mr. Penny.) 'And harmonions,' William continued in a louder voice, and getting excited by these signs of approval, 'har-monions and barrel-organs' ('Ah!' and groans from Spinks) 'be miserable—what shall I call 'em?—miserable——'

'Sinners,' suggested Jimmy, who made large strides like the men, and did not lag behind like the other little boys.

'Miserable dumbledores!'

'Right, William, and so they be—miserable dumbledores!' said the choir with unanimity.

By this time they were crossing to a gate in the direction of the school, which, standing on a slight eminence at the junction of three ways, now rose in unvarying and dark flatness against the sky. The instruments were retuned, and all the band entered the school enclosure, enjoined by old William to keep upon the grass.

'Number seventy-eight,' he softly gave out as they formed round in a semicircle, the boys opening the lanterns to get a clearer light, and directing their rays on the books.

Then passed forth into the quiet night an ancient and time-worn hymn, embodying Christianity in words orally transmitted from father to son through several generations down to the present characters, who sang them out right earnestly:—

> 'Remember Adam's fall,
>   O thou Man:
> Remember Adam's fall
>   From Heaven to Hell.
> Remember Adam's fall;
> How he hath condemn'd all
> In Hell perpetual
>   There for to dwell.
>
> Remember God's goodnesse,
>   O thou Man:
> Remember God's goodnesse,
>   His promise made.
> Remember God's goodnesse;
> He sent His Son sinlesse
> Our ails for to redress;
>   Be not afraid!
>
> In Bethlehem He was born,
>   O thou Man:
> In Bethlehem He was born,
>   For mankind's sake.
> In Bethlehem He was born,
> Christmas-day i' the morn:
> Our Saviour thought no scorn
>   Our faults to take.
>
> Give thanks to God alway,
>   O thou Man:
> Give thanks to God alway
>   With heart-most joy.

> Give thanks to God alway
> On this our joyful day:
> Let all men sing and say,
> Holy, Holy!'

Having concluded the last note, they listened for a minute or two, but found that no sound issued from the schoolhouse.

'Four breaths, and then, "O, what unbounded goodness!" number fifty-nine,' said William.

This was duly gone through, and no notice whatever seemed to be taken of the performance.

'Good guide us, surely 'tisn't a' empty house, as befell us in the year thirty-nine and forty-three!' said old Dewy.

'Perhaps she's jist come from some noble city, and sneers at our doings?' the tranter whispered.

'Od rabbit her!' said Mr. Penny, with an annihilating look at a corner of the school chimney, 'I don't quite stomach her, if this is it. Your plain music well done is as worthy as your other sort done bad, a' b'lieve, souls; so say I.'

'Four breaths, and then the last,' said the leader authoritatively. ' "Rejoice, ye Tenants of the Earth," number sixty-four.'

At the close, waiting yet another minute, he said in a clear loud voice, as he had said in the village at that hour and season for the previous forty years—

'A merry Christmas to ye!'